ISBN 978-0-332-04471-2
PIBN 10004610

PROGRESS

IN

SPIRITUAL KNOWLEDGE

BY THE

REV. CHAUNCEY GILES

AUTHOR OF "THE NATURE OF SPIRIT," "THE INCARNATION AND ATONEMENT,"
"HEAVENLY BLESSEDNESS," ETC.

A MEMORIAL VOLUME

PHILADELPHIA
AMERICAN NEW-CHURCH TRACT AND PUBLICATION
SOCIETY
2129 CHESTNUT STREET
1895

CONTENTS.

CHAUNCEY GILES.*

IT is beautiful, when in the peaceful days at the close of
a long and useful life the thoughts look back over the
way which has been travelled, delighting to see the hand
of Providence in events which at the time seemed unim-
portant and often unfortunate ; and when they turn from
such memory of the past to anticipation of renewed life
in the higher world where the same Divine hand will be
more plainly felt and followed with more perfect trust.
So it was with the Rev. Chauncey Giles, who passed into
the spiritual world at his home in Philadelphia, November 6, 1893.

Mr. Giles's earliest memories took him back to the
hills of western Massachusetts, where he was born, in
Charlemont, on the banks of the Deerfield River, on the
11th of May, 1813. The region is picturesque, and to
one who visits it in summer is most attractive ; but the
hills are rocky for the plough, and farming, the business
of the people, is laborious. The winters, too, are long
and cold, and for months the ground is buried in snow
and the river is frozen with clear ice, often several feet in
thickness.

The parents of the friend whose life we are recording

---

* This biographical sketch is reprinted with slight change from
The New-Church Review of January, 1894, by the permission of
the publishers.

were John and Almira Avery Giles. They were people of ability and of more than usual cultivation and refinement. The father was educated as a physician, but ill health prevented his following his profession. His son Chauncey was the eldest of seven children, and as a boy he became accustomed to hard work, and felt early that some share of responsibility rested upon him for the support of the family and the education of the younger children.

The life in Charlemont was such as belonged to the "good old times" in New England. Children enjoyed out-door sports, especially skating and coasting in the winter. For those a little older, hard work was relieved by the diversions of singing-school and apple-parings and quilting-bees, and by an occasional holiday, notably Thanksgiving Day and the General Muster, when they gathered from far and near to the yearly parade of the men liable to military service. Sundays were kept with the Puritan strictness, and the family spent a long day at the distant meeting-house. From sunset Saturday evening it became sinful to laugh or play or even to walk in the fields for pleasure. The constraint was relieved at Sunday's sunset, when the women brought out their knitting and children began their games. Books were very scarce in those days. There was no periodical literature, with the exception of a small weekly paper which was taken by only a few people. The Bible and hymn-book with the longer and shorter catechism, and perhaps "Pilgrim's Progress" or Baxter's "Saint's Rest" were all that came within children's reach. A copy of the *Spectator* was read and re-read by Mr. Giles, and even a volume from his father's medical library was tried in the hunger for new thoughts. It was at one of the General Musters, while still quite a boy, that he bought a copy of Cowper's ''Poems'' and of Milton's ''Paradise Lost,'' and he spent many a long winter evening reading them over and over again by the bright firelight. Mr. Giles well remembered the intense delight he used to feel when as a small boy he would pore over the pages of a large Bible in a neighbor's house, and the wonderful charm of the story of Joseph arranged for children, a copy of which came into his hands.

The first instruction Mr. Giles received was from his father, and what was lacking in aids to learning was made up in earnestness. He has told me how he was accustomed to do his ''sums'' with a bit of charcoal on the hearth before the fire, and how dearly he prized his first slate earned by chopping a cord of wood. Years after, contrasting the circumstances of his own early life with the larger opportunities of another, Mr. Giles said, '' I had no books, no social influence that tended to develop a taste for literature, or cultivate what I had naturally. It seems as though I was like a tree or shrub in the woods. I was shut out from the light ; I had no culture ; I grew without any direction or assistance.'' In writing of the '' good old times,'' Mr. Giles once said,—

'' They were good times in many essential respects. The people were industrious, frugal, and in the most important affairs of life they were intelligent. If they did not read so much as we do, they thought more. They did not depend so much upon others to do their thinking. They were more self-reliant. Their means of social culture were limited, but they made the best use of those they possessed. If they endured many hardships, they acquired strength by them, and in the struggle for life they gained many of its blessings, and learned how to appreciate them."

Mr. Giles once referred to these early days in remarks made in the Argyle Square church in London, and said that from his earliest recollection he had desired to be a minister, but the idea seemed so improbable and absurd that he said little of it. His father once spoke to him of a situation as a clerk in a store, but he declined it because he did not want to be a merchant. A little later than this, when he was at home on a vacation from Bennington, where he was attending the academy, his father asked him what he intended to do for a living when he had finished school. The young man asked, "What do you want me to do?" His father said, "I would like to have you study law." After a few moments' silence he replied, with a look full of happiness and satisfaction, "Well, if I study law, it must be the law of God." This determination did not leave him, though for many years its realization was deferred till he was led to those doctrines of light and comfort which the Lord desired him to preach.

The education begun at home under the father's care was continued at a "select school" near by. Some time also was spent with a clergyman of the neighborhood, who gave what instruction he could in return for work upon his place. It was a happy day to the young man eager for education, when the opportunity offered to leave his labor in the held, to attend the Mt. Anthony Academy in Bennington, not far away across the Vermont line. About this time he showed his power of application by mastering the Latin grammar in nine days. It is said of him as a young man that "when he was engaged in study he was oblivious of everything about him." At the academy Mr. Giles came under one whom he regarded as a real teacher. He did more than impart a knowledge of Greek, which was his subject; he showed how to study and made study delightful. At Bennington Mr. Giles prepared for Williams College, at Williamstown, near by among the Berkshire Hills, and entered as a member of the class of 1836. He was now nineteen years old. The question of support was still a serious one, and he met his necessary expenses chiefly by teaching in the intervals of college work. Mr. Giles remained with his class till the middle of the junior year, when his health failed—his eyes especially were much affected—and he was unable to continue the double labor of studying and teaching. This illness was, I believe, due to an incident of one of the college vacations. He was at home in the hay-field, and the other mowers were crowding him in his mowing, thinking they would "take down this college youth a peg or two." It was a very hot day, and, having worked till he was exhausted, he drank from an ice-cold spring. Trouble in his head resulted, which for years caused much suffering and interfered seriously with his work. This was probably the origin of a singing or roaring in the head from which he was never wholly relieved, and which at times gave great annoyance.

Mr. Giles received the degrees of A.B. and M.A. from Williams College in 1876, although he never finished the college course. In 1886 he was present at the reunion of his class on the fiftieth anniversary of its graduation. In college Mr. Giles is remembered by classmates as "more than an average scholar, not brilliant, perhaps, but studious, prompt, and accurate. He was a good declaimer, and in the debating society was alert and one of the best speakers. He was strong on temperance and on the anti-slavery question, which was much discussed in those days. In manner he was rather retiring, somewhat shy, friendly with all but familiar with only a few." It is a fact that from boyhood throughout his life Mr. Giles shrank from meeting strangers, and only with great effort went into company.

The interruption of the college course was a great disappointment to Mr. Giles. His desire to be a minister was the motive of his study ; and now as he was about to enter on his chosen work he was compelled to stop his preparation and give his strength to teaching. But in after-years he saw the Lord's providence in this disappointment, for it prevented his confirming himself in the doctrines of the Congregational Church, which were all that he then knew, and kept his mind open to receive and teach the truths of the New Church.

After leaving college Mr. Giles was again in Bennington, a teacher in the academy where he had received his own preparation. At this time religious subjects were much in his mind. ' He was struggling with the hard dogmas of the church," says one who was closely associated with him as a fellow-teacher, " and was at times in a sceptical mood, and more than a mood. He was very conscientious and his mental sufferings were great, and that for years." Probably states of mind were now beginning of which Mr. Giles himself speaks in his little book, "Why I am a New-Churchman." He could not believe the doctrines commonly taught concerning heaven and hell and an arbitrary judgment.

He writes,—

" Doubts having been raised about the truth of one doctrine, they led to the examination of other doctrines and doubts about their truth. I did not doubt because I desired to do so. On the contrary, I clung to every point of the old faith with the greatest tenacity. I clung like a drowning man to the last plank, until I was torn from it, or it failed me, and I sunk into the depths of despair. I have no language that is adequate to express the darkness and horror and agony of the state I lived in, if it could be called living, for years. One hope alone sustained me. I did not doubt the existence, the wisdom, and goodness of God. . . . I settled down to the duties and necessities of life with the purpose of faithfully doing my work and awaiting whatever the future might have in store for me."

A season of feeble health and of rapid changes followed, when Mr. Giles travelled some and taught schools for a short time in several different places. He was for a while a teacher at West Hampton, Mass. Afterwards he taught in Fishkill on the Hudson. He visited Philadelphia, and spent a winter in Middletown, Pa., on the Susquehanna River. He was at this time drifting with no definite aim, and his movements were influenced by a seemingly very trifling thing. It was in after-years a striking example to Mr. Giles of the Lord's use of the smallest means to give direction to our whole life. When a mere school-boy studying his geography he had been attracted by a description of Tennessee, and made up his mind that some day he would visit that State. It so happened that he never saw Tennessee, but for years the purpose was in his mind, and more than once influenced his movements.

From Middletown Mr. Giles journeyed through Pennsylvania and New York, by the slow means of travel which existed before the days of railroads, with the intention of going to Michigan, and then visiting Tennessee. He was moving westward on the Erie Canal. The weather was rainy and unpleasant and the company on the canal-boat disagreeable, and he yielded to the suggestion of a fellow-traveller to stop over for a day at Palmyra. At the hotel where he lodged he saw in a newspaper an advertisement for a teacher. He applied for the position, found friends as if by accident, and was soon settled as principal of the Palmyra Academy, an institution which ranked high among the schools of the State. In Palmyra Mr. Giles met the one who became his wife and his faithful companion in the trials and successes of his life. He used to speak pleasantly of his great indebtedness to a rainy day, but he spoke reverently, for he saw in it the hand of Providence.

Mr. Giles had been in charge of the Palmyra Academy hardly more than a year when he accepted a more remunerative but more laborious position in the Collegiate Institute in Rochester, N. Y. This position he held only a year, and in May, 1840, he was again in Palmyra, teaching a "select school." But in October of the same year, suffering much with his head and dissatisfied with the success of his school, he went to Cincinnati. The intention of visiting Tennessee, formed as a boy, was not forgotten. While in Cincinnati, he one day packed his bag and was going down the stairs to take the steamboat for Nashville, when he was stopped by a stranger who was looking for a teacher to open a school in Hamilton, Ohio, a town some twenty-five miles north of Cincinnati. Mr.

Giles was persuaded to postpone the trip to Tennessee, and the end of November found him settled in a new home. It seemed again a mere chance which brought him to Hamilton, but it was there that he became acquainted with the doctrines of the New Church.

The pages of journal written in Rochester and Palmyra and during the first years in Hamilton show states of mind which are a surprise to those who have known Mr. Giles only since the truths of the New Church became his constant encouragement and delight. He was oppressed with a sense that he was accomplishing nothing. He was conscious of abilities, and was desirous, perhaps ambitious, to make them influential ; but he seemed to himself to make no progress from year to year. His discouragement was in part due to feeble health, for during these years he suffered almost constantly from headache, which at times made work impossible. It is plain also that his depression was somewhat morbid. He underrated the value of his work as a teacher, and was oppressed with a sense of failure where others saw usefulness and success. The contrast of such gloomy, despondent states, which were natural to Mr. Giles, with the hopeful confidence which has been so characteristic of the latter half of his life, shows what the New Church was to him, and goes far to explain his intense desire to spread its light to others. At that time he knew nothing of Swedenborg and his writings, but we find him reading Carlisle and Coleridge with some satisfaction. Though fully occupied in his schools and with no expectation of ever being anything but a teacher, his thoughts dwelt often on religious subjects, and his old fondness for the profession of a minister appears in the interest with which he listened to various preachers, and in the extended criticisms of their sermons and delivery which he entered in his journal. He would observe the effect of a speaker upon the audience and the cause of his success or failure. Self-consciousness in a speaker and any appearance of study for effect were elements of weakness. To him an unassuming modesty, made earnest by sincere conviction, was the truest eloquence, and if art were used, the audience at least must be unconscious of it.

But there were still ten years of teaching before Mr. Giles became himself a minister. These were, in a double sense, years of preparation, for the methods of instruction and of gentle control which he employed in school were what were needed in the church, and at the same time the doctrines of the New Church were brought to his notice and gained a stronger and stronger hold upon his understanding and his affections.

Mr. Giles began his charge of the Hamilton and Rossville Female Academy in December, 1840, and continued it till the summer of 1845. In August, following his settlement in Hamilton, he revisited Palmyra, where he was married on the 8th of September to Eunice Lakey. Her parents, many years before, had come to western New York from Franklin County, Mass., where also was Charlemont, Mr. Giles's native town. It would be pleasant to write of Mrs. Giles and of the qualities which have endeared her to her many friends. In writing of Mr. Giles from this time, we write of both, for they were united in all that we describe. In 1891 their Golden Wedding was celebrated, and in the same year Mr. Giles wrote of his companion of fifty years, "She is and has been a good, faithful, and devoted wife. If I have gained any success and been of any use in the world, it is due to her as much as to myself."

Mr. and Mrs. Giles took their journey from Palmyra by the best means of travel which then existed, the canal from Rochester to Buffalo, steamboat to Cleveland, and from there the stage, day and night, to Hamilton, in all a journey of a week. The winter climate of southern Ohio in those days was soft and mild, a pleasant contrast to the harsh winds of western New York. But Hamilton was unhealthy. It lay on the low banks of the Great Miami River. There was a large basin of standing water for the supply of a canal, and when afterwards water was taken from the river for power, the air was poisoned with miasms from the old river-bed. Sickness was very prevalent, especially the ague. For a long time after going to Hamilton Mrs. Giles was very ill, and before they moved from the town Mr. Giles was brought to death's door by a congestive fever. But in spite of their trials the years in Hamilton were remembered with deep gratitude.

What a contrast it was to their first journey West, when fifty-one years later Mr. and Mrs. Giles took train in Philadelphia to attend the New-Church Convention in Cincinnati! We quote Mr. Giles's description to illustrate both the natural and the spiritual development of fifty years :

"The train left at 4.25 P.M. The day was cool and bright. The car ran so smoothly that it seemed to be at rest almost. The country is looking very beautiful. The apple-trees are in their glory.

As we rushed past them they seemed to spring out of the earth in the beauty and glory of their wedding robes. The earth and the sky were glorious in the smile of the Lord. How beautiful the earth is! What variety of color and form! Surely, we ought to see the Lord's wisdom in everything. How much it would add to the interest of everything around us if we regarded it as the Lord's work to-day, as His gift to us, as a token of His love for us! It would give a new and charming significance to everything if we could see His love in all the means He has provided for our happiness. The ride through the heart of Ohio was beautiful, very beautiful, and I enjoyed it, every minute of it. As we passed Zenia and Morrow and other places, many old associations, some sweet, some bitter, were revived. How wonderfully the Lord has led me! How little I dreamed what He had in store for me when I was working my way along by teaching school! Truly, He leads us by a way we know not."

In the spring of 1843, Mr. Giles's father and mother and sisters came to Hamilton from Massachusetts. His father died there the following year. Two of the sisters afterwards removed to Decatur, Ill., and their mother made her home with them until her death at the age of ninety-two.

We are given a pleasant glimpse of Mr. Giles's school, and of Mr. Giles as a teacher, by one who joined him as assistant when he had been two years in Hamilton. She writes, —

"The first thing I observed in his school was the perfectly good understanding apparent between teacher and pupils, and the courtesy and kindness manifested in their intercourse with each and all. It resembled the home-life in a well-trained family, I thought. Then my attention was called to a wonderful clock which was said to govern the school. A double stroke sounded two and a half minutes before the hour or half-hour. The children knew that they had liberty to speak quietly if they wished to, and the classes took their places for the next recitation of their own accord. Another double stroke announced the hour, and all was still again. Mr. Giles's teaching was noticeable for its thoroughness. His object seemed to be to cultivate a love of knowledge, to form a habit of acquiring it; and at the same time he tried to make it practical in every possible way. He sought to develop the mind and character in a natural and orderly manner, instead of forcing and cramming for display or present results. To illustrate: In teaching a class of beginners in arithmetic, he kept them practising notation and numeration until they each and all could write and read numbers with the greatest ease and correctness. Meantime, to keep up the interest, the exercises were varied by some examples in addition or by learning the tables, etc. They practised on each one of the ground rules in the same way until they could add and subtract, multiply and divide, as fast as they could see the figures. As there are not examples enough given in any arithmetic to cultivate such facility, examples were improvised or taken from other books.

" By this time the multiplication tables and the other tables were as familiar to the children as A, B, C. They take pride in buying and selling wood and coal, building and furnishing houses, making dry-goods and mantua-makers' bills and settling them, all of which they find interesting and rather amusing exercises ; and incidentally the idea enters their minds that this study may be of some use to them in the future. Of course it takes time to go through the arithmetic in this way, but it was never necessary to go through a second time, and as they were not hurried on from one thing to another before becoming perfectly familiar with it, they found the study easy and delightful, instead of hard and disagreeable. And they were thoroughly equipped for the higher mathematics, both by their habits of study and the amount of knowledge already acquired.

" The classes in natural sciences were encouraged in the study of principles presenting themselves in ordinary life. The children became enthusiastic in studying out the mechanical principles involved in the ordinary implements used in their homes and the streets, and the chemical changes taking place under their own eyes.

" The idea that a school-book ever exhausted a subject was never tolerated, or that of finishing one's education on leaving school. The school course was looked upon as only the introduction to an education,—a learning how to learn. If the taste for knowledge has been quickened and developed in the school, and habits of acquiring

b 2*

it are formed there, the business of education is merely well begun. Mr. Giles's methods of teaching were, perhaps, better adapted to the development of a well-rounded, harmonious character than to extraordinary acquirement in any one direction.

"His schools were the most perfect specimens of true democracy I was ever brought in contact with. The only distinction recognized seemed to be moral worth. So far as one could see, all were on a perfect equality. The efforts of the teacher and his interest in their individual progress were unwearied. His patience was not exhausted by the dullest, nor were his interest and pride centred upon the gifted. All he asked was that each should try to improve and do the best he could. You could never guess who were the children of rich or influential patrons. Some of the children of one of the rival churches in town, it is said, were once upon a time told by their parents to notice and see if the teacher were not partial to so and so's children of the other church. In a few days the children reported that they had watched carefully and did not see any partiality. It seems quite surprising, under the circumstances, that the children should recognize Mr. Giles's sense of justice.

"In the primary department Mr. Giles did not insist upon the little ones sitting up straight and still by the hour, neither did he expect them to give their attention to any particular subject more than a few minutes at a time. Their lessons were very short and rehearsals frequent, and their slate and pencil were always at hand ready for use; and they did use them a great deal. There were generally on one of the black-boards some of the capital letters written, or some simple drawing easily imitated, a cup, slate, or book, which they might copy if they chose. They had learned a variety of pretty little songs for children which they delighted in singing, and singing and marching were much relied upon to relieve the little ones of the weariness of long sitting. Mr. Giles's sister Caroline had charge of this department for a time in Hamilton. To see her with her fine voice leading the children's voices in their marching music was something one would not willingly forget. The children were as happy as birds, and as musical. One of the mothers remarked that she did not know but it was extravagant to send all of her children to Mr. Giles, but when she saw the little ones so happy she felt she could well afford the extra expense.

'Why,' she added, 'they sing themselves to sleep every night and awake in the morning singing, and during the day it must be a serious discomfort that a song will not dispel.' "

Mr. and Mrs. Giles, when they came to Hamilton after their marriage, boarded with a Mr. Garrison, a tailor. Mr. Garrison was a New-Churchman and he lent them a book of Swedenborg's. It was "Conjugial Love." As Mr. and Mrs. Giles sat talking in their room one evening the book lay on the table, and as he spoke Mr. Giles carelessly turned the leaves. He glanced down at the book and his eye fell upon the word "heaven" in one of the "Memorable Relations." He read a few lines to see what the author had to say of heaven. The conversation paused as he read on, and when he closed the book it was with the remark that if the crazy man had written nothing worse than that they must have slandered him. Mr. Giles has often referred to the act of the tailor in handing him this book as the greatest service ever rendered him by any man, and has used it to encourage others to do like services.

This beginning of interest in the doctrines of the New Church was in the latter part of the year 1841. The first mention of Swedenborg in Mr. Giles's journal is December 31, 1843, when he writes,—

"If there is anything in the history of the past year worthy of notice, it is that I have become interested in the writings of Swedenborg. They have opened new views of life to me. The world wears a new face. If they are true or false, they will exert a most important influence upon my life."

The next day he adds,—

"If I mistake not, the new ideas of life which I have obtained from the New-Church works will assist me much in overcoming many defects in my character. I think they will give me new strength of purpose, and perhaps in time enable me to overcome and correct some original deficiencies in my nature. I must set myself seriously at work, and though I put no confidence in myself, yet there is One who has strength, and who is ever willing to impart to others if they are willing to receive it. . . . I think the idea that a kind Providence watches over us and directs all things for our good —an idea which has now become a part of my life—will do much to strengthen me in remedying some of the greatest defects in my character."

We see the practical nature of Mr. Giles's interest in the doctrines of the New Church from the first. They attracted him because they promised to give help to overcome his faults and to lead a truer life.

The Rev. Mr. Prescott, or Prescott Hiller as he was afterwards called, was the minister of the New-Church Society in Cincinnati in those days. Mr. Giles heard him sometimes when in Cincinnati, and Mr. Prescott preached in Hamilton occasionally. Both being cultivated men and interested in education, they became warmly attached to each other. A letter of Mr. Prescott's is preserved, dated May 11, 1843, in which he says, referring to a visit to Hamilton,—

"There was a gentleman there who interested me still more than the others. He is a Mr. Giles, a teacher, formerly from Massachusetts. I have been introduced to him and already feel well acquainted with him. He is an uncommonly fine man, one after your own heart on the subject of teaching. He is devoted to it, and means to make it his profession. He keeps an academy here, and the best school in town. I visited the institution and was charmed with his manner of teaching and governing. I am sure you would be pleased with his acquaintance. I have had a great deal of conversation with him. He is already half a New-Churchman in his views. He has also read a little—part of the 'Divine Love and Wis-

dom'—and is much pleased with what he has read. He is now reading 'Heaven and Hell.' I think he must become a New-Churchman
in time.''

On the other hand we find appreciative mention of Mr.
Prescott in Mr. Giles's journal. He speaks of seeing
Mr. Prescott in Cincinnati, and hearing him preach from
"the Parable of the Sower." "His sermon was a very
good and profitable one." Later, when living in Lebanon, Mr. Giles writes,—

"Mr. Prescott came to town and has preached several discourses
on the doctrines of the New Church. It is cheering and comforting
to hear him. I always gain new strength every time I have an
opportunity of hearing him, and when he goes away I feel refreshed
and can enter upon the duties of life with new vigor."

Hamilton is the place which Mr. W. D. Howells has so
picturesquely described in "A Boy's Town." Mr. Howells's father was one of the few New-Churchmen in Hamilton, and for a time he used to meet regularly with Mr.
and Mrs. Giles in their rooms on Sunday for a simple
service. Occasionally one or another was in town who
joined in the worship; but those were days of small
meetings, when four was a large congregation, and five
was a crowded house.

While in Hamilton a feeling of dissatisfaction with
teaching as a permanent profession was working in Mr.
Giles's mind, and in the spring of 1844, when he was
thirty-one years old, he yielded to the advice of friends
and began to study law, still continuing his school. This
was a line of study which, if it had been continued, would
have led Mr. Giles away from his real life work, and he
afterwards saw the hand of Providence in the family cares
and the illness which cut short the study of law after a

few weeks, and turned his attention more deeply to the new spiritual truths. "I have been reading some of the New-Church doctrines lately," he writes in October, 1844, "and if I have health this winter, I think I shall investigate them more fully than I have yet done."

Mr. Giles speaks, in "Why I am a New-Churchman," of the increasing light as he continued his study :

"In this state of darkness and negation the doctrines of the New Church found me, as it seemed to me then, by the merest accident, but as I have since learned to know and believe, by the providence and infinite mercy of the Lord. They came at first as a ray of light which excited interest and attention. Whether it was a solitary ray that gave a little light on one special subject and was limited to that, or a star that was to usher in a new morning and a new day, I did not know. But it was precious in itself, and I rejoiced in it. . . . It was not a solitary ray. It came from a central sun. Special truths harmonized and threw light upon one another. Each one was seen to be a part of a rational and ordered system. Confidence was increased and the way of progress became assured. Mysteries with regard to man's spiritual nature, which had been involved in impenetrable darkness began to give up their secrets. Problems which I had supposed to be beyond the reach of the human mind to solve began to yield to the power of the new truths and assume rational forms. The darkness that brooded over the chaos of conflicting opinions was gradually dispersed, the illusions and fallacious appearances with which the natural mind invests and perverts the form and nature of spiritual truth were gradually dispelled. I could truly say, 'Whereas I was blind, now I see.'"

Mr. Giles writes in his journal, —

"I do not regret coming to Hamilton, though my lot has been one of suffering most of the time since I came here ; sickness and I know not what has laid me low and kept me so, but I have become acquainted with the New-Church doctrines, and I think I have found in them what will be of more value to me than physical health or wealth."

Lebanon was a town of about the size of Hamilton, in an adjoining county. "It was a charming town, which from early times had always enjoyed an enviable reputation for the intellect and cultivation of its people." A new academy had been built in Lebanon, and they were looking for a principal. It was suggested to Mr. Giles to apply for the position, but he was in feeble health and disheartened. He always remembered with gratitude the encouragement received at this time from one of his early New-Church friends. "Go," Mr. Ross said, "and you will get it." "Why do you say I shall get it?" "You will get it because you have some ability as a teacher, and you want to be useful; and when a man wants to be useful, the Lord opens the way for him." Thus encouraged, he applied, and, although the competition was sharp, he got the position and opened the school in Lebanon September 1, 1845, continuing in charge till January, 1848.

Very pleasant memories of this school linger in the minds of many who there came under Mr. Giles's care. One of his pupils speaks most affectionately of Mr. Giles, and says, "Lebanon has never had a teacher so accomplished as he, nor one whose memory is so warmly cherished." The same friend tells an interesting incident. The academy was new, and the grounds nearly bare of trees. The first spring after going to Lebanon, Mr. Giles one day took the boys to the woods, with a large wagon and picks and spades. There was much fun among the boys as each took up a tree and planted it on the academy grounds under Mr. Giles's direction. As the planting was going on, Mr. Giles suggested that some day they might come with their children and sit under the shade of their trees. They were a bright, ambitious, studious set of scholars, and many of them have since held positions of trust and influence. One at least, in fulfilment of Mr. Giles's prophecy, has taken his son to the scene of his own school-days, and sat with him in the shade of the tree which he planted.

In Lebanon the school was large from the beginning, and the duties were exacting. The same friend who has given us the glimpse of the school at Hamilton was still associated with Mr. Giles, and tells us of the wise and pleasant ways in which he awakened a love of learning, and developed the character of the young people under his care. He organized a club which met in the long winter evenings and served a good use in the days when books were less common than now, in awakening an interest in historical and literary subjects. Music was an important feature of the meetings, as it was of the school exercises. Mr. Giles had a happy way of overcoming the difficulties of writing compositions by asking the children to write descriptions of familiar and interesting things. Their exercises were sometimes given the form of letters to real or imaginary people.

" The school day always began with devotional exercises, reading from the Word, music, and prayer, which was often followed by what was called a little morning talk, which never occupied more than five minutes and seldom more than two. A practical suggestion was offered, current events alluded to, or the effects of some historical event were noted. The death of some distinguished man was mentioned, discoveries and inventions were spoken of, anything having a tendency to expand and broaden the visible horizon of these active-minded young people was seized and utilized for this purpose. If the children asked hard questions, he did not hesitate to say that he did not know but would look into it.

"He took educational journals and kept himself abreast of the times in his work. Methods of interesting his pupils were a constant study with him. His heart was in his work, and of course from year to year he was constantly perfecting himself in it."

For a time health was better and life happier in Lebanon than in Hamilton, and interest in the New Church was growing. May 16, 1846, Mr. Giles writes, —

"It is impossible for me to believe as I once did. The doctrines of the New Church have thrown new light upon the Word, upon life, upon everything, and I hardly know what my duty is with regard to an open profession of adherence to those doctrines."

January 1, 1848, he notes that a small society of the New Church has been formed in Lebanon, and that Mrs. Giles and he have added their names as members.

While living in Lebanon the interest in the New Church was much strengthened by acquaintance with Mr. and Mrs. David Espy, who lived some miles nearer to Cincinnati, at Twenty Mile Stand. They were people of lovely character, and beautiful examples of the life to which the doctrines of the New Church should lead.

In the latter part of the stay in Lebanon the sky became overcast. Mr. Giles had suffered severely with pleurisy and with terrible neuralgic pains in his thigh, which interfered with his work in school. The 1st of January, 1848, found him much disheartened, and he resigned his charge of the Lebanon Academy. It was decided to open a family boarding-school for boys, — they had already made a home for a few scholars, — and it was hoped that Mr. Giles might be so far relieved from care that he would recover his health. A pleasant location

was found at Yellow Springs, a summer resort on the line
of the Little Miami Railroad, which had been lately built,
and they moved to the new home in April, 1848. A year
was passed in this place. Mrs. Giles gave the boys a
good and happy home. Mr. Giles, though suffering
intensely much of the time, was with them in their out-
door amusements, arranging excursions into the country,
which was full of flowers, and visits to mills and factories
in the neighborhood. He also gave what personal care
he could to their instruction, taking them into the house
when he became unable to go to the school-room, and
hearing them in bed when he was unable to sit up. After
a time, through long and painful treatment, his suffering
was relieved.

A page of the journal kept in Yellow Springs gives the
first suggestion of Mr. Giles's becoming a New-Church
minister. He writes March 3, 1849, —

"This morning I received a letter from the Rev. J. P. Stuart, in
which he announced his intention to visit us again soon. He has
hinted several times that I would sometime preach New-Church doctrines. If I was free from debt and qualified, I should like nothing
better. But I am neither. [For some years he had been burdened
with debt incurred by endorsing for another.] My intellectual culture has been too meagre, and my habits of thought and reading too
desultory, to enable me ever to be an able expounder of the doctrines
of the New Church. But if I was going to preach at all, I should by
all means wish to preach them. They are so consistent with the
nature of man and with themselves. There seem to be no weak
points in them. They meet every want of the human heart. They
embrace every idea that is rational concerning God and the spiritual
world, and embrace in their noble philosophy every atom of matter."

This was a season of great discontent with himself, of
many regrets that he was not more useful and that he had

had so little system or perseverance in his efforts to educate and train himself. But the sunshine of trust in Providence soon returned. Occasional visits from Mr. Stuart were a source of much pleasure and comfort. Reed's "Growth of the Mind," Noble's "Lectures," and Swedenborg's tract on "The Infinite" were among the books which were read with pleasure. "I consider the greatest blessing of my life," Mr. Giles writes, March 25, 1849, "that I became acquainted with them [the doctrines of the New Church]. They have removed the darkness which enveloped many objects, and made them a matter of reason, when before they were only cognizant to the eye of faith. They have done more than this. They have presented the Lord in such a light that the whole universe has become changed, and is radiant with His love."

Mr. Giles had not been long in Yellow Springs when a proposition was made to him, through the father of one of his scholars, to remove his school to Pomeroy, a mining town on the Ohio River. In April, 1849, he took his family to Pomeroy, and the old Pomeroy mansion, in a commanding position above the river, was prepared for the uses of home and school. The Pomeroy family, the owners of the mines, were cultivated people, and their large "connection" formed a delightful society into which Mr. and Mrs. Giles were cordially received. This was their home till their removal to Cincinnati in the autumn of 1853. The stay in Pomeroy was delightful in many ways. The home was charming and healthful, the society was pleasant, the school prosperous, and when leaving was spoken of, Mr. Giles was told that if he wished for more money, he could remain and have whatever he wanted. A friend who had charge of the common schools of Pomeroy during Mr. Giles's stay, and had good opportunity to know his abilities as a teacher, says, "As an educator he had no superior and few equals. He held to the view that love and justice will control where force would fail."

Mr. Giles continued his study of Swedenborg. After a time there was opportunity to be useful in conducting services, and a friend suggested that he obtain a license as a reader. Accordingly he was ordained May 23, 1852, with authority to lead in worship, and on Sundays he conducted services in turn in several places within reach of Pomeroy. At Rock Spring, two miles from Pomeroy, he preached in summer in a barn ; at Rutland, seven miles distant, in the Universalist church ; and at Kygersville, twelve miles away. He held service also occasionally in the school-room at Pomeroy. In undertaking this work Mr. Giles expected to read the sermons of others, but he had not read more than one or two when he began to write for himself. The first attempt pleased him so little that he threw it away. The first sermon of his that was heard was from the text, "The leaves of the tree were for the healing of the nations," delivered in 1852. Mr. Giles used often to recall a meeting at Rock Spring at which he delivered this sermon. It was in a log house on a summer evening. The only light was a tallow candle, around which the insects fluttered, and all that he could see of his audience was their eyes shining out of the darkness.

The Sunday rides to the places of meeting are remembered with pleasure by one who often accompanied Mr.

Giles. There were others who attended the services in the several places, and enjoyed the same sermon four Sundays in succession. Mr. Giles had preached in this way for a year, when there was desire that he should perform the marriage service and administer the sacraments. He was therefore ordained with the full powers of a minister of the New Church, May 29, 1853, by the Rev. David Powell, in Cincinnati, who also performed the first ordination. Thus far he had given most of his time and strength to his school, and the preaching took a secondary place. The time was near when he must choose between the two.

In the summer of 1853, Mr. Giles took some of his scholars to their home in Cincinnati, for the vacation, and was invited to preach one Sunday for the New-Church Society. He often recalled with amusement the disappointed look of the congregation when he, a schoolteacher from the country, entered the pulpit. But it gave place to intense interest before he finished. From that time his call to Cincinnati was talked of. He continued his journey to St. Louis, where he was engaged to preach for a few Sundays, and returning, he took back his boys to Pomeroy for the opening of the fall term. In September an invitation came to Mr. Giles from the First New-Jerusalem Society of Cincinnati, to officiate as their minister for one year at a salary of one thousand dollars.

The question was a hard one. On the one hand were a pleasant and healthful home, and an assured support in a profession in which he had long experience. On the other hand were city life, a greatly reduced income, and a profession which was almost untried, and for which he

3*

had no regular preparation, but which offered the possibility of greater usefulness.   He decided in favor of the
change, and removed with his family to Cincinnati in
November, 1853.

From a worldly point of view the step was most unwise.
Some of Mr. Giles's friends almost doubted his sanity ;
others were sorry for the change, knowing his excellence
as a teacher, and feeling that his best use was in that profession.   But the step was taken, and Mr. Giles entered
into the active work of a large and long-established
society, at forty years of age, with no theological training,
with less acquaintance with the doctrines of the church
than many in the congregation, having written but twelve
sermons, and having seen the sacraments administered in
the New Church but a few times.   He began at once to
preach twice each Sunday.   He was called here and there
to long distances to attend funerals.   Within the society
he found conflicting elements to harmonize and an almost
utter lack of young life.   It was not an easy task which
he had undertaken.

Mr. Giles, in beginning his work in Cincinnati, made
special effort to meet the needs of the young people and
to interest them in the services and in the practical uses
of the church.   His long acquaintance and experience
with his scholars prepared him to succeed with the young
people and the children of the church ; and his cheerfulness and pleasant humor helped to endear him to them.
His efforts were successful, and the society was soon
strengthened by a large body of active and earnest
younger members.   The affection of the young people
for Mr. Giles and their devotion to him were very strong

in Cincinnati. One of the "young people," writing of
a time a little later, when Mr. Giles lived at the top of one
of the hills which circle Cincinnati about, says,—

"It was a walk of a mile and a half from where most of us lived
to the hills, and another half-mile climb to the house, up a steep path
with rough stone steps a part of the way. It was before the days of
inclined planes or even of street-cars or omnibuses. And every
week a party of the young people would go over this toilsome route
to see him and have a meeting of a young people's class."

Mr. Giles's relations with the little children were also
very happy. He was usually present in the Sunday-
school ; for a time he was the superintendent. But his
part at the Christmas and Easter festivals was what the
children especially enjoyed. The stories, "The Wonderful Pocket," "The Magic Shoes," and many more,
which have since been printed in several little volumes,
and which have interested so many children, were most
of them written for these occasions. They are especially
dear to those who associate them with Christmas happiness and Mr. Giles's charming manner in addressing the
children. There was never in the stories any exciting
plot, and rarely much action or incident, but they always
expressed some truth of our inner life in simple and
amusing form, in which it was at once recognized by the
children. "Those who were scholars then and have
since grown into mature men and women tell us they
were the most interesting stories they ever listened to,
and they never lost a word of them as they were read."
So writes one who heard them, and adds, "I think
there never was a man that came closer to children than
he did, and when he spoke every one listened. These

little stories were gems that every child remembered, and on any Christmas could tell just what the preceding Christmas gift was and all about it." The custom of putting thoughts for the children in story form at Christmas and Easter was one which Mr. Giles continued, and his stories were enjoyed no less by the children in New York and Philadelphia.

As for the old dissensions in the Cincinnati Society, Mr. Giles treated them as he almost always did such things,—he ignored them altogether. He declined to listen to complaints of one against another. He was watched to see with what party he would side, but it was as it had been in school when the children tried to detect partiality,—there was none to find. Under such treatment dissensions could not live.

At the end of one year's ministry in Cincinnati, the society voted to employ Mr. Giles for another year. As the second year drew to its close in the autumn of 1855, Mr. Giles received an invitation to go to Boston to act as assistant to the Rev. Thomas Worcester. The invitation was declined, but the thought of losing Mr. Giles seems to have awakened the Cincinnati Society to the need of making his relation with them more permanent, and they asked him to become their pastor. He accepted the position October 6, 1855. He records in his journal his desire and intention to be a devoted pastor, to enter upon a more thorough course of study, to perfect himself as much as possible as a preacher, and to become better acquainted with the people, and strive to do all that he can for their spiritual good.

The work in Cincinnati was laborious. It was usual

for Mr. Giles to teach a class in the Sunday-school; "hear a class," he always said, which suggests that with him scholars were not passive listeners. The morning service followed. In the afternoon he often drove to Glendale, a suburb of Cincinnati, and preached, returning to lecture in the evening. For a time he gave lectures Wednesday evenings, and a class of ladies met Saturdays at his house. Calls to attend funerals were frequent ; it was the exception when a week passed without one, and on many Sundays a funeral was attended before morning service or between services. It was not the custom in those days to take long summer vacations, and the work in the hot weather, with short intermission, was exhausting. For some years Mr. Giles suffered with his throat, and feared that the trouble would interfere with his work. The most serious interruption was in the winter of 1860, when on account of feeble health he visited New Orleans, being absent two months.

In 1858 a new responsibility came to Mr. Giles in his election as president of the Urbana University. He never made Urbana his home, but for several years exercised a general oversight of the institution and visited it occasionally.

A tone of discouragement is noticeable in Mr. Giles's private record of his early ministry, but it was not felt by others. His influence in the society, in the Sunday-school, and at home was uniformly cheerful. He was dissatisfied with his extempore speaking, and thought himself too old to learn to do it well. He also concluded rather hastily in those days that he never should be able to write an interesting course of lectures. He was sometimes disheartened when the attendance at service was small, and would fear that his usefulness in that place was nearly ended. Indeed, he never could quite overcome a little depression when he was obliged to speak to "empty benches."

Mr. Giles wrote, August 9, 1863, when thirty years of his best work were still before him,—

"I now begin the work of another year with many doubts and misgivings and with little apparent strength for the work. I do not think I shall accomplish much, and I fear I shall not do much more in this world. How little, oh, how little I have done!—almost nothing it would seem. And I feel that my powers are failing in some respects. I may preach better perhaps. But I do not know. There ought to be ten or fifteen years of good hard work in me yet."

But another spirit was gaining strength which over-came any natural despondency. A week later than the above he writes,—

"I am trying to bring myself into a state to do my duty and leave the results with the Lord. I know that the Lord requires only my duty. Results are with Him alone. We have nothing to do with them."

To this trust was added, as years went on, an undoubt-ing confidence in the triumph of the truth, and in the real success of every effort to advance the cause of the Lord's church, which was inspiring to all who felt its influence.

Mr. Giles, soon after he became a minister, was recog-nized as one of the ablest preachers in the New Church. His preaching from the first possessed the same elements of strength which afterwards made it so effective in other fields. He felt the need of "more plainness and directness in preaching and talking about the spirit;" and spiritual things, as he spoke of them, became substantial realities. Subjects often treated in a vague and abstract way he made clear by regarding them from universal principles. He was fond of speaking of religion as a spiritual science, and of showing that spiritual truth has the same logical unity and the same certainty as truth of natural science. Knowing that the same Divine laws rule in all realms of the creation, in mind and matter, in heaven and earth, he looked to nature and to natural life for illustration of spiritual truth. He had remarkable facility in such illustration. He also made frequent use of the principle that the Lord works always like Himself. By studying His methods in a plant which we hold in our hand we may learn of man's regeneration. "How often," writes a friend, "has he taken as his illustration an egg, a seed, the eye, a watch, an engine, and presented it in such a way that the spiritual truth he wanted to teach blossomed in the mind as he talked of the natural image!" Mr. Giles had no taste for minute study of fine points, and never burdened his sermons with them, but set himself to teach the great essential principles of the New Church with all possible clearness and force. A hopeful, joyful spirit pervaded his preaching,—a deep sense of the wonderful goodness of the Lord and of the beauty of the heavenly life. He did not threaten and condemn, but won the heart to the goodness of living with the Lord. He was not discouraging to weak and sinful souls, but inspired them with new hope and resolution. Mr. Giles's manner in the pulpit was simple and earnest ; his voice was of unusual strength and of a sympathetic quality.

There were times when the tenderness of his own feeling made it difficult for him to speak. Some would say that Mr. Giles was persuasive. It was not so in any artful sense, but his manner was tender and at the same time expressive of his own intense conviction of the truth of what he said.

Mr. Giles was always in the effort to improve his preaching, and often expressed the belief that there are new and better ways of presenting spiritual truth yet to be discovered. Early in his ministry he wrote,—

"I am more and more dissatisfied with the effect of preaching; it does not seem to me to be as efficient and well directed as it ought to be, certainly not if its main object is to teach spiritual truth. No system of science could be taught in such a hap-hazard manner with any success. There is certainly great room for improvement in my mode of preaching, and I mean to effect it."

A year later he writes, —

"It does seem as though more might be made of the sermon in the New Church. But I have not found the way yet, and I do not know who has. Very little good seems to grow out of it yet."

And once more, —

"I am satisfied that ordinary sermons are but little use. They are too fragmentary. They give truth in bits without showing its relation. We are yet far from the true method, and I am too old to do much in finding or practising a better."

It was probably his desire to make preaching more connected and systematic which led Mr. Giles often to write sermons in connected series, keeping the thought of the congregation upon one subject for a considerable time. The expressions of dissatisfaction are interesting as illustrating Mr. Giles's desire for improvement, for he did not become too old to enjoy trying new things and new ways if they gave promise to be better than the old. But no one will accept his own estimate of his preaching.

Though Mr. Giles excelled as a preacher, he was perhaps equally helpful to the church in other ways. He was always a peace-maker. His almost overwhelming sense of the greatness of the work intrusted to us by the Lord made all personal feelings and dissensions seem wholly out of place. All our time and strength are needed for the work. He was wonderfully successful in finding money for church uses, and he did it not by begging, but by helping people to realize that they have no money of their own, but that what they have is intrusted to them by the Lord to make useful.

Mr. Giles was a leader always, but a leader whose rule was scarcely felt. He never forced his will upon others, but taught the true principles of action and waited patiently. He prepared the ground and sowed the seed and gave it time to grow. An example of this is found in his relation with the first church of which he was pastor.

The Cincinnati Society, when Mr. Giles became its pastor, was not connected with the General Society of the New Church in Ohio, nor with the General Convention in the United States. Mr. Giles believed that association is orderly and useful; that so a power and freedom of action are gained which an individual or a society does not enjoy which stands alone, but he was willing to wait till the usefulness of union commended itself to others. He had himself been received as a member of the General Convention at the meeting in Boston, June 30, 1855. In 1857, through Mr. Giles's influence, the

Convention met in Cincinnati ; and September 5, 1860, his patience was rewarded by the society's voting to join the General Society of the New Church in Ohio, which was a member of the General Convention. "This I have long desired," Mr. Giles writes, "and I have no doubt it will be of great use to the church generally." It is remarkable that a similar experience was repeated in New York, and again in Philadelphia. The society in New York had withdrawn from the Convention, and had worked alone twelve years when Mr. Giles became its pastor. Some one remarked to Mr. Giles when he went to New York, "You need not expect to induce this society to join the Convention ; it never will." To which he replied, " I shall not try to induce you, but you will do it." A year later the society joined with others in the neighborhood to form the New York Association, which after another year united with the general body of the church. The situation in Philadelphia was peculiar. For years the President of the Convention was pastor of a society which was not connected with that body ; but patient waiting and the principle of use prevailed.

The society in Cincinnati, at the time of Mr. Giles's coming, occupied a church on Longworth Street, which was dark and noisy and unsuitable. Mr. Giles was earnest that they should have a better home. Finally he preached a sermon in which he contrasted the elegance of the people's dwellings with the poorness of the house provided for the worship of the Lord. A friend remarked to him at the close of the service, " Mr. Giles, that sermon will do one of two things : it will drive you out of this church, or the whole congregation." It had the latter effect, but not immediately. The society took up the question in earnest in the spring of 1860. A lot on one of the most central corners in the city was bought, and plans were being considered when the breaking out of the Civil War put a stop to all enterprise, and the ground was returned to its former owners. But before Mr. Giles left Cincinnati a better home for the society was provided. The church on the corner of Fourth and John Streets, now occupied by the society, was bought, and January 17, 1864, it was dedicated.

At the same time that the new church was being prepared, Mr. Giles was considering a proposition to remove to New York. He had declined the invitation to Boston some years before, and had already declined an invitation to New York. This time he decided to go, and on February 1, 1864, presented his resignation, to take effect the 1st of the following May. The reasons which led to this change are shown in letters written by Mr. Giles to the society. Referring to the lighter work in a new field, he says,—

"This would give me leisure for more pastoral duty and time to prepare some works for the press, which I have long contemplated and which men of good judgment think might be of much use. And it is a question with me whether I might not be more widely and permanently useful to the church if by using the materials already accumulated I could find time to prepare my discourses with more care, and address a wider audience through the press."

He speaks most affectionately of his relations with the Cincinnati Society,—

"I feel bound to the society by many strong and tender ties, and the thought of leaving you is always attended with pain. I have preached for you nearly one-fourth of the existence of your society, and I cannot recall an unpleasant word that has passed between me and any member of the society or congregation during this time."

His letter of resignation shows that the consideration mentioned in the former letter prevailed,—

"I know I could not much longer perform the duties which the society requires and which the wants of the church demand. My health is good now, but I know that I have not the power of prolonged labor that I had a few years ago, and I see unmistakable signs that the power is constantly diminishing. I think I can be more useful to the church and to my family to accept the way Divine Providence has opened for me, to get relief from the great and continued pressure of writing, and so use my remaining strength and direct it in such channels that it may be the most available for the use of the church."

The last months of Mr. Giles's stay in Cincinnati were especially happy ones. The society was occupying the pleasant church lately provided, the attendance at worship was large, and many persons united with the church by baptism or confirmation. On Sunday, April 17, thirty persons, ten adults and twenty children, were baptized ; and on the following Sunday, which was the last on which Mr. Giles preached as pastor of the society, eighteen persons were confirmed. "It was a most beautiful and interesting sight," he writes, "and rejoiced my heart greatly. I seemed to be reaping the harvest of my past labors." The Holy Supper was administered to one hundred and twenty-five communicants, although the day was stormy. "This is four or five times as many as were present when I administered it the first time. The Lord be praised for it all."

While connected with the Cincinnati Society, Mr. Giles

received the powers of Ordaining Minister or General Pastor at the meeting of the General Convention in Philadelphia, June 14, 1863.

The affection between Mr. Giles and the Cincinnati Society was strong and always continued so. There was in it something of that friendliness which belongs to a new country where people have been drawn closely together by the hardships of pioneer life. But a short time before his death he wrote,—

"I cannot tell you how much it gratifies me to know that I still hold a warm place in the hearts of my old and new friends in Cincinnati. I think the members of the New Church there seem nearer to me than they do at any other place. They were my first love in the church, and I think of them as they were when we lived there and they became a part of my life"

The work in New York began in May, 1864, and continued for nearly fourteen years. It could hardly be called lighter than the work in Cincinnati. It did, however, lead to the printing of articles and books, the use which Mr. Giles had especially in view in making the change. Until this time very few of Mr. Giles's sermons or lectures had been printed, though for years the manuscripts had been borrowed and read in several small societies which were without ministers.

The winter after going to New York Mr. Giles lectured in the church on Thirty-Fifth Street on Sunday evenings, from October to March. He began in November a series of six lectures on the spiritual world. The first lecture of the series was entitled "The Answer of the New-Jerusalem Church to the Questions: What is Spirit? What is the Spiritual World? Where is it? and What are its Relations to this World?'' Mr. Giles notes that the house was completely filled and some went away. The church was crowded throughout the course. After the delivery of the first lecture the suggestion was made that it should be printed and be ready for distribution the next Sunday evening. This was done, and the experiment seemed so useful that it was continued through the course, five hundred copies of each lecture being printed for free distribution. These lectures as printed from week to week became afterwards the basis of the little book '' The Nature of Spirit, and of Man as a Spiritual Being,'' which has proved the most popular of any book of the New Church. It has been issued in several languages and editions, and its circulation has probably reached one hundred thousand copies. The lectures were written from week to week for the next Sunday's use, with no thought of making a book ; and when they were first published Mr. Giles was too busy to revise them, and they were seen through the press by a friend. This was characteristic of Mr. Giles's literary work. Of all that he has published very little has been written originally for that purpose, or has received the careful finish which an author expects to give to a book. He wrote right along, with a plan of what he intended to say, but allowing his subject to grow and develop as he went ; and as it was written, so it usually stood, with little change or revision.

In closing the lectures of the first winter in New York, Mr. Giles says, —

" They have been the most successful course I have ever delivered. The attendance has been good throughout, and the interest quite profound. Eleven of them have been printed and very extensively circulated through the country. They have been read in many societies and sent to a great number of individuals, and I trust something has been done to help forward the cause of humanity, and to establish the kingdom of God upon earth."

The success of the first season's lectures in New York led to a bolder attempt the following year to bring the truths of the New Church before the public. The great hall of the Cooper Union was secured for a course of five Sunday evening lectures. The subjects were "Death," "The Resurrection of Man," "The Life of Man after Death," "Swedenborg," and "The New Church a New Dispensation of Divine Truth." The hall was well filled at every meeting; probably fifteen hundred people were present at some of the lectures, and the attention was good. But the visible effect of the lectures was disappointing. A few persons were drawn to the society, and doubtless a use was done in introducing the New Church to the community and removing prejudices against it. "Mr. Giles did his work well," writes a friend; "his heart was in it; he was satisfied; for, as he encouragingly said, 'No one knows the result of the planting.'"

Further remembrances of Mr. Giles in New York by the same good friend are too pleasant to withhold, —

"There was nothing dramatic in the life of Mr. Giles, neither did he pose for effect before the world. His motives and purposes were far beyond such littleness. His purely pastoral life can be compared to the smooth flowing of a brook through grassy meadows and flowering shrubs. The turbulent stream from the mountainside had no counterpart in his nature. This phase of his being is beautifully illustrated by his writings: classic in style, apparently simple, they have a power and directness which go to the very core of his subject, sounding depths of truth brought to the surface by great minds only. Dignity and self-control governed his character, while composure and gentleness marked his daily life ; add grace and a quiet humor in his intercourse with others, and the true gentleman is in view. The world is the better for his living, and the New Church a gainer by his faith and love for her doctrines, which were intense.

" His calmness and self-possession may be illustrated by two incidents in his New York pulpit. The usual services had been completed, and he rose up to deliver his sermon, but could not find the manuscript ; all of his pockets were explored in vain. He quietly left the desk, went to his house a square off, returned with the missing manuscript, and delivered a very able sermon, not at all disconcerted by the singular circumstance. The congregation waited his return quietly, but with a bit of suppressed amusement.

" On another Sunday morning the congregation had assembled, the time had arrived for the service, but Mr. Giles had not been seen. One of his sons was sent to look him up. He was found in his study writing, and deep in thought ; when told the congregation was waiting his presence, 'Bless my soul !' was the reply. His opening words at the service betrayed no flurry over the delay."

It was during his stay in New York that Mr. Giles delivered in the church on Thirty-Fifth Street his lectures on "Our Children in the Other Life." They were at first printed as leaflets, and have now for many years been published in more convenient form. They are full of comfort. With the tenderest sympathy they lift up the thought to heaven, and tell of the homes prepared by the Lord for His little ones, where, secure from every danger, they develop under angels' care in the eternal spring. They have brought consolation to thousands of sorrowing hearts.

A new avenue of usefulness was opened to Mr. Giles in 1865, when he was associated with Mr. Thomas

Hitchcock in the editorial charge of the *New-Jerusalem Messenger.* From May 1, 1873, to January, 1878, Mr. Giles was sole editor. He was also editor of the *Children's New-Church Magazine* from 1868 to January 30, 1872, when it was discontinued. This editorial care added greatly to his labor. There is no more exacting master than a periodical, which must be ready each week on time whether there are contributions or not, whether one is sick or well. Mr. Giles often was obliged to write a considerable part of the paper himself, and for a time he attended also to the details of proof-reading and the making up of the paper. He also contributed generously to the *Children's Magazine,* and told to a wider circle of children such pleasant and instructive stories as had been enjoyed by his Sunday-schools.

In 1875, while Mr. Giles was pastor of the New York Society, he was elected president of the General Convention of the New Jerusalem in the United States, succeeding the Rev. Thomas Worcester ; and he held the position until his death, a period of eighteen years. In the general body of the church, as in the societies with which he was connected, Mr. Giles was a warm supporter of practical uses and a leader in them. The missionary cause was especially dear to him, and the printing and publishing of the doctrines. His earnestness in the work of the church, his confidence in the support of the Divine Providence, and in the ability of the people to supply the means to do their part, were inspiring, and led to substantial results. Mr. Giles's annual addresses as president of the Convention presented in practical ways the principles which should guide the church in its

work. The address seemed to sound the key-note of
the session, and it was a note of harmony and practical
usefulness. His very earnestness that the church should
be at work actively furthering the great uses intrusted
to it made Mr. Giles impatient of obstruction, and even
of parliamentary forms, when they seemed to retard the
uses which he had so much at heart. He recognized
this quality in himself as a defect in a presiding officer,
and it was his custom of late years to intrust the conduct of the business to the vice-president. He thought,
however, and probably with truth, that his own ignorance
of rules had been useful to the church in leading to less
regard for mere technicalities. Mr. Giles's presence
always seemed to give ·deliberations a higher tone, and
when he spoke it was often to lift discussion above minor
differences to the more spiritual plane of use, where all
could unite, and where the light of heaven shines. Mr.
Giles's influence in public meetings and at all times was
for peace. He avoided controversy, especially upon
sacred subjects, usually preferring that attacks upon
himself or his views should go unanswered. He bore
no malice towards those who opposed him, and remembered nothing against them when they showed a desire
to join helpfully in the common work.

The same year that Mr. Giles became president of the
Convention he made his first trip abroad. He landed in
Liverpool, and, after some pleasant days in Scotland,
went to London, where he received a warm, even enthusiastic, welcome at the Argyle Square church. He
found himself at once among friends, for his sermons,
and especially the lectures on "The Nature of Spirit"

and on "The Incarnation and Atonement," had been widely read on the other side of the water. The members of the New Church in England were glad to see and hear and know personally one whose writings they so highly valued. Mr. Giles felt very deeply the kindness shown him on this and subsequent visits, and close friendships were formed with his English brethren. Writing home to the *Messenger*, from England, he once said, —

"I found I was not a stranger. I could not make myself one. They not only took me by the hand, but by the heart. I was a friend and a brother and at home. A feeling would sometimes come over me that I must have seen them and known them before. I hope the cordiality of my welcome and the impossibility of feeling that I was among strangers may be accounted for by the great law of spiritual association, according to which those of a homogeneous nature feel as though they had always known one another when they first meet. I am sure I shall always remember their kindness and unremitting efforts to make my visit a pleasant one, with profound gratitude. I feel that I have been greatly benefited by my intercourse with them. It has enlarged the horizon of my thoughts and affections, and enriched my mind with many charming scenes and pleasant memories, which will be a comfort and delight during my whole life."

On his first visit, in 1875, Mr. Giles attended the New-Church Conference in Manchester, as the official messenger of the Convention, and received the kindest hospitality. He continued his journey to the continent. Availing himself of the kind escort of a friend to Germany, he afterwards wandered alone into Italy, and, tempted from place to place, feeling that this was probably his only chance to see the historic cities, he visited Venice and extended his journey to Rome, seeing something of Switzerland and Paris before his return.

But the first trip to Europe was not the last. Mr. Giles visited his friends across the Atlantic five times in all. In 1878, which was the summer following his removal from New York to Philadelphia, he made his second voyage, accompanied by his wife and youngest son. The chief mission of this visit was to the New-Church friends in Paris. It is difficult for us in a country where religious thought and expression are so free, to realize the discouragements under which the little circle of New-Churchmen in Paris were struggling, oppressed by the influence of the Church of Rome, and by the government, and by their own fears. Mr. Giles was much touched by their position, especially by the noble and untiring efforts of Mlle. Holmes, now Mme. Charles Humann. He secured the kind offices of the United States government and obtained a letter to the French government from President Hayes, testifying to the orderly character of New-Churchmen in our country, which was the means of securing permission for the little circle in Paris to meet for worship unmolested. At this visit Mr. Giles assisted in the organization of the Paris Society, addressing them through an interpreter. The little circle, lonely, timid, and oppressed, received strength and hope from Mr. Giles, with his free American spirit, and his sublime confidence in the truths of the New Church and their triumph in the world. There was a delay of several weeks in receiving the necessary permission of the government, and the time was spent in part in travel. The journey included a trip to Scotland with a delightful visit in Paisley. Mr. Giles was again cordially welcomed in London ; he attended the Conference in Salford, and before sailing for home he received the warmest expressions of affection and esteem in Birmingham and Manchester.

The following year Mr. Giles again made a vacation trip to England, accompanied by one of his sons. The experiences of this journey are fully recorded in a series of interesting letters written by Mr. Giles to the *Messenger.* He preached on the steamer on the outward voyage, as he did on several of his voyages, and this time awakened a somewhat remarkable interest. He attended the Conference in Dr. Bayley's church in London. He visited Paris again, and encouraged the faithful little group of New-Churchmen in that city, baptizing some of their number. Before sailing for home he visited the beautiful church lately finished at Birmingham. The next year, 1880, Mr. Giles crossed again, accompanied by Mrs. Giles, and they enjoyed many pleasant experiences among their new and old friends in Birmingham and Manchester, and attended the Conference in Liverpool. The journey was extended to the continent, and Mr. Giles visited Mr. Mittnacht in Frankfort.

The last trip to Europe was in 1883. The chief purpose of the visit was to dedicate the new church nearly completed by the society in Paris. Mr. and Mrs. Giles sailed to Antwerp. Some time was passed at Aix-la-Chapelle, where Mr. Giles sought relief from rheumatism by using the hot baths. They visited England and found themselves among old friends, and afterwards crossed to Paris, where the new church was dedicated by Mr. Giles, assisted by the Rev. John Presland, of London.

These visits abroad, which were enjoyed through the

kindness of a friend, gave Mr. Giles rest after seasons of hard work, and the memory of them was a constant pleasure to him. They served also a very real use to the church in England and America, in strengthening the bonds of sympathy between its branches.

The first visit abroad was made while Mr. Giles was pastor of the New York Society, but before his second visit he had removed to Philadelphia. In performing the double duty of pastor and editor, Mr. Giles worked beyond his strength, and in the autumn of 1877 he was very ill. Before his health was fully restored he received an invitation from the First New-Jerusalem Society of Philadelphia to become its pastor, and he began work in the new field the 1st of January, 1878. There was an apparent lack of worldly wisdom in the change. The society in Philadelphia had been through hard experiences, and at this time was weak and distracted by conflicting elements. Its most earnest and devoted members were discouraged, and many persons who were stanch believers in the New-Church doctrines held aloof from the society. There was little interest in the public worship, and the means to support it were raised with difficulty. Of this society Mr. Giles was invited to become pastor, at a salary much less than he was receiving in New York. Why did he accept? "Because," to use his own words, "I had an assured feeling, that amounted to a certainty, that it was a call of the Divine Providence, to do a work for the New Church which I could do in no other way. I had no expectation of doing anything more than help you to become more united and work together more harmoniously and efficiently for your own spiritual good and the prosperity of the church. But so sure was I that it was a call from a higher source than your society, that I had no doubt, and no hesitation in accepting it." Mr. Giles also had in mind some books which he had not found leisure in New York to put on paper.

What Mr. Giles hoped for in coming to Philadelphia he saw accomplished, and much more. But he was far from taking credit to himself. It was the Lord's work, and if he was the leader in it, he was supported by faithful, devoted helpers, without whom nothing could have been done. .

It is useful to notice the more important steps by which harmony and active life grew in the society. A beginning must be made. It chanced to be the decoration of the windows of the church which the society then occupied, on the corner of Broad and Brandywine Streets. Next the purchase of a new organ was undertaken, with many misgivings. "The difficulties of paying for it," to use Mr. Giles's words, "were not overestimated. The whole machinery and all the motive power of the society were brought into requisition to raise the money. We had suppers and sales, strawberry festivals and concerts and lectures until every one was weary of them, and almost of the organ itself, which began to remind us of the necessity for renewed effort to pay for the music. I think the movement was useful to the society. It was movement, and that of itself was worth more than the organ. It awakened a more general interest in the society, brought its members together and gave them some practice in working together, and prepared them to take another step when the time came for it."

When Mr. Giles had been in Philadelphia a year the society recast its by-laws, providing for quarterly business meetings, and for a Church Committee of nine members, who should meet weekly with the pastor, to care for the spiritual welfare of the society.   In the Church Committee almost every new movement originated, and was carefully considered before being presented to the society.   Mr. Giles kept the committee on the alert to find new and better ways for the society to do its work.   It must move on, it must improve, or it would go backward.   The freest expression of opinion was encouraged in the committee, but its members learned to differ kindly, and to set aside personal preferences for the good of the society. The same spirit extended to the larger body.· No important step was taken in the committee or in the society till it could be taken with practical unanimity.

In the autumn of 1879 the New Church in Philadelphia came into unexpected prominence.   It had already been found that Mr. Giles's lectures attracted larger audiences than the church building could well accommodate, and in opening the autumn course it was decided to secure the hall of the Young Men's Christian Association, where Mr. Giles had once before lectured.   Unexpectedly the hall was refused on the ground that the New Church is not "evangelical."   The first lecture of the proposed series, on "Spiritual Death," was accordingly advertised to be given in the church, though the advertisement referred to the disappointment in not obtaining the hall. Dr. E. L. Magoon, pastor of the Baptist Church at Broad and Brown Streets, generously, and not without bringing censure upon himself, offered Mr. Giles his church.   He put his offer in writing, and with characteristic bluntness addressed Mr. Giles as "My dear Fellow-Sinner," saying, "They may deny that you are evangelical, but they will admit that we are all sinners." The newspapers of the city published the incident widely, which gave opportunity to make it generally known that "the doctrines held by Swedenborgians are evangelical in the sense of affirming and teaching the supreme and sole Divinity of Jesus Christ, and the absolute dependence of every one upon Him for salvation ; the absolute necessity of faith in Him as the Redeemer, Regenerator, and Saviour of men ; and the verbal and plenary inspiration of the Sacred Scriptures." Dr. Magoon's church was crowded to overflowing on two Sunday evenings to hear Mr. Giles. It was impossible to invite the crowds now attracted to the lectures to the little church at Broad and Brandywine Streets, and the course was continued in the Horticultural Hall, then the largest hall in the city. It needed a strong voice to fill the hall, and a clear presentation of the truth to hold the attention of the increasing audiences which gathered to hear. But Mr. Giles was fully equal to the occasion.

The same winter Mr. Giles delivered in the church a series of discourses on "The Garden of Eden," and the house was overcrowded throughout the course. These were followed by another series of discourses upon the Lord, beginning with one entitled "Who was Jesus Christ?" delivered April 4, 1880. We note the subject and the date, because in connection with this lecture a new step was taken, which, though small in itself, led to great results.

In a Church Committee meeting Mr. Giles asked what new work could be thought of to extend the influence of the society, and keep the interest of its members awake and active.   He mentioned the plan of publishing a few discourses from week to week as they were delivered, which seemed to work well and to be useful in New York. Mr. T. S. Arthur said, "Let us try it for two or three weeks at least." It was done, and the first discourse printed was the one named, of which many thousands have since been distributed.   From that time it became a custom with the society to publish Mr. Giles's discourse of one Sunday for distribution the next Sunday.   Hundreds were taken away each week, and some persons who did not attend the church received them regularly. The members of the society made it their duty to distribute the sermons wherever they might be useful.

The large attendance to hear Mr. Giles was meantime suggesting the necessity of a new and larger church. Reminding the people some years later of the beginning of this movement, Mr. Giles said, "None of you will forget how impossible of accomplishment it seemed at first to almost every member of the society.   It was too absurd to consider for a moment.   There was not sufficient money in the society to do it.   Those who put the mildest construction on the idea regarded it as most visionary and impractical, and if it had been pressed at first with any degree of pertinacity it would have been promptly rejected.   But the seed was quietly planted and began to grow."

By the 1st of June, 1881, a lot had been bought, and March 11, 1883, the church at the corner of Twenty-

second and Chestnut Streets, now occupied by the Philadelphia Society, was dedicated.   It is a beautiful church
of ample size, with a connecting building in which are a
cheerful Sunday-school room and parlors and library and
book-room.   The whole, when finished, cost about one
hundred and fifty thousand dollars, and there was practically no debt upon it at its dedication.   Still better than
this was the harmony which prevailed throughout the
work.   Mr. Giles writes,—

" There were differences of opinion about some minor matters of
detail, but they were amicably adjusted to the general satisfaction
of all.   It is said that no workman in the erection of the buildings
was seriously injured.   The same can be said of the feelings of the
members of the society.   It is not often that so large and important
an enterprise is carried to completion with so little friction and with
such apparent ease and general satisfaction."

The success in raising the large sum of money was due
largely to Mr. Giles's teaching that we are stewards of
the Lord's goods, which it is a duty and privilege to use
for the best interests of His kingdom.   The money for
the church was more cheerfully and probably more easily
raised than the money for an organ had been a few years
before.   The harmonious spirit of the work was also due
largely to Mr. Giles's wisdom.   When small differences
arose he laid personal preferences aside, and helped the
society to decide every question on the ground of use.
Should there be one reading-desk or two?   Mr. Giles
was here to preach the truth ; he would do it from a
music-stand if need be.   Let not any trifling external
thing cause the great spiritual use to be forgotten.

In a little more than five years Mr. Giles had brought

the Philadelphia Society from a state of discord and in-
activity to one of harmony and usefulness.   It had left a
small and unattractive church for one commodious and
beautiful.   It had become known and influential in the
city.   And not in the city alone.   A characteristic of
Mr. Giles, to which some members of the society attribute its prosperity under his care more than to any other,
was his desire to reach out to help others besides ourselves.   He recognized it as a law of life and growth that
what we have must not be enjoyed selfishly : it must be
passed on for the blessing of others.

Mr. Giles saw great value in the library and reading-
room connected with the church, and did all that he
could to develop their usefulness.   Here members of the
congregation and strangers could find New-Church books
and tracts ; and here they could meet for study and various church interests through the week.   The uses of the
book-room were organized under the name of the New-
Church Book Association of Philadelphia, of which Mr.
Giles was made president.   The work of the American
New-Church Tract and Publication Society was also
transferred to these rooms, and Mr. Giles rejoiced to see
its increasing business giving regular employment to
many of the young people of the church.   These active
uses he saw would do much to strengthen the love for
the church and to extend the influence of Sunday through
the week.

The Tract Society had been organized in 1865, some
years before Mr. Giles came to Philadelphia.   And
through the generous co-operation of the publishing
house of J. B. Lippincott & Co., at a time when the

works of Swedenborg were almost unknown to the public, and were regarded with prejudice by religious teachers, the society had done a great use in publishing the books in handsome form through the usual channels of trade. Mr. Giles was connected with the society from the time of his coming to Philadelphia, and upon the death of Mr. T. S. Arthur, in 1885, he became its president. During the years of his association with the society, and largely through his influence, its work greatly increased, especially in the publication and distribution of tracts. The printing of Mr. Giles's sermons from week to week led to a regular weekly distribution through the mails, which in time became so large that in 1888, for convenience and economy, the tracts were given the form of a periodical, with the title of *The Helper.* The work continued to grow, till a recent report of the Tract Society showed an average distribution of *Helpers* and other tracts for the year of over one thousand a day. The publication of books was meantime not neglected. In all this work Mr. Giles was the leader. He always advocated printing as the most economical and effective means of reaching the public, and did much to awaken the church to the importance of this mode of teaching. In recording their appreciation of Mr. Giles's service in its work, the managers of the Tract Society said, "He has furnished the most useful sermons and lectures and books for publication ; he has, by his broad sympathies and by his knowledge of the church throughout our country and abroad, done more than any other to lift the society's work above mere local uses to such as are of service to the church at large. His annual reports, so full of love for the cause and of confidence in its success, have called forth a general co-operation in the work of the society, till it now has friends and supporters wherever the New Church is known."

The last years of Mr. Giles's ministry were passed with the Philadelphia Society, who were his devoted friends and his faithful helpers in every enterprise. As his physical strength grew less with advancing years, he felt the need of a helper in his work. In May, 1885, the present writer was called, and for eight years and a half was his assistant and a member of his family. Mr. Giles's kindness in this relation was most generous and absolutely unfailing. He gave wise counsel, yet allowed the fullest freedom. He was patient with shortcomings, and was always ready with sympathy and encouragement.

For some years Mr. and Mrs. Giles spent their summer vacations at Lake George, in New York State. Comfortably housed in "The Sagamore," Mr. Giles enjoyed the society of friends who had cottages near by, or who came and went among the summer guests. The hotel stands on an island in the lake. The green lawn which slopes to the water is shaded by forest foliage, through which the sunshine falls upon the grass and white birch stems. Across the water rise wooded mountains, and in the lake are islands crowned with forest trees which dip their overhanging branches. The air is cool, and the scene one of peaceful beauty. Mr. Giles rested in the shade or enjoyed a drive over the hills with friends ; or he would row out into the lake, and, fastening his boat to an overhanging tree, spend an hour in reading. He wrote long and careful letters to his friends, full of the peaceful beauty of his surroundings, and including, as his letters always did, uplifting, encouraging thoughts.

Sunday frequently gave opportunity for the work he loved. Service, for some seasons, was held in the woods near the hotel, where the tree-trunks and arching branches were the cathedral columns and roof, and the squirrels listened with the audience. In later years, services were held in a room of the hotel, and Mr. Giles took his turn with other ministers.

The enjoyment of natural beauty was very deep with Mr. Giles. It was to him not merely natural beauty, but he saw in everything tokens of the Lord's love and wisdom. This habit of thought, which grew with every year, had much to do with the ready illustration of spiritual truth by objects and phenomena of nature, which added so much of clearness and beauty to his preaching. He delighted also, as he looked upon the flowers or the ripening fruit, to think, "The Lord is doing this for me to-day. See His love and wisdom working before my very eyes."

On an August day, in his quiet retreat, Mr. Giles wrote in his journal,—

"Another of those calm, sweet, peaceful, and lovely Sabbath days. A perfect type of peace and heaven. I have never seen such days anywhere else. There are quiet and bright days everywhere. But here are so many concomitants, so many things that conspire to the same end. The lake sleeping and gently breathing in the bosom of the hills. The hills, steadfast and quiet in their strength, looking down and smiling upon the lake. The trees that stand as sentinels to guard the islands and lawns, and with their shade and beauty make secluded places for the people to sit and muse and let the beauty of the earth and the glory of the heavens melt into the soul.

The fleecy, gently-moving clouds whose motion suggests peaceful
rest.   All nature suggests harmony, innocence, and peace."

One July day he wrote, —

" The ground is covered with the blossoms of the chestnut-trees.
The workmen are raking them off, and they make quite a windrow.
They have done their work, and now they pass away and cease to
hinder the work of forming the fruit.   Is it not so with the natural
facts, the material ideas, in the growth of our own minds and in
every deed we do?   We gain the reason, the way of doing things.
We learn facts ; we arrange and compare them, and use them in
accomplishing our work.   But when we begin to work our mind is
not occupied with the reason, but with the work.   The natural ideas
and reasons have faded away, and are set aside.   The same principle applies to the decay of the material body.   It is a blossom
which performs an essential service, and when it has finished its use,
when it has done all it can for us, it fades and falls away, and leaves
us free from its encumbrance.   'We all do fade as a leaf.'   In this
way we can see in nature as in a perfect mirror the principles and
the methods of Infinite Wisdom in accomplishing His purposes.   The
Lord is continually working out the problems of life before our eyes."

Equally beautiful thoughts of the Lord's ever-present
love were suggested by the white summer clouds :

" They moved so gently, and their soft edges, bright with the glory
of the sun, melted into each other so tenderly, that they seemed the
perfect type of peace.   I like to think that the Lord is doing all this.
He is in all His works.   His tender mercies are over all His works.
How different nature looks when we regard it as what the Lord is
doing now !'"

It was a trial to Mr. Giles to spend weeks and months
of every year in what seemed useless idleness.   But he
found comfort in the reflection that our spiritual growth,
like the growth of a tree, is gentle and unconscious.   It
must have its times of rest :

"If a tree could keep a daily record of its life, what could it say? 'A day of sunshine. I felt warm and comfortable. A pleasant breeze moved my leaves and sent a gentle thrill through my body. But I have done nothing but breathe and exist. I do not see that I have done any good or gained any strength. Some children did come and play in my shade, and a lady remarked how tall and beautiful I was. So by the silent growth of many years I have been able to perform some use.' So it must be with men. They are collecting the natural and spiritual substances which the Lord forms into vessels for the reception of life from Him."

The peaceful beauty of the mild summer days constantly turned Mr. Giles's thoughts to the land of eternal spring. Again and again he spoke of it :

"How beautiful it will be to live where the climate is exactly suited to our tastes, where the restraints of time and space and a suffering body are removed, and there is the freest opportunity for the development and exercise of every good affection! And that life is eternal, everlasting! The spiritual world grows nearer and more substantial every day. The idea is overwhelming. To live forever! To find employment and the means of happiness, an employment which does not weary, and which is a constant source of ever-increasing delight! Can it be possible! How good and merciful the Lord must be! Why am I not more grateful? Why does not my heart open to His love? Why am I not more devoted to His service? I am old and weak, and yet I might do more. I must do more."

Rheumatism had caused Mr. Giles almost constant pain for many years. In the winter of 1890–91 he experienced for some weeks extreme suffering. Twice within a few years a slip on the ice resulted in serious injuries. But, in spite of suffering and advancing years, Mr. Giles retained remarkable strength and vigor. As late as November, 1889, he made a missionary trip to Savannah and Jacksonville, and the meeting of the Convention in 1893 was the first at which he was unable to be present and take an active part.

Mr. Giles observed the failure of his physical powers not wholly with sadness, though it was a sore trial to him to give up any useful work. It was interesting to him to study the gradual process by which one is withdrawn from the natural world. "A man is born into the world gradually," he would say, "by the development of his natural senses and faculties through many years. So he dies by the gradual closing of the means of communication with the outward world." He noticed the increasing difficulty of remembering words and bits of knowledge, and saw that in writing he could draw only from that which had become, as it were, a part of his life. He felt that he was gradually coming into the state which belongs to the spiritual world, where the external memory is closed and one retains only what has, by his living it, become a part of himself.

It was impossible for Mr. Giles to be idle. He was very industrious, and his heart was in his work. He studied and wrote as much as he was able, sometimes all day continuously, and for a few moments at a time when he could not longer hold his mind to the work. He sometimes set himself a stent, to do so much each day. In the winter of 1889–90 he wrote the little book, "Why I am a New-Churchman," in which he tried, by reference to his personal experience, to show others what blessing may be found in the truths of the New Church. The book was useful, but perhaps would have been more so if he had not through modesty made the personal references so brief. Some of Mr. Giles's earlier books we have mentioned. "The Nature of Spirit," "Our Children in the Other Life," and "The Incarnation and Atonement" were among those published while he was in New York. "Heavenly Blessedness," published in England, is a series of sermons upon the beatitudes, which I believe were delivered in Cincinnati. "The Second Coming of the Lord" and "Perfect Prayer," a series of discourses on the Lord's Prayer, were published soon after coming to Philadelphia. "Evolution" is a course of lectures delivered in Philadelphia, showing the origin of creation and development to be from above and within. "The Forgiveness of Sin," a study of the passage in Luke describing the anointing of the Lord's feet, was among the later books. "Why I am a New-Churchman" followed, and "Consolation," a message of comfort to the bereaved. To these must be added five volumes of children's stories,—"The Valley of Diamonds," "The Gate of Pearl," "The Wonderful Pocket," "The Magic Shoes," and "The Magic Spectacles,"—and sermons and lectures printed separately, some three hundred in number. There were also left in manuscript about five hundred and eighty unpublished discourses. From these the chapters of the present book have been selected ; other series of discourses may also be published as small volumes.

Mr. Giles was permitted to continue his active usefulness almost to the end of his earthly life. In the autumn of 1892, on his return from Lake George, he began a course of lectures on death and the spiritual world, which were the last discourses that he delivered. On the 20th of November he spoke extempore on "The World of Spirits," the introductory state of the other life, and he was not again able to preach. He, however, performed several services at the church and at his home during the following winter. Easter Sunday, April 2, he was present at church, and we find the note in his journal,—

"I confirmed ten young ladies this morning. It was an interesting sight. The Holy Supper was administered to over two hundred communicants, the largest number who ever partook of it at one time in our church, except at some meeting of the General Convention. I am very thankful that I was able to administer it."

The last entry in his record of official acts is under date of May 12, when he baptized a little child in his study. It was the day after his eightieth birthday, and the flowers which decorated the room in honor of the anniversary added to the beauty of the simple and impressive service.

From time to time during the winter and spring, as he had strength and relief from suffering, Mr. Giles worked upon the little book, "Consolation," in the desire to share with others the bright thoughts of death and heaven and the confidence in the Lord's eternal mercy by which he was sustained. As he received expressions of gratitude from friends and strangers for the help they had found in his preaching and writing, he felt sincerely that it was the Lord's doing, and was amazed that the Lord had been able to make him an instrument in His work of comforting and saving human souls. His cheerfulness and the pleasant humor which had always helped to lighten care for himself and others were unfailing.

The summer came, and Mr. Giles was not able to go to Lake George, but remained at home in Philadelphia.

He grew gradually more helpless in body, though his mind was clear. He had known for some years that his heart was weak and irregular in its action, and he expected that when he passed away from the natural body it would be suddenly. "I think I can see signs of it that are unmistakable," he wrote in April, 1891. "That will be pleasant. I can conceive of no way in which the transition could be more natural or more easily made. But it will be as the Lord pleases, and not as I will."

Contrary to his expectation and hope, the failure of physical strength was very gradual. It was at first hard for Mr. Giles to be waited on, but with wonderful patience he learned to intrust himself wholly to the Lord and to those about him. He became truly as a little child, and "of such is the kingdom of God." The interest in things outside of himself, especially in the church, was always active. On Sunday morning, the day before his death, greetings were received by telegram from the Boston Society, which was holding anniversary meetings. He heard the message with interest, and desired a reply to be sent. Mr. Giles counted it as one of the blessings of his illness that it brought about him his children. He had four sons and two daughters, all married and away from home. It gave him delight in his extreme weakness to remember the Lord's assurance that He gives His angels charge over us to keep us. "The Lord needs means and instruments in caring for us," he would say. "My children and the good friends about me are His angels on the natural plane." If now and then he felt himself impatient for release, he would stop and count his blessings, and say, "What am I that I should long for something better ; that I should feel that this world is not good enough for me?   I am ready now to go or stay, in the Lord's own time, as He wills."   On the 6th of November, 1893, he passed quietly away.

Mr. Giles himself once wrote,—

" Death, blessed, lovely death, opens the prison doors to the soul, breaks off our chains, and with gentle hand and smiling face leads from this land of night and storms, from this cold, inhospitable, desert land to a bright, eternal home ; a home in which we shall find those who love us ; a home to rest in, a beautiful, lovely home to live in, to love in, to find free play for every faculty, ample means for the gratification of every heavenly taste and the attainment of every heavenly purpose.   This is the blessedness to which death leads us.

" He is the most loving, gentle, and beautiful of the angels.   He comes to cherish, not to destroy; to transplant, not to kill; to awaken us from sleep, and lead us into life."

WILLIAM L. WORCESTER.

Every blessing comes ac-
cording to a law of the
Divine order. It is in the
nature of things.

When we stand in that
order we put ourselves
in the way of help -

MR. GILES'S HANDWRITING, FROM NOTES FOR AN EXTEMPORE LECTURE.

PROGRESS IN SPIRITUAL KNOWLEDGE.

"I have yet many things to say unto you, but ye cannot bear them now.

"Howbeit when he, the Spirit of truth, is come, he will guide you into all truth: . . . and he will show you things to come."
—JOHN xvi. 12, 13.

IN these words our Lord teaches us a lesson which has a most important bearing upon the condition of the human mind which is unfavorable to all progress in knowledge. We are constantly tempted to mistake the limits of our knowledge for the limits of the truth. The more ignorant men are, the greater the temptation to do it. It requires some knowledge to discover our own ignorance. Scientific men were much more disposed in former times, when there was but little knowledge of nature, to be dogmatic, and to claim that they had reached the summit of knowledge and had explored all the secrets of nature, than they are now.

We see the most remarkable exhibition of this tendency in the disposition to limit knowledge upon the most important subjects of human interest, to what has already been attained, to what was attained, we might say, centuries ago. The belief among Christians is almost universal that we have reached the limits of our knowledge of spiritual truth ; that no further progress is possible while we remain in this world ; that the doctrines of

Christianity, as they are accepted and understood in the so-called evangelical churches, are absolute truths, which cannot be superseded, and from which no advance can be made. They are the limit of our possibilities. New facts may be discovered about them ; there may be new ways of stating them, new illustrations of their truth, but there can be no advance beyond them. They mark the farthest boundaries of our knowledge. So determinate and fixed is this belief that it has passed into a maxim, that "what is true is not new, and what is new is not true."

If it is true that no farther advance in spiritual knowledge is possible, it is well to know it, that we may not waste our energies in struggling against the inevitable, but may rest and try to content ourselves in the darkness and uncertainty of our present attainments. If it is not true, then we ought to know it, that, without fear of danger to our eternal interests, we may freely and fearlessly examine all questions relating to our spiritual nature, and use all the means in our power to advance into clearer light and higher attainments. The bare possibility that we can gain a clearer and more rational light upon all the great questions of man's spiritual nature and destiny ought to be sufficient to stimulate us to the diligent use of all the means in our power to attain so important a result. Let us, then, examine the subject in the light of reason and revelation, and see what ground we have for believing that we can continually advance in spiritual knowledge, into clearer light and more certain attainments.

There is nothing in the present attainments in spiritual

knowledge so complete and satisfactory as to lead to
the conclusion that nothing more is desirable. On the
contrary, the present state of religious thought proves
directly the contrary. There has never been a time,
since the truths of Christianity were first revealed, when
there was so much difference of opinion with regard to
them, and so little heartiness in their reception as stated
in the dogmatic forms of the various churches, as there
is now. The fundamental doctrines of Christianity as
they have been held, which have been regarded as essential to salvation, are not taught with the clearness
and distinctness and directness in any of the churches
that they were formerly. The ministers themselves have
not the undoubting faith in them which the ministers of
former times had. The intelligent members of the church
do not believe them in their naked and unmodified form
as they were once believed. The doctrines formerly
accepted are not now held with that unquestioning belief
which a good Presbyterian lady once told me she had in
the Bible. "If the Bible had said that Jonah swallowed
the whale instead of the whale swallowing Jonah," she
said, "I would believe it."

There is an uncertainty, a diversity of opinion upon
what have been regarded as the fundamental doctrines
of Christianity which is increasing rather than diminishing. The Trinity, the Atonement, the Resurrection, the
nature of our own existence after Death, the Inspiration
of the Bible,—questions which form the basis of all religious belief, are discussed with greater zeal than they
ever were, and there is a greater variety of opinion upon
these doctrines, among those who believe in them in

some sense, than ever before.   The opinions range
through all shades from a merely nominal acceptance of
the doctrines to that belief which admits of no doubt because it admits of no examination.   Is it rational to suppose that this confusion of tongues, this variety of opinion
and even contradiction of belief, this uncertainty and
doubt upon questions which relate to man's highest interests, is the best which man is capable of attaining?
Is he forbidden to advance beyond the twilight and confusion of mere opinion?   It seems to be contrary to the
nature of the human mind and the purposes of the Divine
love and wisdom that it should be so.

But if any one is disposed to deny that there is this
diversity of opinion, and to assert that the fundamental
doctrines of Christianity, as formally held by Christians,
are generally accepted without any doubts as to their
truth, it still holds that they go only a very little way in
spiritual knowledge.   It is acknowledged that the doctrines themselves are not and cannot be understood.
They are great mysteries which the human mind, in this
life, cannot fathom.   The Trinity is a mystery, and the
more it is discussed and explored the greater the confusion.   The Incarnation of God, and the manner in which
He effected human redemption by assuming a human
nature, is a mystery which, it is generally acknowledged,
cannot be understood.   The Resurrection is a mystery
which must be simply accepted as a fact, but which cannot be explained.   We are taught that we are to live forever, and at the same time we are told that we can have
no certain knowledge of the modes and forms and nature
of the life after death.   These great facts are affirmed in

the most positive manner, and just enough is taught
about them to awaken interest and lead to their examination, and then we are told that they cannot be understood ; we must accept them by an act of faith. Suppose the doctrines are true, how little they have done for
man !

Now, I ask, is it reasonable to suppose that the Lord
intended this to be the extent of human attainment upon
these great themes which relate to man's highest interests? Does it accord with the nature of the human
mind? Is it consonant with His oft-repeated declaration
in His Word that a true knowledge of God is of vital
importance to man, that to know Him aright is life everlasting? Does it seem to be consistent with the goodness and wisdom of God that He should tantalize us with
expectations which He forbids us to realize, and give us
problems impossible of solution, which rend the soul
in its efforts to reach the unattainable? What else does
He leave in such a fragmentary and unsatisfactory condition? It is like bringing the tree to leaf and bud, and
arresting its progress before attaining the glory of blossom and the blessing of fruit ; it is causing hunger and
thirst and providing no means to satisfy them ; it is giving to the material body the power of growing into the
beauty of womanhood and the strength of manhood and
withholding the means of growth, leaving it in helpless
infancy, cursed by eternal feebleness ; it is endowing
man with the power of perceiving a few rays of the morning twilight, and awakening in him the expectation of
the coming sun, and then leaving him in that expectation
while its coming is withheld. It is contrary to every

principle of the human mind, and to all the Divine methods so far as we have any knowledge of them. We conclude, therefore, that the Lord never intended to arrest man's progress in the knowledge of spiritual truth, and stay his footsteps on the threshold of knowledge, while the whole universe of truth lies waiting to be explored.

But we are not left to conjecture or to our own reasoning upon this subject. The Lord has declared, as clearly as human language can express a truth, that it is the purpose of His heart to communicate His love and wisdom to men. He desires to communicate Himself. He gave the Word for this purpose. He came in the flesh to be a light to the world. He attributes every loss and sorrow to ignorance of Him, and every possible attainment and joy to a true knowledge of His nature and relations to men.

The words of our text are an explicit declaration of the fact that progress in spiritual knowledge is possible. "I have yet many things to say unto you." We cannot suppose that these words applied to the disciples alone. They must be of universal application. They are as true of the highest angel as of the child just born. The Lord is infinite, man is finite. The Lord has a perfect knowledge of all causes in all their possible forms and relations and effects to eternity. He knows the influence of every affection, thought, and act upon our whole future, in all its combinations and its relations to every other thought and act and being. He sees the end from the beginning of every particular in our lives.

How little the wisest men know, even of natural forms

and substances! Our knowledge is limited almost entirely to appearances and to a few links in the chain of cause and effect. We know that when light flows into the eye we can see, but we do not know how such a force, flowing into such a form, produces such an effect. We know that the undulations of the air flowing into the ear cause hearing; we know some facts about the relation of the air to the ear, but why its inflowing should produce the effect it does no one can tell. Great progress has been made in natural science during the last century, but the relation of the known to the unknown is no greater than the smallest fraction to the infinite. Swedenborg says that the wisest angels see that their knowledge, compared with what there is to be known, is so infinitesimal that they simply say they do not know anything. Every finite intelligence, however great its advancement in knowledge,—and in the coming eternity that knowledge must be so great that we have no words to express it or power to conceive of it,—will stand upon the shore, while the ocean of truth stretches away into the infinite distance before it. The time can never come when the Lord will not have many things to say unto us.

This idea, at the first view, may appear to be discouraging. Must we be learners forever? Shall we never get to the end of our lessons? What is the use of learning if we can never reach the goal? We know it to be true that the more we know the more we see there is to be known. The higher we rise, the wider the horizon. This should not discourage us, because the acquisition of knowledge upon every subject which interests us is a source of pleasure. Knowledge is also intellectual and spiritual power and wealth.   People never complain because they have more chances of gaining power and riches.   Every new truth enlarges man's means and capacities for happiness.   Why, then, should he desire to have the sources of truth, and his ability to gain it, exhausted?   The fact that they can never be exhausted, that the Lord will always have many things to say to us, is the hope and the assurance that the means of happiness will never fail.

Limited knowledge does not necessarily imply false knowledge.   If we know but little, that little may be true as ·far as it goes.   When the school-boy has only learned that two and two make four, he has not made much progress in the science of numbers, but he has learned something which he will never need to unlearn.   So it is with regard to every subject of human knowledge.   When we have learned the single truth that God is one in essence and person, we have not advanced very far in a knowledge of His attributes, but we have learned an absolute truth which we shall never find occasion to unlearn.   It is as true for the highest angel as it is for the little child.   Every new fact adds new clearness and interest to those we have already learned.   For this reason our interest in learning and our happiness in gaining knowledge will continue to increase forever.

The fact, therefore, that the Lord has many things to say unto us, and will always have many things to say unto us, holds out to us the grandest hopes for the future.   He will always have something new to tell us, and there will always be the zest and joy of learning from Him.   He will always have many things to teach us about the laws of our own nature, about our relations to others. He will always have many things to reveal to us concerning His own love and wisdom, and His infinite tenderness and care for us. He will always have many things to reveal to us concerning the excellence and beauty and grandeur of the world around us, and concerning His infinite wisdom in adapting it to human wants, and in making it a means of support and culture and happiness. The instructed mind sees a multitude of substances and forces and beauties in the material world which no one saw a century ago ; and when we pass out of the twilight of this dead, material world into the brightness and the perfections of the substantial, living, spiritual world, He will show us innumerable things ineffably more beautiful and nicely adapted to all our wants, ministering to a higher culture and a more exquisite happiness.

The reason is often asked why the Lord does not speak to us more plainly. The question is often put to New-Churchmen, why the Lord did not make known the truths of the New Church before, if they are so great an advance upon former knowledge upon spiritual subjects. Our Lord gives the answer to all these questions in the words, "But ye cannot bear them now." The Lord reveals the truth to us as fast as we can bear it. What He can tell us is not limited by His knowledge or power or willingness to communicate, but by our ability to receive.

The word translated "bear" may mean to understand. "I have yet many things to say unto you, but ye cannot understand them now." We have conclusive evidence in the Gospels that the disciples did not understand many things which our Lord spake to them. This is true of all disciples.   It is true of natural and of spiritual knowledge.   When a child takes its first lesson in mathematics, in its ignorance and innocence it might say to the teacher, "Tell me all about the whole science of numbers."   The teacher could only reply, "I cannot do it."   "Why can you not do it?"   "Because you cannot bear such knowledge now.   Mathematics is a great and complicated science, and it requires much study and severe discipline of the mind to understand it.   I will tell you about it as fast as you can bear it."

If this is true of a natural science, how much more must it be true in relation to the great problems of man's spiritual nature and destiny !   They lie above the senses and the appearances of nature ; they relate to interior and hidden things.   Man's progress in the knowledge of the outer world has been remarkably slow, though its phenomena have been continually present to the senses, and its forces have been continually offering themselves to his service, to fight his battles, bear his burdens, and do his work.   The wind and the rain, the sun and the earth, were constantly whispering their secrets in his ear, but he could not hear their voice.   How, then, could we expect that man could understand those higher truths which relate to his spiritual wants and destiny?   If it was many thousands of years before man could discover the forces in steam, the existence and use of magnetism, and the nature of the substances which contain so many elements which contribute to his comfort and happiness, is it incredible that it should require an equal number of years before he could be prepared to receive interior spiritual truth?

But the words "ye cannot bear them now" mean more than inability to understand : they mean indifference and hostility to spiritual truth. There is an inherent repugnance in the natural mind to spiritual truth. It is more than ignorance, or incapacity, or indifference : it is hostility ; it is opposition of nature. It is like the repugnance which we find in the material body to certain substances. We use this very term concerning them. We say we cannot bear the smell or taste or sight of them. The natural degree of the mind has fallen. All its tastes have become perverted. It looks downward and outward to material things. It does not act in harmony with the spiritual mind. It does not like to hear anything about a spiritual world. It cannot conceive of a distinctly spiritual existence. Something akin to nausea is excited by hearing about the spiritual sense of the Word.

When our Lord said to His disciples that He had many things to say unto them, He evidently did not mean that he had many more natural facts to teach them about Himself or His mission in this world, because He never did speak much more to them about these things. His meaning was more plain as He went on to say, "But when he, the Spirit of truth, is come, he will guide you into all truth. . . . He shall receive of mine and shall show it unto you." He shall show you the spiritual meaning of the words which have been spoken unto you, for they are spirit and life. They could not bear their spiritual import then.

Many Christian people are in the same state now. They can talk about religion ; they can pray with fervor and sing with delight. But they cannot bear to think that the Bible has a spiritual meaning. The idea that the spiritual world is a substantial and really-existing world ; that man himself, as to his spirit, is in the human form and fully organized as a man seems absurd to them. The idea that the old, familiar Bible is luminous with infinite truth, and that they have drawn their doctrines and formed their opinions from the appearances of truth in the letter ; that their minds are veiled and over-shadowed with the clouds of the letter, while the un-veiled and glorious sun shines in clear radiance about them, they cannot bear. But when the spiritual truth, not the letter of it, but the Spirit of truth, comes,—and He will come when men will open their minds to receive Him,—He will show them many things which they never dreamed of before. He will show them things to come. These things are not natural events that will occur in the church in after-times, as most commentators have sup-posed, but spiritual things. A new and more accurate knowledge of the Lord,—"He shall receive of mine, and show it unto you ;" a more accurate and a larger knowledge of our own nature and destiny. He will show you things to come in the spiritual world. He will reveal to you the laws of the spiritual universe, and show you how surpassingly beautiful and glorious it is. He will make real to you your eternal home, and lead you into it.

When the Spirit of truth begins to shine in our under-standings, a new and glorious day is dawning upon us ; a sun is rising which will never set. As the mind opens to the reception of this light, it enlarges, and can receive more of the many things which the Lord has to say to us. It also improves in strength and quality. It can receive higher truths, clearer light ; it has a more comprehensive and delicate capacity for reception ; it can receive larger and richer and more ·exquisite joys. It will continue to advance towards the Lord with constantly accelerating velocity ; its power of reception from the Lord will continue to increase, and yet the Lord will always have many things to say that are more glorious and that will fill the soul with a constantly deeper and more exquisite joy. May we be among the number of those who have clear eyes and listening ears and open hearts to receive the many things which the Lord has to say to us, and which His Spirit of truth is ever ready to show unto us.

THE DOCTRINES OF THE NEW CHURCH
A SPIRITUAL SCIENCE.

"Behold, I make all things new."—REVELATION xxi. 5.

WE live in a miraculous age. Our lot has been cast
in the midst of those tremendous changes in man's
spiritual condition which could be fitly typified only by
the most stupendous convulsions in the material world,
—by the darkening of the sun in the heavens, the falling
of the stars from their places ; by conflagrations and
cosmic storms ; and by the creation of new heavens and
a new earth.

It is our happiness as New-Churchmen to know the
meaning of these prophetic symbols, and, secure from
harm from these convulsions, and unterrified by the
noise and wild fury of old systems falling to ruin, and the
collision of chaotic forms of belief, to stand upon the
new earth rising fresh and fair from the ruins of the old,
and to see the new heavens, clear and serene, overarch-
ing human life,—heavens whose moon is brighter than
the sun of the former age, and whose sun shines with
seven-fold splendor.

I ask your attention to one of the distinct and peculiar
characteristics of this age. one which clearly entitles it to
the claim of being the fulfilment of the Divine promise,
"Behold, I make all things new ;" which will make it

enduring as the power of the Lord to create human souls,
will give it the excellence of heavenly graces, the beauty of
heavenly forms, the power and glory of Divine truth, and
imbue it with the blessedness of heavenly peace ; which
will make it the Lord's kingdom on earth. I say, "will
make it," for this new day of the Lord, even to the most
advanced minds, is yet only in the gray of the morning.
Its full-orbed sun is yet below the horizon, and the mass
of the people are still asleep in the shadow of the valley.
Some of them are indeed stirred by a new breath of
power, but "whence it cometh and whither it goeth"
they cannot tell. It is the unconscious influence of the
Divine force which precedes the light, which opens the
eyes and prepares them for its reception. But enough
of the light has been seen by some minds, watching for
the morning, to reveal its true nature and to give undoubted assurance that it is not the twilight of an age
passing away, but the morning of a spiritual age which
is new in spirit, new in form, new in power, and will be
new in life. The characteristic of the new age to which
I invite your attention is one peculiar to its genius, which
gives it a surpassing excellence. I propose to speak of
the truths of the New Church as a spiritual science.

By science I mean the laws of the Divine order as they
exist in the creation, the methods of the Divine wisdom
in effecting the purposes of the Divine love in their connections and relations. The Lord's methods of working
in nature constitute natural science. When we discover
those methods and the relation of one substance and of
one form to another, and of causes to their effects, that
knowledge constitutes science. Science treats of sub-

stances and forces and forms in their connections and relations, and reveals the laws and methods by which many things make one. Science is spiritual when it · relates to spiritual subjects. The same conditions are essential to a spiritual as to a natural science. Let us consider what those conditions are.

First, science must be based upon facts. It is as impossible to construct a science without facts as it is to build a stone wall without stones. Science cannot be constructed with fancies, or opinions, or of facts even as they appear to the senses. Nor can it be formed by a mere accumulation of facts. Science is formed by insight into the intrinsic forms and qualities of isolated facts, by which their relations to other facts are seen, and the higher laws and qualities common to all the particular facts are discovered. It is now known that all the kingdoms of nature, and all the individuals in each kingdom, are bound together, penetrated, and moved by substances and forces of a finer and more subtile nature than the coarse concrete forms which clothe and hide them. The knowledge of these forces and the laws according to which they act upon every particular object, and of how the stone and plant and animal welcome and treat, receive or reject, use or reflect these, to them, heavenly visitors, is the science of nature.

Spiritual science requires spiritual facts. These are given us in the doctrines of the New Church. Swedenborg's introduction into the spiritual world, and his statement, from living experience, of what is done there by the Lord and angels and spirits, was just as necessary to a spiritual science as a man's introduction into this world and the ability to see and hear what the Lord is doing here, and what men are doing, and how they are doing it, is an essential condition of any natural science. The claim of Swedenborg to have done this, a claim to which men take strong exceptions, is absolutely essential to the work he performed. His doctrines of man's nature and relations are not based upon fancies or opinions, but upon facts, upon what takes place in the spirit. He has also rendered to men this further service and given this larger evidence of the truth of his claims ; he has shown us how to descend from the palaces of spiritual truth into the paradise of nature, and to find the higher laws of the spirit ruling in corresponding forms and working by similar methods in animal, plant, and mineral.

One of the causes which has made the endless discussion of religious questions so fruitless in results is the want of any fixed and clearly-defined subject of spiritual knowledge. The New Church stands on the solid basis of spiritual substance. It deals with realities. The spiritual world is the real world, the spirit is the real man ; its laws of culture and development are as definite and immutable as the laws of nature ; they are also ascertainable and capable of precise application. We have the same basis for progress in spiritual knowledge and life that we have for progress in natural knowledge and life in this world. The spiritual body is presented to us for examination, as real and substantial as the material body which is presented to the physiologist for his study. We are introduced into a distinct and substantial world, and we are furnished with true principles for our guidance. So far as regards a substantial basis, therefore, we are as thoroughly equipped for progress in spiritual knowledge for the attainment of some distinct and desirable end as the men of science are for knowledge of physical laws and their use in our natural progress.

There is also no dearth of material for endless advance in spiritual knowledge. The science of correspondences, which reveals the definite relation between natural effects and spiritual causes, opens in nature, and especially in the natural symbols of the Sacred Scriptures, exhaustless depths of spiritual knowledge. Every natural object and act mentioned in the Scriptures is the outward form and expression of a spiritual fact or a series of facts, one lying within the other, and all so connected and related that they reveal the means and the order of man's spiritual creation and of his relations to the Source of life. We shall never want for facts, therefore. Science will sooner exhaust nature than any finite mind can exhaust the forms of spiritual truth contained in the Sacred Scriptures.

The doctrines of the new age possess also in an eminent degree the second essential of a true science ; they are organized truth. They are not assertions made upon personal authority ; they are not detached and unrelated truths ; much less are they conflicting statements which destroy one another. They bear the same relation to spiritual facts that a house does to the materials of which it is constructed, or that the wonderful structure of the body bears to the food which nourishes it. They are a symmetrical whole, composed of intimately related parts, a house fitted to be the home of heavenly affections and the indwelling life of the Lord.

Science teaches us how to use facts. Rational knowledge shows the ratio or relation of one thing or of one being to another, by which the unity of life is discovered. The plan and form and function of the various mental faculties are shown by true spiritual science. In this respect we are better equipped for spiritual progress than the scientific man is for natural progress. Here we find again the inestimable service which Swedenborg has rendered us. He has given us the laws of spiritual life as they are derived from the Lord and exist in man. We have only to learn them and to examine spiritual facts in their light to see their true nature and relations. We can verify the general law by particular facts. The principle is seen at first in outline more or less distinctly ; but every new particular fills up the outline, brings new light to it, and is a new witness to its truth. Having rational knowledge we know how to dispose of the facts as we learn them. We see their relations to other facts and to the central principle which underlies the whole. They fall into their places and tend to unity. Beneath the illusion of appearances we see order, harmony, and the most powerful forces working according to immutable law for human good.

This is a new and distinct step, and gives man the same help in spiritual progress that a rational knowledge of the substances and forces of nature has given him in natural progress. It forms a basis on which he can stand. It gives him power to wield his materials, to build up his life, and to come into orderly and helpful relations to others. His knowledge changes from a thicket, in which he gets entangled by a multiplicity of apparently unrelated and incongruous forms, to a garden with sure paths which lead from blossom to fruit, from labor to attainment. ˙He comes out of confusion and chaos into harmonious and established order.

The doctrines of the New Church are a statement of the laws of man's regeneration, spiritual culture, and growth in heavenly life, and of his relations to the Lord, to angels, spirits, and men ; to the spiritual world on one side of his nature, and to the material world on the other. They possess all the qualities of a true science of the spirit ; they will meet every requirement for the most varied and fullest development of our spiritual faculties and the attainment of every natural, spiritual, and heavenly good which man can conceive and the Lord can give.

Science not only introduces us into a world of new truths, gives us clearer light, enlarges the horizon of thought, and reveals to us the beauty and harmony of the Divine order, but it teaches us how to employ the substances and forces we have discovered for our own use. We are all familiar with the achievements of natural science in this respect. It has discovered and brought into common use tireless forces of exhaustless power which bear our burdens, run upon our errands, do our work, and minister to our comfort in manifold ways. Science has not only revealed them, but it has taught us how to use them. It has harnessed them to our service ; it has put the reins into our hands by which we can control and guide them. Spiritual science will render the same service to us on the spiritual plane of life. It not only introduces us into a new world of spiritual truth, illuminates the understanding with its light, and charms the soul with its beauty ; it not only places us in the midst of the Divine harmonies and unveils the forms of spiritual substances and forces as much superior to natural forces in power and capacity for human good as the soul is more excellent than the body, but it teaches us how to use them to overcome our spiritual enemies, to remove the obstacles to our progress, and to help us in the development of our noblest faculties and the attainment of our highest good.

There is conclusive evidence that men, urged by their needs and stimulated by their hopes, are demanding a knowledge of spiritual truth which is based on facts, which is logically consistent, and leads to practical results. Wearied with fruitless labor, distracted with doubts, tormented by conflicting passions, despairing of help from the past, hungry for meat that will feed their famished souls, and with aspirations for a higher life than they have found the method and means of obtaining, they are waiting in despair or turning with hope to a new day. They find that all things in the material world are related and indissolubly bound together ; that unconnected existence, even for the stone, is impossible. They see method, order, subordination existing in all things great and small, and immutable law governing all the Lord's operations in nature, and they logically conclude that the same principles and methods rule in the realm of spirit. They see that the Lord does not work at random in the creation and development of the plant and the material body, and they pertinently ask why He should do it in the formation of the spirit. All the tendencies of the age, all its movements, its hopes, and even its doubt and denial and despair, and all those subtile and delicate but powerful currents which sway the feelings before they awaken thought, which kindle hope and turn the face in the direction of the new light, point with unerring finger to a scientific and rational knowledge of spiritual truth ; they prophesy the existence of an order, method, and law of the spirit, of the same nature as those which exist in the material universe. The claim that a spiritual science is possible does not come from a few minds alone disaffected with the confusion and comparatively fruitless religious doctrines of the past ; it comes from every form and movement in nature ; the stone embodies it, the grass and the vine and every tree of the forest speak of it, the instinct of the animal proclaims it. Every principle in man's nature declares the possibility of a spiritual science, because it is itself the embodiment of it. But especially the rational faculties of the mind demand rational knowledge as the eye demands light, the fin water, the wing air, and the body food ; and whatever the Lord has given man the power to want, He has provided the means to supply. The existence of a Divine order in spiritual growth and attainment is certain, and the ability of man to receive and understand the knowledge of it and come into the life and joy of it is as sure as that plants will blossom and bear fruit, and that seedtime and harvest will continue.

Let us then notice some of the effects which a rational knowledge of spiritual truth and a life conformable to that knowledge must legitimately and certainly produce. Fortunately we are not left to conjecture concerning these results. We have a complete demonstration of the power of rational knowledge in the miracles which science has wrought on the natural plane of life. If a true knowledge of the forms, forces, and qualities of nature can change the face of the world, modify all human conditions, and bring into the service of man a multitude of powerful, tireless forces to bear his burdens, run upon his errands, and in manifold ways minister to his wants, what limits can we assign to the power of a rational knowledge of spiritual substances and the laws of their activities and relations? The results of such knowledge must be as much greater and more beneficent in the spiritual realm of life as the knowledge itself is higher in degree and more excellent in its forms. It is not possible to over-estimate its beneficent effects, for it is a knowledge of causes, of vital forces ; it deals with the sources of power ; it is the true knowledge of God and of man and of their relations to each other.

The effects of a rational knowledge of spiritual truth will be both negative and positive. The truth not only gives man power and light, but it frees him from many obstacles to his progress. The truth makes him free.

It frees him from groundless fears. When we do not know the way we fear that every step may lead to danger. It is natural for us to fill the unknown with terrors. Before the light of science had dawned upon the earth, any deviation from the accustomed order of nature, as an eclipse of the sun or moon, filled the minds of men with superstitious fears. They trembled at the dire calamities which they supposed such phenomena to forebode. The same occurrence now gives pleasure to millions, and is the means of much useful knowledge. In spiritual life men are tormented and held in cruel bondage by groundless fears. There is the fear of coming evils which never come and have no existence ; the fear that the Lord is our enemy when He is our infinite and unchangeable Friend ; the fear of death as the most terrible calamity, when it is an orderly step in life ; and a multitude of other fears, wholly groundless, which destroy man's peace and paralyze his power. A knowledge of spiritual truth will disperse the darkness of ignorance in which these spiritual fears are bred, chase them away as the coming sun dispels the night and all its hideous forms.

Again, genuine spiritual knowledge will free the mind from doubt. Man's progress in spiritual life is constantly retarded by doubts. He goes to and fro instead of moving on to new attainments ; he stands still instead of advancing ; he rejects the truth when offered to him ; his steps are halting, his courage weak ; he hesitates and lingers and is distracted by conflicting influences, misses the chances of life, and fails of any great attainment in spiritual development, because he is not sure of the path which leads to it. The misgivings, the fears and torments which the noblest minds have suffered from this cause are one of the most mournful phases in the sad history of humanity. Men do not doubt about what they know ; it is when they do not know, or when they see in the twilight only the flitting forms of appearances that they doubt. Genuine knowledge carries the conviction of certainty with it. This is the effect of the doctrines of the New Church upon those who know them. This benign power will increase until all doubts are dispelled, and man will walk in the freedom and joy of the new light, with firm and sure steps, in a straight path to the attainment of the highest ends.

A result of rational knowledge is constant increase of light. Every new truth verifies the principle to which it relates. Every new truth is a new star in the firmament of the mind. All progress in knowledge, natural as well as spiritual, is from evening to morning, and from morning to bright day. Many have accepted the doctrines of the New Church, at first with a hope tremulous with fear that they might come to a point where they would find their way obstructed with insoluble problems and darkness again gathering over them. But it has been their blessed experience to find the way becoming clearer; difficulties vanish, problems which were supposed to be beyond human skill to solve yield readily to the new power, paths open into broad spaces which seemed closed to human approach, mysteries are understood, and light increases at every step. When we come into the harmonies of the Divine order we begin to see truth in the light of truth. Genuine truth is its own witness; it shines with its own light, it reveals its own nature, and it fills the mind with light. This is the history of science, and it accords with the experience of every man and woman who has come into the light of the new age.

This gradual and constant increase of light also produces a conviction, which finally amounts to a certainty, that we are on the right road to the attainment of the end we are seeking. When we discover new truths in harmony with those already known, we get new and stronger confirmations of what we have already learned;

we are attracted by the new beauty, we are stimulated
to new activity, we are always attaining ; new gates open
into broader fields of truth, and the certainty of convie-
tion that we are on the right path which leads to the ever-
receding goal of perfection fills the mind with a sweet and
profound peace.   We are coming into the order of the
Divine wisdom ; we see the way to make ourselves a part
of the Divine harmony.   .

It is a remarkable fact in the history of humanity that
men have regarded those who were the most friendly to
them as their direst enemies, and those steps in life which
have been provided by infinite love and wisdom for their
highest good as the most terrible calamities.   They have
fled from their friends, they have been blind to the richest
treasures of truth which lay before them, they have been
tormented with groundless fears, have wandered in darkness when the light was shining all around them, and
have been crushed with self-imposed burdens when almighty power was offered to lift them from their shoulders.
The rational knowledge of the new age clears away all
these shadows, dispels the appearances which have surrounded human life with illusions, and places man in the
midst of forces of omnipotent power friendly to every
human interest, and teaches him how to use them for the
development of the highest plane of his being.   It gives
him definite, practical knowledge.   It reveals to him the
true ends of life, puts the means of attaining them into
his hand, and shows him how to use them.   It must,
therefore, render him the same service as a spiritual being,
as a citizen of a spiritual world in which he is to find his
home and to dwell forever, that a knowledge of the finer

substances and forces of nature has rendered him as a material being and son of earth and time. It must change the whole aspect of human life ; it must give an immense impulse to progress in spiritual knowledge ; it must give fulness, clearness, directness, and precision to every effort for spiritual culture ; it must bring man into such relations to the Lord that he will know what to do and how to do it to come into orderly relations with Him, and to open every faculty of the soul to Divine influence, to be with the Lord where He is, and thus to dwell in the centres of life and move in the peaceful currents of the Divine order to the attainment of new joys and the rest of an ever-deepening peace. It must make all things new.

We stand in the morning of this new day ; its privileges and its responsibilities rest upon us. No men ever had greater interests committed to them ; no men ever possessed larger means and grander opportunities for their own spiritual attainment and to make themselves a blessing to humanity. Much has been given to us ; much will be required of us. Let us be faithful to our trusts ; let us counsel wisely and labor diligently to make known to men those spiritual and Divine truths in which the Lord is making His second coming to men, and by which He will subdue all things unto Himself.

GOD AND MAN.

" So God created man in his own image, in the image of God created he him."—GENESIS i. 27.

THERE are two vital questions which lie at the foundation of every religion and give quality to it. These questions are, first, Who is God, and how shall we think of Him? Second, What is man, and how are God and man related to each other? Neither of these questions can be understood without some knowledge of the other. They are reciprocally and intimately related. It is impossible to gain a true idea of God without some true knowledge of man, and it is impossible to gain an adequate conception of man's nature without some correct knowledge of God. Man was created in the image of God. We must, therefore, look to man to get our first hints of the form and nature of God. I propose to state, as far as I can in limited space, what the New Church teaches upon this subject.

The doctrines of the New Church are Unitarian in the assertion that there is one and only one Supreme Being. They are Trinitarian in teaching the Divinity of Jesus Christ. They differ essentially from both in showing that the whole Trinity is embodied in the one person of our Lord and Saviour Jesus Christ, and that these three essentials of His nature constitute His Divine personality. This is in accordance with all that He says about Himself in the whole of Scripture when rightly understood. The

94

apostle declares it in the plainest manner when he says, "In him," that is in Jesus Christ, "dwelleth all the fulness of the Godhead bodily." The Lord Jesus Christ affirms it when He says, "The Father dwelleth in me." "He that hath seen me hath seen the Father." "The Father is in me, and I in him." By this He means that there is a reciprocal and organic union between them, like that which exists between man's soul or mind and his body. The Father is the Divine nature as it is in its uncreated and infinite essence; the Son is the human nature, glorified and made Divine, both united in one person, one being, and making one God, as man's spiritual nature and his physical are united in one human being and make one man. The Father, called in the Old Testament Jehovah and God, is within the Son, as man's mind is in his body. The Divine and the human natures are distinct and yet so closely knit together that they form one person, one being. This union is not one of sentiment, or agreement in character or purpose, like that which may exist between two men who desire to accomplish the same purpose and agree in the means of doing it. It is an organic union; it is of the same nature as that which exists between the mind and the body, between will and act. Such being the intimate, organic, perfect union between the Father and the Son, we do not divide them in thought or affection. When we think of the Son we think of the Father, as we think of the whole man when we think of his body. We think of Him in the human form, and we have a distinct object of thought. When we love the Son we love the Father, and we have a distinct object in our minds for our affections to rest upon. They are not divided between two. They are centred in one. Only one person can be supremely loved.

Having gained a distinct conception of the personal unity of God, we can see that the Divine attributes cannot be divided between two persons. They must all be combined in one person, in the one person of our Lord Jesus Christ. Mercy and truth meet together in Him. Righteousness and peace kiss each other in Him. Mercy and justice join hearts and hands in His Divine person. This new doctrine solves the problem of the unity of person and the trinity in the Divine Being. It harmonizes all the Divine attributes, and presents to us one Divine Being in the human form, animated with human love and doing all things for human good. We may no longer pray to one Divine person to grant us favors for the sake of another, for there is only one Divine person. We no longer fear the wrath of an angry God, for there is no angry God. Jesus Christ is Immanuel, God manifest in the flesh, and He is not angry. His infinite heart is full of love for men. We only fear to sin against such infinite wisdom and unchanging love. Every one must be able to see that such a clear, distinct, harmonious, rational knowledge of God and His Divine attributes must clear the mind of its doubts and conflicting opinions, must quiet its groundless fears, and tend to bring it into harmonious, orderly, and more intimate relations with Him whom to know aright is life everlasting.

The New Church gives us new, rational, and satisfactory knowledge concerning man as a spiritual being and his relations to the Lord, who is his Creator, Redeemer, Saviour, and the constant source of all his power and life.

The human spirit has generally been regarded in the Christian world as a force, as an unorganized, unsubstantial, formless essence, as a breath, an influence, bearing somewhat the same relation to the man himself that steam bears to the engine. All conceptions of it have been vague and unsatisfactory. There has been but little advance beyond the mere affirmation of its existence. Consequently all ideas about its nature and modes of operation have been vague, indistinct, and unreal.

The New Church regards the spirit in an entirely new way. According to its doctrines the spirit is the man himself in the human form, and the seat of all his power and life. It is organized of spiritual substances, as the material body is organized of material substances, and possesses all the organs, external and internal, in general and particular, that compose the material body. It has a head, trunk, and limbs. It has eyes and ears, brain and face and vocal organs, heart and lungs, arteries and veins and nerves. The spiritual organs perform relatively the same functions that the material organs perform. Spiritual lungs breathe a spiritual atmosphere ; the heart propels a spiritual blood through arteries and veins ; the nerves give sensation and power ; the hands can grasp spiritual objects, and the feet can walk upon a spiritual earth ; the eye opens to the light which flows from the spiritual sun, and the ear vibrates in harmony with the modulations of the spiritual atmosphere.

As a whole and in each least part the spirit is in the human form. The common idea has been that the body was first formed and then the spirit was breathed into it, as men make an engine and then set it in motion by steam. The new doctrine teaches that the spirit itself moulds the body into its own form, weaves its fine and delicate textures in its own loom, and clothes itself in every least part with it, making it a medium of communication with the material world, the house in which it dwells, a complicated and miraculous instrument adjusted with infinite precision to all the forms and forces of matter, for the purpose of gaining natural ideas and delights to serve as materials for the development of the affections and the intellectual faculties.

But this is merely a temporary service. The material body renders the same service to the spirit that the husk does to the corn, the chaff to the wheat. The spirit is immortal. It was made, and by its very nature ordained, to dwell in a spiritual world corresponding to its own nature. But it must have a basis to rest upon. It must have vessels to hold its fine and fluent substances while they are being prepared for distinct and permanent existence.

According to this idea the spirit is the real, substantial man and the seat of all human power. It is the spiritual eye that sees. The material eye only serves as an optical instrument to bring it into such relations to material light that images of material things can be formed on its delicate canvas. The material ear cannot hear. It is the spiritual ear within that becomes moved by its vibrations and perceives harmonious or discordant sounds. The same is true of all the senses. They are simply the material instruments which the spiritual senses use to gain entrance into the material world and accommodate themselves to its substances and forces.

Men have so long been accustomed to regard the spirit as a formless essence, a merely abstract entity, that it is difficult to disabuse their minds of the error and convince them that the spirit is organic and substantial. It is generally supposed that the way to gain any true conception of spirit is to deny it all the qualities of matter. It seems to be taken for granted that only matter possesses substance and form, and that when we attribute these properties to spirit we materialize it. But this is not so. There are some attributes that are essential to existence. It is impossible to conceive of the existence of any object that is destitute of substance and form. The essential idea of existence is that of standing forth in substance and form. Every one will acknowledge that God is the most real and substantial being in the universe. He must be substance and form in their origin and essential qualities. There can be no power without some substance that embodies it. It inheres in the nature of things and in the nature of human conceptions, that if there is a Divine Being, there must be Divine substances ; if there are spiritual beings and a spiritual world, there must be spiritual substances and spiritual forms. To deny their existence is denial of God and of everything that is not material.

But we have ocular demonstration that spirit is substance and form and possesses power. This is a kind of testimony that men have often demanded. "Show me a spirit," they say ; "let me feel it. Let me see spirit exert itself and produce some sensible effect." The truth is, all that is done by the body is done by the spirit's power. There is no power in the material substances that compose the material body to organize themselves into the human form and acquire the faculty of seeing, or hearing, or feeling. Do oxygen and hydrogen and carbon and the insensate, inorganic mould possess any such power in themselves? The material body is continually wasting away, and if it were not supplied with new substances, it would soon become dissipated. What power and miraculous skill weaves the new substances into the old forms without any mistake, and preserves the body from annihilation? Can the food we eat do it of itself?

But this is not all. When the spirit leaves the body, all power and consciousness cease. The eye may be as perfect in its organization as ever, but it cannot see. The ear and the other senses have lost all power of consciousness. Have lost it, do I say? No, they have not lost it, for they never possessed it. The material eye never saw ; the material ear never heard ; the material hand never felt ; the material heart never beat, of themselves. If you were in a factory where all the wheels were humming with motion, would you not know that some power not in themselves was driving them? And if they stopped, would you not know that the power had been withdrawn from them? Have we not just as certain evidence that the organs of the material body have no inherent, self-derived power in themselves to act ; that they must be moved by some spiritual force ; and when that force is withdrawn they must return to dust? It seems strange that rational men will ask for evidence of the existence of spiritual substances and forces when they perceive them in constant operation within and around them.

We have the evidence of our own consciousness also of the substantial and permanent nature of the spirit. It is now a generally-accepted fact that thought and affection are indestructible. No one can divest himself of ideas or truths he has once gained. They may be for-gotten, as we say, but they remain in the mind and can be recalled. If the mind or spirit were a mist or a form-less essence, it could be dispersed like a vapor, and all the ideas and affections that were embodied in it would be dissipated. But they are not, and never can be. Amputate a limb and it ceases to be a part of the human body. But a thought or an affection cannot be ampu-tated. Destroy the body and the spirit is not injured. The material body is evanescent ; it is constantly passing away like a flowing stream ; but the spirit remains un-touched, substantial, immortal.

If the relation of the spirit to the body is such as I have represented it to be, the spirit must be the man himself. It must be in the human form, because the material body is cast into its mould. All the organs are woven into a garment to clothe the organs of the spirit. The spirit must therefore be composed of a series of organic forms or organs, which, combined into one, be-come the human form. What, then, is the spirit? It is a human being in a human form as a whole and in its least particulars. It is substantial, and the substances of which it is composed are untouched by the dissolution of the material body ; the human spirit endures forever.

Having gained a clear and true idea of what the human spirit is, and of the distinction between the spiritual body and the material body, we have gained the point of view from which we can see the trinity and unity in man which are essential to personal beings, and from this we may see more clearly the nature of the Divine trinity in the one person of our Lord Jesus Christ.

We have good grounds for looking to man to find the trinity in God, because man was created in the image of God and after His likeness. If man was made in the image of God, we must find in him a likeness of God. God must be in the human form. The Divine nature must be composed of attributes corresponding to those which compose man. The Divine faculties must sustain the same relations to one another which human faculties sustain. If there is a trinity in God, there must be a trinity in man. If there is a trinity in man, there must be a trinity in God. If the trinity in man makes one person, one human being, the trinity in God must make one Divine Person, one Divine Being. If this trinity in God makes three persons, each composed of the same substance and possessing the same attributes, the trinity in man must make three persons, each composed of the same substance and possessing the same qualities. An image must have the same form as the original, and so far as it is an image it must be like it.

What are the three essential factors of a human being? Are they not the soul or spirit, the body, and the power of the man reaching forth to affect objects and beings outside himself? These three are perfectly distinct. The spirit is not the body, and the body is not the spirit, and the influence or operation of the man is not the spirit or the body. But the three make one person, one man. If either were absent the other two would not be a man.

We may regard the subject in another way. Man is essentially composed of love, intelligence, and the union of these factors in thought or deed. The love or will is not the intellect, and neither of them is thought or act. Love does not make a man ; action does not make a man. A human being is the product of the three. But the three do not make three persons. There is the same trinity of Divine love, Divine wisdom, and Divine operation in God.

To return to man, the image of God. The spirit or soul is the father of the body. It begat it and formed it and continually creates it. If the material body had consciousness and power of its own, it could truly say, I came out from the spirit. I can do nothing of myself. The spirit does the works. It could say everything that the Saviour says concerning His relations to the Father ; and yet the spirit and the body make one man, as the Father and Son make one God.

Look at the subject in another way. The soul is in the body. Jesus Christ says, "The Father is in me." "No man cometh unto the Father but by me." There is no way in which we can get access to a man's mind or spirit but by his body. If the body could speak, it could say in truth, No one can come to the spirit but by me. I am the way, and the only way.

Here is a larger and more important truth than may at first appear. By coming to the Father something more is meant than coming to Him in space, as one man approaches another. It means that we cannot come to Him in thought,—that is, we cannot think of Him truly in any other way than as He is manifested in Jesus

Christ.   How is He brought forth to view in Him? In
the human form, as a Divine Man.   The agnostics are
right when they say that God as an infinite and formless
spirit, "without body, parts, or passions," is unthinkable.   There is no image, no idea in the mind, no distinct subject for the thought to rest on.   We can only
think of things and beings that have substance and form.
There are no beings or things destitute of these essentials
of existence.   If I should ask you to think of a tree or
an animal or a man that had no substance and no form,
you would say it was absurd, because you know it to be
impossible.   For the same reason we can only come to
Jehovah, the Father, in thought as He appears in Jesus
Christ ; and He appears in Him as a man, in the human
form.   " He that hath seen me hath seen the Father."

For the same reason we can come to Him in our affec-
ions in no other way than by Jesus Christ.   No one can
love a being of whom he can gain no conception.   We
cannot love a formless essence, an abstract virtue or
power.   Think of the absurdity of loving an abstract
child, a woman or a man without substance or form !   It
may be said that we do love an ideal person.   There is
some truth in that.   But our ideal is the image we form
in our minds.   So, doubtless, every one has some conception in his mind of God.   He makes an image of
Him, even while denying that He has any form.   But
here the image is formed for us.   The Word is made
flesh, and dwells among men.   " God manifest in the
flesh."   God manifest in the human form.   God come
down to men, associating with them, teaching them by
word of mouth, by precept and example ; the tender,

merciful God, healing their diseases, sympathizing with them in their sorrows and sufferings ; a kind, patient, pure, unselfish, noble, wise God ; and yet a man. He has a human heart ; He works in human ways ; He has human sympathies. This is the way He is revealed to us in Jesus Christ. He is revealed not merely by example and formal instruction, but He is embodied in the form of Jesus Christ. Jesus Christ is His form, His body, His love, His wisdom, His way of working among men and saving them. The love and wisdom of Jesus Christ are the Divine love and wisdom. God reveals Himself in Him even to the human senses, in a form comprehensible to the child. When we think of Jesus Christ we think of the Father ; when we love Jesus Christ we love the Father ; when we pray to Jesus Christ we pray to the Father ; when we worship Jesus Christ we worship the Father. We think of Him in the same way and in the same sense as, in thinking of the bodily form of a friend, we think of his mind ; when we speak to the body we speak to the soul.

According to this doctrine we have the whole Divine trinity in one personal Being, in Jesus Christ, as we have the whole human trinity in every man. We have the whole trinity united in the human form, of which we can gain a distinct idea. The mind is not confused and discouraged by trying to think the unthinkable ; it is not distracted by thinking that there are three Divine persons and saying that there is but one God. We do not pray to a being of whom we say we can form no conception—but to whom we speak and of whom we try to think—to grant us favors for the sake of or in the name of another Divine person. We go to Jesus Christ, who is God manifest in the flesh, as a little child goes to his father, in a plain and simple way, without trying to make any metaphysical distinctions, and ask Him to grant the help and blessing we need for His own love and mercy's sake. We can think of Him ; we can love Him ; we can trust Him. He is the way, the truth and the life.

If Jesus Christ was really God Himself manifest in the flesh, and not merely an ambassador from God, or a distinct person standing between men and Him, you can see what an important bearing a true conception of His character and mission will have upon the conditions and means of human salvation. It places it on new grounds. It takes it out of all that is merely formal, legal, technical, and arbitrary, and demonstrates to our senses how the one and only Divine Being loves and pities His children, and what practical work He has done and is doing to save men from sin and misery and raise them up to holiness and eternal life. God has generally been represented as an austere, inexorable embodiment of that natural, mercantile form of justice which demands the full measure of punishment for every offence. But justice has a higher meaning than this. Divine justice is not vengeance ; it is Divine love directed by Divine wisdom to secure the highest good to men. There is an immense difference between sending some one to do a painful work and doing it yourself. If Jesus Christ was God Himself, clothed with a human nature and a material body, by means of which He came down to human comprehension, living, laboring, teaching, and dying as to His material body among men and for them, every one can see in what a beautiful and attractive form it presents the Divine character. We can know and love and delight to serve such a Being.

This is the light in which the doctrines of the New Church present the Divine character. They dispel the cloud of misconceptions which have obscured it. They bring the Lord down to men, and present Him in such simple and clear form that a child can understand something of Him and learn to know and love Him. They take nothing away from His sanctity. They do not destroy the law or the prophets ; they help men to understand them. They do not break the force and sanctity of the least of the commandments, or teach men to break them. On the contrary, they show that they are the immutable laws of the Divine order, and, consequently, that they cannot be broken without loss and suffering. Their whole scope and tendency is to assist men in solving the problems of life ; to make the way to the attainment of the highest good plain and easier to walk in ; to reveal the Lord to men in a clearer and more attractive light ; to give man a truer and nobler conception of himself and of the capacities of his own nature for happiness, and to show the means that lie within his reach to attain the highest good.

THE DIVINE METHOD OF CREATING.

"By the word of the LORD were the heavens made; and all the host of them by the breath of his mouth."—PSALM xxxiii. 6.

THERE is but little said in the letter of the Word concerning the creation of the universe, except the bare announcement of the fact that the Lord is the Creator of all things, and that all things were created by "the word of the LORD" or the Divine truth. The conclusions we form concerning the creation, from this declaration, will depend upon the idea that we have of "the word of the LORD" and "the breath of his mouth." If by "word" we understand a mere vocal expression, we shall come to the conclusion generally entertained upon the subject, that the Lord spoke the universe into existence. He said, Let it be, and it became. "He spake, and it was done; he commanded, and it stood fast." According to this idea the universe was created without any modes or processes from cause to effect. There were no steps in it. It is true, science demonstrates pretty clearly that our earth has been gradually evolved from a chaotic state, and for many thousands of years continued to advance towards a condition suitable for the habitation of man. But the theologian evades the difficulty by supposing that the act of creating was speaking into existence the elements out of which the universe was gradually formed.

This idea of the creation practically severs the universe

from any living, present connection with the Creator. It implies that He once created it and committed it to the keeping of certain laws which men call the laws of nature, and now He stands as it were aloof from it, watching its operations somewhat as a man makes a machine and then watches its movements.

But this is not the idea of the New Church. Our doctrines teach us that the Lord is an everlasting or continual Creator, and that He creates all things from Himself. The universe is a perpetual creation, continually renewed and increased and held in existence by the same power which first gave it being. The universe was not created out of nothing by a vocal expression, but from the Lord Himself by the continual operation of His Divine love and wisdom. It is not in any sense fixed and independent of Him. It is not cut off or severed from Him and held in form and existence by laws. Laws have no power. They are merely the Divine method of working. The Lord works in, through, and by them. There is not a single thing in the universe that can maintain itself a moment when severed from the Lord. The hardest metal or stone would vanish from sight and from existence as quickly as light vanishes from the room when you remove the luminous body from which it flows, if its connection with the Lord were severed. The outflowing of light from a luminous body well illustrates the momentary dependence of every created thing upon the Lord for its continued existence.

According to this idea the universe is a constant creation. All its forces are continually derived from the Lord. Nothing acts of itself. The force of gravity is

not inherent in matter.   It does not originate in the earth
or the sun.   It comes momentarily from the Lord.   The
attraction of cohesion is not a power of itself, but the
Divine method of forming individual things and holding
them together, and the exercise of power is as constant as
the effects of it.   Suppose the power we call cohesive
attraction should be in part withdrawn from solid substances, they would all fall asunder, and there would be
no individual forms or things.   The earth would be a
fluid mass.   Withdraw it still further and there would be
nothing but gases, and if the process were still continued
matter would be annihilated.   This truth is perfectly
illustrated by an analogous process in the human body.
The body is organized by the soul and kept in existence
as an organized form by it.   If you sever any part of the
body from its connection with the soul, disorganization
begins to take place, and the severed part is dissipated.
So it would be with the material universe, only more fully
and instantaneously, if it could be severed from the ever-
creating power of the Lord.   We arrive, then, at this
important truth, that the universe is a perpetual creation
from the Lord, and has a living connection with Him.

Such being the case, the question naturally arises,
What is there in the Lord from which or out of which
the universe can be created?   The Lord in His essential
being is love and wisdom or goodness and truth.   It
must be from or out of goodness and truth that the universe is created.   Most persons conceive of love or goodness as a mere affection or state of the soul, and of wisdom
or truth as knowledge or simply knowing.   But this is
not the true idea.   The Divine love and wisdom are sub-

stance and form itself. The Lord exists in Himself, not from another. He must be substance itself, for He gives subsistence to everything. If substance is that which stands under, is the origin and support of all things, surely the Lord must be that substance ; and if He gives form to everything, there must be something in Him that gives the form. He must be the Former of all forms. He must be form itself. The inmost essence of the Lord is Divine love, and the form of that love is Divine wisdom or truth, and from Divine truth all things were created. The declaration of the Sacred Scriptures, then, that "by the word of the LORD were the heavens made," is literally true, when we have a correct idea of what "the word of the LORD" or Divine truth is.

It is true we can form no adequate conception of what the Divine goodness or truth is in itself. The intensity, power, and perfection of the Divine are altogether above the conception of the highest angel, much more that of man. We are so weak and ignorant that we do not know what anything, even the most common object that is daily before our eyes, is in itself. We should find it as impossible to define what matter is as what spiritual or Divine substance is. It is enough for us to know that all things have their origin in the Lord and flow from Him as the only real and essential substance.

When we say the universe is an emanation or outbirth from the Lord, it must not be understood that gross material forms come directly from Him, but those substances and forms from which the material universe was created. The creation proceeds from the Lord by distinct steps or degrees. This may be illustrated by the

creation of the planets from the sun. Granite and iron
and diamonds do not proceed immediately from the sun.
The first emanation from the sun is matter in its purest
forms, as an aura or ether; then it becomes a gas, a fluid,
and finally a solid. A part of this process we know from
actual observation. For instance, oxygen and hydrogen
gases by combination form water, and water becomes a
solid in ice. Here we can trace the formation of a solid
down three steps. We do not yet know much about
light and heat and electricity, or those substances which
are called the imponderable agents in chemistry. But we
know that they act a most important part in all the
changes and activities of matter. They are doubtless to
the grosser forms of matter what the soul is to the human
body, and from analogy and experiment there is good
reason to believe that the grosser forms of matter are
created from them, as water and all other fluids and
solids are created from gases. Solids are the last step
in the creation, where the living forms and substances
become inert and dead.

The first emanation from the Lord is not matter, nor
even spiritual substance in its lowest forms, but a sun so
intense and glowing with the Divine love and wisdom
that even the angels cannot bear its heat and light except
as it becomes modified and adapted to their states. This
Divine sun flows from the Lord and encompasses Him,
as light and heat flow from our sun and encompass it.
This sun is pure love and wisdom as they flow from the
Lord. It is also the substance from which and out of
which the spiritual world is created, in the same manner
relatively as material worlds are created from the material

sun. That sun appears to the angels remote, as our sun does to us. It is also the centre of the whole universe, both spiritual and natural. From it the spiritual world is created, and the souls of men are formed. Thus man is a being organized of spiritual substances derived from the Lord, and is kin to all things in the spiritual world.

As the spiritual world was created from the spiritual sun, of spiritual substances, it is a more substantial and real and living world than this. But it is not a simple world in which all parts are alike; it exists in various forms and degrees. The Divine substance ever flowing from the Lord descends in distinct degrees. The first emanation from the Lord is the spiritual sun by which He is encompassed; the first emanation from the spiritual sun is the celestial heaven, in which the highest angels dwell, who can receive the Lord's love and wisdom in their highest degree and in the purest created forms. This heaven is as distinct from all the others as the air is from the solid rock.

The next remove from the spiritual sun is the spiritual heaven, which is a degree lower than the celestial heaven, and is distinct from that heaven as it is distinct from the spiritual sun, or as our earth is from our sun. This heaven is the abode of spiritual angels. They are called spiritual angels in whom a degree of life has been opened corresponding to the substances of which the spiritual heaven is composed.

The next remove from the spiritual sun is the natural heaven, which is the lowest form of the spiritual and is only one degree above the material. Thus there are three heavens, each distinct from the other, and formed

h   10*

of spiritual substances in three distinct degrees. The main truth I wish to present now is that the creation proceeds from the Lord by distinct steps, each lower plane being formed from and through the next higher and thus all from the Lord.

From spiritual substances matter is formed. Not gross and solid matter, but matter in its purest forms. The first step from the spiritual to the material is the suns of the various systems in the material universe. According to the philosophy of the New Church, these suns are pure fire, from which issue light and heat. This pure fire is the most subtile form of matter ; so subtile and pure that we can obtain but little if any knowledge of it through our gross and material senses, and yet it is inert and dead compared with spirit. From the suns the various planets or earths are formed by a process exactly analogous to that by which the various spiritual worlds or heavens are formed. The Divine love and wisdom, which we must remember are not names but real substances and forms, flow down from the Lord by distinct degrees, until that which was Divine and infinite and above all created reception and comprehension, becomes dead and solid matter, as the metal and stone. Thus there is a living connection between the rock and the inmost Divine of the Lord ; there is a chain of causes and effects running from the highest to the lowest, binding all together into one whole.

Reasoning from analogy and from the very nature of the Divine love and wisdom, I think we are forced to the conclusion that the material universe is not yet complete, and never will be. The Lord is now creating new worlds, and will continue to create them to eternity. There are discoveries in astronomy which seem to confirm this conclusion. The Lord is not idle. Life must continually flow from Him. He is continually creating new souls, must He not be continually creating new worlds?

The truth that the universe is a perpetual creation from the Divine sun answers the question which is often asked, and which has been supposed to be unanswerable, What keeps up the heat of the sun? It is known that all heated bodies gradually give off their heat and grow cooler. And it has been argued from this that the sun must eventually cease to shine and give off heat, and become opaque like the earth. Others have imagined that the comets supply the sun with fuel, and in some unknown way keep its fires continually burning. But the truth is, the fire of the sun is perpetually created by the Lord from the spiritual world. The suns themselves are an emanation from Him, as light and heat are an emanation from them, and they cannot cease to shine, for they are perpetually fed from the exhaustless fountain of the Divine life. Thus the stability and perpetuity of the universe does not depend upon any laws or relations of matter, but upon the immutable order and infinite sources of Him who is life and substance and form itself.

This sublime truth, that the universe is a continual creation from the Lord, reveals to us, if we can correctly understand it, how the Lord is everywhere present in the universe. There is not a stone in the street that is not connected with the Divine by the presence within it of living forces from Him. As the universe descends from the Lord, or, what is the same thing, recedes from Him

by distinct steps or degrees, it always retains a vital connection with Him, upon which all its activity and life and
its very existence depend.   It is a common idea that
the Lord created the first plant, and gave to it the power
of propagating itself, and then His direct agency ceased.
But this is an entire mistake.   Power cannot be communicated in that way.   A machine can only be kept in
motion by the continual application of the motive power.
The Divine agency is just as necessary to the creation of
the last plant as the first.   The actual presence of a substantial and living element from the Lord through the
spiritual sun and the spiritual world forms the plant in
every part of its progress.   It is the same in the animal
kingdom.   The organization of the animal form, and all
its instincts and life, are also the effects of the spiritual
element from the Lord working from within.   One animal cannot create another.   No animal can form its own
instincts.   I repeat, therefore, that the creation of the
material universe, as a whole and in all its parts, is due
to the spiritual presence and agency of the Divine sphere
of the Lord through the spiritual world.   The spiritual
world, then, in its relations to this, is the world of causes,
not only as a whole, not only as a first cause, but in each
particular and at every moment.   Wherever you see a
form or motion, growth or change, you may know that
there are spiritual substances and forces at work, just
as certainly as you know when you see a machine in
motion that some power is moving it.

The very deadness and inertness of matter fit it to
serve an essential use in the Lord's creation.   The material world forms the basis on which the spiritual world

rests, and from which it reacts. Creation requires a passive and an active. There must be something to act and
something to receive the action,—to be acted upon. We
see this principle clearly in exercise in this world, and
the Lord always works like Himself in all parts of His
creation. The earth was first created from the sun, and
now the sun acts into it and sets all its forms in motion.
It acts upon the atmosphere and causes all its currents
and winds. It acts upon the water and lifts it from the
ocean and the land into the heavens, in the form of
clouds, which descend in rain and form rivers, and thus
the element of water is kept in perpetual play. It acts
upon all vegetable and animal forms, and keeps them in
a state to be acted upon and moulded by the spiritual
forces which reach them from within. If there were no
earth the sun's rays would be dissipated in space, and,
like a blow upon the empty air, produce no effect. The
spiritual world is the real and substantial world, the world
of causes and forms, and is everywhere present and op-
erative ; and the material world was created to be a basis
for its operations, to arrest the outflow of living forces
from the Lord, and reflect them back towards their original fountain. They flow from Him as love and wisdom
in substance. They return towards Him in human souls,
organized in His own form and likeness, and capable of
receiving His love and wisdom in ever-increasing fulness
and joy.

The truth that the Lord is an ever-living, present, and
perpetual Creator is one that men are very slow to learn.
Men will not believe that the Lord is now doing what He
has always done, that He is unchangeably active. '' My

Father worketh hitherto," said our Lord, "and I work." This truth brings the Lord near to us as a present, living God, and not merely an historical being.   The whole universe is the effect of His working to-day, is made up of the forms which His love and wisdom have assumed and do assume to-day ; and they are as truly tokens and messages of His love as the work which any man does is an evidence of his present, living power and of his wisdom and skill.   It is the Lord who feeds the blazing furnace of the sun by emanations from Himself, and every ray of light and heat that falls upon our world comes from the Lord through the sun, and is a message of the Lord's love and wisdom.   It is the Lord who creates from a living, spiritual sun the innumerable hosts of stars that gem the heavens and fill the immeasurable space.   With this truth in our minds we look up to the sky on a cloudless night, and our thoughts do not travel back vast ages to admire and wonder at a mighty power once exerted, but we are filled with amazement and awe at what He is now doing.   The stars are now creating and created from Him.   He now marshals them in their harmonious order, and sends them on their shining way.   "See," says the devout soul, "what my Father is now doing."

As he looks over the earth in the spring and sees the bare trees and dead mould clothed with the beautiful garment of organized forms ; as he sees the beautiful flowers bursting from the cold clod, and delicate petals gently unfolding from the hard, woody stems until the valleys are clothed with a new beauty, and the hills with a new glory, "See," he says, "how my Father works." It is His hand that weaves the delicate texture of leaf and blossom. It is His hand that distils the farina of wheat and the sweet juices of the various fruits, and rounds them into such beautiful and graceful forms, and paints them with such delicate and various hues. It is not dead nature ; it is not primal and abstract law ; it is not gas or electric fires. Matter is but the thin veil beneath which He works. Galvanic forces are but the swift shuttles with which He weaves the web of organic forms. The falling stream falls not of itself, but runs and sings in sweet accord with His attractive power. The dewdrop does not round itself, but the fine particles of mist leap and cling to each other's embrace by His will. The bird does not organize itself, or sing an idle, senseless song. It sings His praises in a voice which is one chord in the harmonies of His nature.

Look up, the worlds are not rushing on aimless errands by self-impelled forces, but each pursues its swift and shining way by certain paths for certain ends. Look around you, the whole earth is tremulous and living with His all-pervading presence. He speaks to you in the loving voice of wife and child ; He smiles upon you in their sweet lips ; He ministers to you in their gentle hands. Look, I pray you, my brother ; look through the thin veil of nature and the sweet disguises of material forms and see the presence and power of your Heavenly Father. For He is present and working there. From Himself, by instruments formed from Himself, He now creates all.

MAN A FORM RECEPTIVE OF LIFE.

" I am the vine, ye are the branches. He that abideth in me, and I in him, the same bringeth forth much fruit; for without me ye can do nothing."—JOHN XV. 5.

THE general truth contained in this portion of the Divine Word is this: that man's life consists in his conjunction with the Lord, and that severed from Him he is nothing. The doctrines of the New Church teach the same truth when they declare that "man is a mere organ of life." It is this truth to which I wish to invite your attention, a truth fundamental to all knowledge of man's own nature and of his relations to the Lord.

Let us look first at the truth itself. "Man is a mere organ of life," or as it is expressed in other words, "a form receptive of life." This is not a figurative or relative expression. Man is just as truly a mere form or organ of life as a tree. He has no more life in himself—that is, no more life that has its origin in him—than a piece of granite has. For there can be only one being who has life in himself, —that is, underived life, — for to have life in one's self is to be self-existent, and to be self-existent is to be uncreated, and to be uncreated is to be Divine, to be God.

All men who acknowledge a God assent to this truth in some form. But still it is generally supposed that man is endowed with certain faculties or powers and then left to himself in some measure to work out his destiny, or to live ; and thus the idea is entertained that man has independent and self-acting power, though in the beginning he was created. The Creator gave him a start, as it were, made him to be self-existent, and then left him to himself so far as mere living is concerned, and only teaches him from without, as we teach one another, how to live. Most men who think at all upon the subject doubtless suppose that the Lord made man somewhat as a man forms a machine, with the difference that man is a self-acting machine, and when once created they suppose that he goes on perpetuating himself without any immediate, special agency of the Creator.

The practical effect of this doctrine is the denial of the immediate and constant agency of the Lord in life. We rarely, if ever, think of the origin of our life, and remember only that we now live and seem to live of ourselves. Now, the plain, simple truth is that man is a mere organ of life, or a form by which life from the Lord is manifested, and it is by a constant action of the Divine life upon or through this form that man has any life. It is the Divine influx or inflowing that gives life to this form that we call man.

So far as our observation extends we know that this is a universal law. No finite thing that we have any knowledge of has any life in itself, and all that we call its life is a constant inflowing into it. If we look at the human body we shall find abundant illustration of the principle.

The human eye is a mere organ of sight. It has no light in itself. No phenomena appear until the eye is acted upon, until it is set in motion by the influx of the ether. When its waves flow in, this organism is set in motion, and the result is sight. When they cease, sight ceases.   So the ear is a mere organ or form of hearing, and is adapted in every respect to the air.   When the waves of the air flow in, the organ is set in motion, and the effect is a sound.   It is with the ear just as it is with the pipe of an organ ; when the inflowing wave ceases, then the sound ceases.

The same is true of taste and of touch.   No sensation is excited unless something acts upon the organ formed for that sense and excites it, and when the action ceases the sensation ceases.   So the whole human body, in every part, from the least to the greatest, within and without, is made up of mere organs.   They are not all organs of sensation.   The brain is the organ of thought, the tongue and larynx are organs of speech, the heart is an organ for propelling the blood, the lungs for breathing, the feet and legs are the organs of locomotion.   Not one of them has the least life in itself, or acts unless it is impelled ; when the motive power is shut off the organ ceases its motion, as a wheel ceases to revolve when the propelling force ceases to act.

The heart does seem to expand and contract of itself, but we know that it does not ; for when the spirit leaves the body the heart has no motion.   If it were really self-acting it would keep on.   The human body, then, is a series and congeries of organs, and every action, motion, and affection that we can predicate of it is caused by some force flowing into these forms and setting them in motion.

This law or mode of the Divine operation is universal, so far as our observation extends.   Is it rational to suppose that the action of the law is limited by man's powers of observation? Certainly not. As far as observation extends, it teaches us that the Lord never contradicts Himself, that He works after the same general plan everywhere. Reason, then, may take up the thread when observation can go no further, and show by the laws of analogy and correspondence how the Lord works in degrees or planes of the mind entirely above our observation.

When we pass from the study of man's body to his spirit, we conclude that as the combination of material organs compose the body and make the material form of man, so, as to his spirit also, man is a mere organ of life, an organ composed of a series and congeries of spiritual forms, which in their combination make up the human form. There is no more life in itself in the spirit than there is in the body. It is an organ receptive of life. There is a spiritual eye and a spiritual ear and heart; there are spiritual lungs and hands and feet, and all the other organs, internal and external, that make up the human form, and they are composed of spiritual substances, and are as perfectly adapted to a world composed of spiritual substances as the material man is to the material world. The eye is set in motion by waves of a spiritual ether, the ear vibrates to a spiritual air, the lungs breathe a spiritual atmosphere. The heart propels spiritual blood. When the natural body is laid aside, the spiritual senses are affected by contact with spiritual forms; the foot treads upon a spiritual earth, which is composed of a greater variety of forms than the material earth. Men live in spiritual houses and wear spiritual garments and engage in various uses suited to the world

they are in, and yet that whole world and all who are in
it are mere organs of life, having the same relations to
one another that material forms have.   If we ascend to
the highest angel we shall find him a mere organ of life,
having no more life in himself than a string or pipe of a
musical instrument, and no more power to set himself in
motion or to live from himself.

We come to this conclusion, then, that the whole universe of angels, spirits, men, animals, vegetables, and
worlds is a vast complicated organism, having no life in
itself in any of its parts or forms.   It is created by the
Lord to be the organ of life which flows into it from Him,
and sustains and animates it.   The Lord constantly
creates and gives ; all that created things or beings can
do is to receive.   And this is the next principle which I
wish to notice.   The measure and quality of the life we
receive depend upon our capacity or ability to receive.

This is also a universal law.   The Lord is omnipresent
in all His fulness, but He can only be received according
to the capacity of the recipient form.   This diversity of
ability is illustrated in the human body in the same
manner as diversity of form.   The vibrations in the air
that produce the sensation of sound are just as much
present to the hand and eye as they are to the ear, but
they are received and perceived only by the ear because
that is the only organ whose form is adapted to the purpose.   The modulations of the ether float all around us
and fall upon us from every direction, but the eye only
has any knowledge of them, because it is the only organ
formed to receive them.   All the causes which excite the
sensations of sight, smell, taste, and hearing may be

present to the hand ; all their undulations may fall upon
it, but it does not discern their presence, though one of
the most wonderful organs in the body, simply because it
is not fitted to receive them. Place a person destitute of
eyes in the midst of a beautiful landscape. The flowing
stream, the quiet valley, the gently-rising upland, and
the varied outlines of a wide sweep of hills, diversified
with innumerable forms of tree and rock and animal,
canopied by the blue sky or the ever-shifting forms and
hues of the clouds lighted up by the glories of the rising
or the setting sun,—all this infinite variety of form and
color and beauty is a blank to him, though the causes
which should reveal its presence, the undulations in the
ether reflected from them, fall upon him from every
point. The only want is in him. He has no organs to
receive these motions, and consequently they are to him
as though they were not. What is true of the eye is
true of the ear and of every material organ. All material organs are made and adapted to be acted upon by
material agents, and the manifestations, effects, or phenomena are in exact accordance with the power and
degree of reception. The higher the form of the organ,
the nobler its functions, the more excellent the forces of
life which it receives and to which it responds.

If, now, we ascend to the spiritual forms, we shall find
the same general law, only varied in its effects with the
capacity of the form. The Lord is present to every
man's spirit with all His love and wisdom, but He can
communicate only what can be received, and what can be
received depends upon the quality of the organ. The
phenomena or the resulting effects of influx into the

spiritual organs which compose the man are thoughts and affections. Thoughts and affections are changes of state and activities of spiritual forms, just as sound and light are the effects of the air and ether falling upon and setting in motion the organs of the ear and eye. And the thought and affection are exactly according to the measure of reception.

We should rationally expect that forms composed of substances so eminent in excellence would be susceptible of corresponding effects, and we find it is so. Our observation also, as far as it extends, teaches us that the higher the form and medium, the more varied and noble the results. The rock receives only sufficient influx, which we call attraction, to hold its particles together. It is a mere mass. In the vegetable world we first find organized forms, but each form is fixed to one spot. It has growth within certain limits, but no sensation. The animal kingdom possesses locomotion and sensation, and it possesses them by virtue of its higher organization. Man possesses all these, and within and above them a spiritual and celestial organism, and it is these highest forms which really constitute his humanity and elevate him above the animal.

The pre-eminent quality of a spiritual form is that it is not subject to the laws of fixed time and space. Organs formed of matter grow chiefly by increase in size. But a spiritual form grows by perfecting its state. Spiritual forms are as clearly defined and distinct from one another as material, and appear to be, and are in one sense, in space, as much as material forms ; but the spaces are not fixed and independent of the mind, but conform to it.

From this quality of spirit it will be readily seen that there are no limits to its growth. A spiritual form may increase in the quality of its state to eternity,—that is, without any limitations as to time and space. Nor can it be destroyed or dissipated as a material form can, which can communicate itself only by giving away a part of itself. A sum of money, a piece of land, or a body of water is diminished by whatever is removed from it. But with the spiritual forms it is not so. It matters not how often a thought or affection is communicated to another, it still remains in the mind, and has even been increased by the efforts to communicate it. Thus it can be readily seen that it is impossible to dissolve and disperse a spiritual form. Spiritual death is not the dissolution of the soul, its ceasing to exist as a form, but its malformation, its disorderly action.

Another peculiar and prominent quality of the spiritual forms which constitute the human mind is, that they retain every motion that is communicated to them. This quality, with the power of reproducing every motion and change of state which has ever been excited in the mind, we call memory. Thus all our states return, and may return to eternity, though modified by all succeeding states.

Another quality peculiar to the most perfect spiritual forms is that their activities are attended with consciousness. We know that we love and think. The rock does not know that it exists, the tree does not know that it grows, nor has the animal any power to reflect upon the fact of its existence.

Another quality of the highest human faculties is that

they act in freedom. Their freedom is just as much a gift of the Lord as the power of motion or thought, or any other power. We can act as of ourselves. While it is true that all life comes from the Lord, it so comes that we do not perceive its influx. Our first intimation of it is in its effect upon ourselves. Thus we seem to live of ourselves. This is of the Lord's love, that man might not be a mere machine, but a free and intelligent agent. Thus man has the power constantly given to him to receive or to reject the Lord's influx into him. He can turn himself away from Him, or he can turn himself towards Him. He can live in order or disorder.

Man's spiritual form is constantly perfected by right action and injured by wrong action. It is at first a mere possibility, but constantly unfolds and develops by use. And it develops in two ways ; each organ becomes more perfect, and new degrees of life or higher spiritual forms are constantly coming forward. Every new truth received into the mind, and woven into its tissues by the affections, becomes a new organ for the reception of a larger measure of the Divine life. And every heavenly affection of charity to the neighbor or love to the Lord is, in itself considered, an harmonious modulation of the whole spiritual form, and has a permanent effect. It tends to induce a state of such orderly and heavenly action that the form is more easily set in motion in the same way again. In time a habit, as we term it, is formed,—that is, the form takes on these motions spontaneously without any effort of the will, whenever the existing cause is present, as the æolian harp rises and falls in harmonious chords when the wind breathes upon it.

The highest attainable perfection, then, of any created being, is this ability to receive the Divine life in the largest measures and highest forms. To be a recipient of the Divine love and wisdom is the very end for which man was created. The Lord made him in His image and likeness, that he might be a form in every respect adapted to the reception of life from Him. Man is a mere organ, but an organ after a Divine pattern. All that the Lord asks of man is to receive Him and to enjoy the blessedness of conjunction with Him.

This is a great practical truth of paramount importance to every created being. Let us state it clearly. "Man is a mere organ of life." He is a combination of forms connected together in series and degrees, one within another, and all so related, though indefinite in number and degree, that they form a one, which in the complex we call man. All the phenomena of life, all affection, thought, sensation, all that we perceive as pleasure or pain, every possible quality that we can predicate of man, is caused by influx into this wonderful combination of forms. The influx, with its effect and manifestation, is always determined by the form, as the quality of a musical sound is determined, other things being equal, by the nature and quality of the instrument.

The Lord is present to every created being and to every created thing with all His love and wisdom, to the highest angel in heaven and to the lowest devil in hell, to the wisest sage upon earth and to the infant just born, to every animal and tree and rock ; but each one can receive only that which its form adapts it to receive.

The Lord is present to each one of us now, but we see

Him not, because we do not receive Him. We should not any of us need to move from our places to see the ineffable splendors of the celestial heaven and groups of angels of a loveliness and beauty beyond our conception, and to hear harmonies such as never fell upon mortal ear, if we had the organs to receive such a revelation. We stand in the universe like a statue in a garden. The sun pours his mid-day splendors, his rising and his setting glories, upon it; those motions in the ether which would communicate to the living eye the forms and colors of all surrounding objects fall upon the stony eyeball; the fragrance of a thousand flowers is wafted on every breeze, and the minstrelsy of a thousand winds plays around the well-cut ear, but it stands with dead and stony gaze through summer's heat and winter's cold, unmoved by the beauty of spring or the golden wealth of autumn. Why? Because it has no organism within to receive and be played upon by these manifold forces. So we stand in the midst of the spiritual world because we deny our higher life. We turn away from the Lord and refuse to receive Him.. He stands at the door and knocks; He presses upon every avenue as the air presses upon us. But we can only receive what we have the organs to receive.

There are in every human soul the possibilities of only less than infinite power and blessedness, but they remain mere possibilities, like the germ of a seed before it begins to grow, because we do not suffer life from the Lord to flow into them and bring them out into definite form and fill them with the activities of His own love. By our evils and falses we bar every access of the Lord to our souls, over which we have control, and by the perversion of our spiritual forms we change all that does flow in, from the perfect order, beauty, and harmony of heaven into infernal ugliness and grating discords. We suffer the cursed dust of mere earthly loves to settle down upon the fine but unused tissues of the higher faculties within us, and the damp mould of earthly passions to gather upon them, or the scorching fires of selfish and worldly loves to sear and wither their fair forms. We are dwarfs in spiritual stature, and our life is poor and mean, because we will not admit the Divine love and wisdom into our souls. We are like the stunted shrubs of arctic climes because we turn away from the sun of heaven.

How poor and disjointed and lean is even the best life compared with what it might be, and would be if we would receive what the Lord wishes and strives to give us! Here we stand in the midst of the infinite : organs of life after the image and likeness of the infinite. The Lord calls to us in every conceivable form, "Ho, every one that thirsteth, come ye to the waters, . . . yea, come, buy wine and milk without money and without price." But we heed it not. The sweet, heavenly melody of His voice is swallowed up and lost amid the din and roar and harsh discords of worldly life. We are hurrying to and fro to get something to satisfy the clamorous appetites of selfish and worldly desires. We give free access to the influx into the organs of sensual and natural life, and they grow strong and huge and many-handed, grasping and crushing on every side, while the angels, who come to bring us heaven and eternal life, sit alone, unheeded in the dusty, dwarfed, and desolate upper chambers of the mind.

The Lord has created us forms receptive of life,—of
His life.   He has so made us that we are free to receive
it in true order or not.   We can receive it into the
lower or the higher forms of our mind.   He offers us
the highest good and the lowest.   We can receive either
only by becoming its form.   The question for every man
and every woman to determine is this, and it is of all
questions the most important : What kind of a form shall
I become?   What shall I be?   It is not a question of
words, but of life.   Here is the life of infinite love and
wisdom, freely offering itself to become formed and ulti-
mated in me.   Shall I admit it only in inverted order
into the lowest forms of my mind, the natural plane of
life?   If I do, I shut it out from all above, and the highest, noblest, most capacious and fruitful portion of my
spiritual organism is severed from the Lord and becomes
a withered branch.   And all that is received is inverted.
It is changed from life to death.   The loves of self and
the world reign, mad passions rage.   The mind becomes
a cage of unclean birds, of pride and envy and malice
and low cunning and the greed of gain, ambition, cruelty,
malevolence, and a fruitful swarm of low, vile, sensual
delights, which bite and sting and poison in the end.
All its motions will be discords.   All its activities will
clash and war with one another.   All its truths will be
lies, all its loves evils.   It will be to the spiritual sun
what the deadly nightshade is to the natural sun, turning
all its pure light and heat into poison.   Who wishes to
become such an alembic, to distil infernal poison out of
the sweet and fragrant blossoms of heaven?   Doubtless
there would be a prompt and unanimous denial in words

of any such wish. But what says that higher and truer voice, the life? What did you do when you spoke evil of your neighbor? when you forgot his interests in your eagerness to secure your own? when you coveted his goods or his place, or when you were puffed up with self-conceit, or elated with pride at some possession? What answer did you give when you let the serpent of any sensual love breathe lies into your ear? No evil can come into the mind and be loved unless the mind is itself the form of that evil. What we receive and love we are.

If we receive the Divine life into the highest forms of our mind, into the will, the love, it will flow down into all the lower forms of the mind in order and harmony. It will enlighten the understanding with truth, it will flow down through all the affections, and out in every act, transforming everything into its own likeness. We shall be filled with the fulness of love. There will be love to the Lord and to the neighbor. There will be a clear light in the understanding, and a sweet, serene peace will flow like a river through every channel of the soul. We shall be formed after the pattern of heaven. Heaven will be within us. Every form will grow into its ineffable beauty. The soul will be built up in all its fair proportions, and every fibre of every form will be tremulous with its harmonies. The Divine love and wisdom will flow into us unimpeded. We shall abide in the Lord, and He in us. We shall be conjoined with Him, and He will withhold from us no good. All our activities will be free, because they will flow from our loves ; and the life of to-day will be but the bud which will blossom to-morrow and the next day ripen into fruit. And thus we may go on to eternity, making each attainment and each measure of blessedness the starting-point for a nobler height and a fuller measure of joy. Is it not, then, the question of questions? Should we not propose it to ourselves every morning? What life shall flow through me to-day? And every evening should we not ask ourselves the question, Of what have I been the organ to-day?—life or death? Stand up bravely to the question. Let it echo and re-echo through every chamber of the soul; for on its answer will depend how much life you will receive, and what will be the quality of that life.

THE KINGDOM OF GOD WITHIN YOU.

"Behold, the kingdom of God is within you."—LUKE xvii. 21.

IT is one of the sad consequences of man's fallen, degenerate state that he looks without for happiness rather than within. He looks down to the world rather than up to the Lord ; to things rather than states. He takes the lowest form of good as his standard, and measures all things by it. The material world, natural life, earthly possessions, honors, joys are the balances in which he weighs all that he calls good. Wealth, wisdom, honor, beauty, power, glory, all are estimated by the standards of earth and sense. And man himself, the crowning work of the Lord, with faculties of measureless capacity, is valued for what he has of earthly things rather than for what he is.

A little reflection must show us that it is an entirely false estimate which is formed in this way. The lower can never be a measure for the higher. Light, heat, magnetism cannot be measured by the cubic foot or valued in dollars and cents. The body is no measure for the soul. A heavenly, eternal good cannot be estimated or expressed in the terms of any earthly good. "What shall it profit a man, if he shall gain the whole world, and lose his own soul ? Or what shall a man give in exchange for his soul?" The most of the stars are so remote from the earth that their distance cannot be measured. The diameter of the earth's orbit is not great

enough to produce any apparent change in their position.
So no earthly good, no wealth, no wisdom, no honor or
power embraces within its orbit any dimensions or anything so precious that its value has any ratio to a heavenly
good.   The least spiritual good divided by the earth
itself and all that encircles it would, in its final analysis,
be reduced to the mathematical formula of one divided
by zero.

Not that the things of this world are valueless.   This
world is the kingdom of the body and the senses, and a
beautiful and glorious kingdom it is.   When subordinate
to the kingdom of God and an instrument of its service,
it is of inestimable value.   It becomes of no value, or
worse than valueless, when it is placed in competition
with heavenly good and is destructive of it.   All material things, all worldly possessions and natural delights,
are given for the soul, and not to take its place, and their
value is always measured by the use they serve for man's
spiritual needs.   The body was made for the soul and
the earth for the body, and, through that, for the soul
also.   Thus the world is only a remote province of the
soul.   Every lower degree of life was formed to serve a
higher, and all degrees of life were made to be the recipients of life from the Lord and to act in harmony with
Him.   The higher the degree, the nobler the faculty and
the more blessed its activities.   The higher the degree,
the nearer we approach the Divine.   The Lord seeks to
communicate all of His own to man, and man's true glory
and happiness consists in his reception of the Lord's
gifts.   The kingdom of God is within us, and if we
would enter into that kingdom and take possession of its

immeasurable good, we must permit the Lord to form it within us, and co-operate with Him in doing so.

I propose, then, to consider specifically what constitutes the kingdom of God, and to show how it is within us. And, first, that part of the kingdom of God which is in man's physical body.

The eye is the kingdom of light. For there is a subtile ether pervading the material universe, and the eye is a form organized to receive it and act in harmony with it. All the motions and qualities of the ether, all colors and shadows, in their infinite variety, and all forms dwell in the eye. The kingdom of color, of light, of form dwells in it.

The kingdom of sound, of harmony, is in the ear. It is a kingdom small in size, but wonderful in capacity. What harmonies dwell in it! It takes up and repeats the modulations made by all instruments, by all human voices and all material things, from the faintest whisper to the loudest thunder, through every shade of modulation and combination. Each of the other senses is a kingdom within itself, embracing everything relating to it.

I have alluded to this relation of the senses to the material world as illustrating how the kingdom of God is within us, for the analogy between the soul and body is perfect. The spirit is the kingdom of all affection and thought, with their delights, in the same way that the eye is the kingdom of light and the ear of sound. But spiritual forms are more exalted and excellent in all their qualities than material forms. They are susceptible of an indefinitely greater variety of changes, and of a continually increasing development. They are formed to receive

12*

life from the Lord in higher and more perfect degrees, and hence to be the subject of more exalted delights,—to be indeed the kingdom of God, which He rules, which He beautifies with all heavenly loveliness, which He fills with all heavenly delights, and in which He sets up His throne, the theatre on which He displays His glory, and the home in which He dwells.

To a partial view the human soul may seem to be too contracted a kingdom for the display of omnipotent power and the diversified operations of infinite wisdom, and too small in capacity to satisfy the desires of infinite love. It has indeed no size that can be measured by natural standards, and yet the material universe is not large enough to contain it or satisfy it. When measured by the highest standard, the human soul is the largest and the most capacious and varied receptacle of the Divine life of any created form. We shall find it so even if we limit its development to this life. To gain some idea of its capacity we have only to consider for a moment how vast and varied are the contents of any well-filled and highly-cultivated mind. In some minds the whole history of humanity, so far as it has been recorded and can be known, is written in clear and living characters ; the lives of individual men, the rise and fall of nations, the battles, the heroism, the civilization, the struggles of truth with error, the hopes, the successes, and the despair. The vast evolutions of humanity gradually unfolding from age to age, and the little incidents, the trifles light as air, of the passing hour, all, in every variety of form and relation, can be embraced within the compass of human thought. If life were long enough, and the conditions of space would permit, every fact, every motion, every deed that has occurred upon this globe might be treasured up in the human mind.

If it were possible to construct a panorama of every physical change that has taken place on our earth from its first emergence from chaos until the present, or any future time ; the slow formation of its rocky crust through ages of ages, its upheaval into mountains and subsidence into valleys, the everlasting battle between the ocean and the rock, the formation of strata by millions of years of unending strife, the silent, slow but sure growth of continents from the life and death of coral and microscopic insects, the sprouting of the first blade of grass, the blossoming of every flower through all the floral and arborescent generations until the present time, the creation of the first insect and animal and all the swarms of ephemera and all the birds that have ever carolled and spread their wings in the air, and all the beasts that have lived and died upon the earth,—if the whole history of the animal, vegetable, and mineral kingdoms, in every isolated fact, in every particular form, and in all their relations and combinations, could be made to pass before the mind, they could all be retained and comprised in one memory. And when this picture, with its almost infinite details, had been transferred to the canvas of the memory, you might begin again, and on the same canvas photograph the history of humanity in all its movements, embracing the lives of every man, woman, and child that has ever lived, in all their actions and relations to one another, the life of nations and the gradual changes of centuries, and not a line or shadow in this picture would interfere with the other, but all would become more distinct from the presence of each. When you stand upon an eminence and cast your eye over a wide expanse of earth, everything within the circuit of your vision is clearly pictured upon it, every mountain and hill, valley and stream, city and dwelling ; all things even to the down upon the blossom and the mote in the sunbeam, with their shadows, colors, and forms, are distinctly delineated. Could you see a thousand landscapes, one after the other, and then look up and sweep the circuit of the heavens, one picture would not interfere with another ; one would not obliterate the other. You might shut your eyes and see them all. Hour after hour, during our whole life, myriads of forms are drawn upon the retina of the eye, and yet no one interferes with another. Such is the perfection of a material form ! What, then, must be the capacity and perfection of a spiritual form to receive and to retain? No impression ever made upon the memory is lost. We never forget. We may not be able to recall, but what we know once we know forever.

But the mind is not only capacious to receive and tenacious to retain ; it is not merely a kingdom of dead facts and forms ; it has also the marvellous power of rearranging and combining them, and of creating out of them an ideal world, and peopling it with ideal forms of surpassing loveliness and beauty. The facts of history and science are to the mind what air and water and earth are to that invisible and plastic power that decomposes and reconstructs them into the various beautiful forms of vegetable and animal life. It is perpetually rearranging and recreating objects and living forms, with which it enlarges and adorns its kingdom. From facts it eliminates knowledge and thoughts of a higher form, and from these again it deduces principles of more general application.

And these principles and lofty ideals the mind can re-embody in material forms. The artist first stores his mind with a multitude of beautiful forms, and from these extracts their essential beauties and recombines them in a perfect whole, or rather in a multitude of ideals, which have no bodily realization upon earth. All that poets and artists have expressed existed first in their own minds. The noble form was in the mind of the sculptor before he could see it in the marble. The marble was only the mirror in which he saw the child of his own fancy reflected. The imagination first paints the picture upon its own canvas, and that which lives and glows upon the material canvas is only an imperfect copy of the mental original. The vast cathedrals were first erected in the architect's brain, from foundation to pinnacle, and the beautiful creations which poets have embodied in numbers through all time were still more beautiful as they lay in fair ideal worlds in their own fancies. All that they have expressed, much and wonderful as it is, is only the rude sketch of what dwelt within them. What beautiful worlds compose the poet's kingdom, and what fair women and noble men dwell in them! But who ever saw on canvas or in marble, in poem or in song, the full embodiment or realization of his ideal? No, the kingdom within is larger than the kingdom without; profounder oceans roll, grander mountains rise to loftier heights, and lovelier valleys lie between.   Groves and gardens and gently swelling hills and shining rivers, and paradises of fruits and flowers that have no antitype and can have no embodiment on earth ; cities of wide streets and marble palaces sparkling with diamonds and shining with gold ; and all the fair world peopled with beings of corresponding excellence, innocent and lovely women, pure and noble men,—all these dwell in clusters and constellations in the kingdom within.   And there, too, exist Utopian governments whose rulers are wise men, consulting the public rather than their private good, and whose people are obedient, intelligent, and happy.   In the wide and populous realms and starry heavens of the mind innumerable sciences and systems come and take up their permanent abode ; arts flourish, kingdoms rise, people are born that never die.   And yet there is room.   Every thought enlarges the boundary of this kingdom ; every new science or art is a new province.   The more you put into the human mind the more it is able to receive.   Is it not a kingdom worthy of a heavenly King?

But I have yet spoken of only one grand division of this kingdom, the intellectual and rational.   There is another realm, twin to this, as large in extent, as various and beautiful in the forms that compose it, and that is the kingdom of the will, whose provinces are affections, and whose immeasurable riches are joys.   There is an affection for every thought, and there is a delight for every affection.

These kingdoms run parallel with each other, and everything within them joins hands.   They are halves of one whole.   The heart is as capacious of joy as the head of truths. Every relation which the soul sustains to the outward world, to thoughts and deeds, was intended to be a highway for the entrance of joys into the heart. The will is an organ of countless pipes and stops, and every act was intended to excite some affection and produce some delight. We know that this instrument is now sadly out of tune, and it often produces terrible discords ; but we know enough of its nature to conclude that, if it were in perfect harmony, there could be no limit to the variety and blessedness of the delights it is capable of receiving. How many quiet and peaceful delights flow into the heart through the senses, through our daily labors and casual contacts with our fellows ! Who can enumerate the delights of social life? delights that spring up as flowers by the dusty way-side of traffic and business ; the familiar greeting, the pleasant smile, the cheerful look. The cheering word dropped into the soul awakens harmonies that linger and play around it through the day of toil and in pleasant memories forever. How manifold the joys that are awakened while we contemplate the beauty with which the Lord has invested the whole earth !

But what are all these compared with the deeper and purer joys which are awakened by the relations of home ! Home ! There is no other sound in human language that awakens so many chords as that. Brother, sister, parent, child, husband, wife, all cluster around it, and the human heart has chords that vibrate in wonderful harmony with every one. Who can enumerate and estimate the joys that are created by these relations ? And yet the human soul can contain them all. If every thought and every act were an instrument of myriad strings, and every vibration a distinct joy, the soul could receive them all. And yet there would be room. Every delight that has blessed a human heart from the creation of man could be compressed into one heart, and yet there would be room. One of the fine globules of water that float about as mist contains all the circles, arcs, and dimensions that can be found in all spheres. It has its centre and circumference, its diameter and poles, its radii and zones, its arcs and curves, as complete as the earth or the sun itself. So each human heart has in it the capacity for the joys of all human hearts. Oh, the inestimable worth, the inconceivable grandeur of the human soul! Though enclosed in the compass of a few feet of flesh, it is a kingdom that stretches away beyond any assignable limit, whose depths are fathomless to any human power, and whose heights rise above the conceptions of any finite intellect. He who rules this kingdom alone knows how vast it is in its extent, how boundless in its capacities for joy.

But I have not yet spoken of the higher degrees of this kingdom. I have referred only to the natural degree of the mind, the most remote and barren province of this kingdom, the frigid zone of the soul. The kingdom of God is a spiritual kingdom, and all its forms and delights are so far exalted above natural delights that human language is totally inadequate to describe them. They are therefore called ineffable and inconceivable. If the human soul is capable of so many thoughts and affections, with their attendant delights, in the natural plane of life, how immeasurable must be its capacities in the spiritual and celestial degrees!

The human soul is made to receive life in three degrees, .
each one rising so far above the other in the extent of
its capacities and in the variety and perfection of its attributes that the activities and delights of the higher can
be expressed only in general terms, and by remote analogies in the lower.   And yet there is not a joy that thrills
the inmost life of an angel that may not thrill yours.
We have sometimes a foretaste of these joys here that
comes to us as a prophecy and hope of what we may be.
A peace glides over the soul and fills it with a sweet calm
and quiet joy ; and again it may be exalted and thrilled
with a heavenly delight.   But it is a delight muffled and
deadened by the weight of flesh.   It is rather a dream
of heaven than heaven itself, a strain of harmony floating
down to us from its remote glories rather than the full
chord of its harmonies.   What, then, must those joys be
in their fulness and perfection !   And the kingdom of
all these joys is within you.   And however large and
varied, however exalted and incomprehensible, it is ca-
pahle of indefinite extension.   This is the kingdom in
which the Lord dwells, and which He fills to its fullest
capacities with His Divine love and wisdom.   This kingdom, I repeat, is within you.   Every one of you is heir
to all its riches, glory, and blessedness.   All thought,
all affection, all delight is within us, and we have and
possess only what we can receive.   However destitute
you may be in worldly riches and honors, the kingdom
of God is within you.   The Lord has made every human
being in His own image and likeness, and consequently
capable of receiving life from Him in every possible variety and form.   What, then, can compare in worth, in

greatness, in capacities for blessedness with the human soul?

The kingdom of heaven is within you. Not actually in all, nor in any in full development and power; but it is within all in possibility, as the harvest is in the grain of wheat, as natural affections and physical powers and natural science are in the infant. The germs of all heavenly joys are within us; the possibilities of the three heavens lie wrapped up, fold within fold, in our spiritual forms, and only await development. And as the seed in good ground is surrounded on all sides by substances specially adapted to its growth, through which forces are continually flowing into it and moulding its possibilities into actual forms, so the Lord has placed the soul in the midst of spheres, relations, and forces that are in the continual effort to call all its forms into actual existence, to create the heavens and the earth within it. All the relations of the soul to the body, and through that to the material world; all the relations of human beings to one another, which grow out of their wants and pleasures, their labors and rest; all social, civil, domestic, and spiritual relations were specially instituted by the Lord to be instruments in forming this kingdom within us, and mediums of filling it with life from Him; and its fitness to accomplish this end is the true measure of value for every earthly and every heavenly thing.

Let us not, then, count ourselves rich and happy, so much for what we have of worldly good as for what we are and may obtain of heavenly good. Let us look to the kingdom within us as our real and only invaluable and imperishable possession.

HUMAN BEAUTY: ITS ORIGIN AND NATURE AND THE MEANS OF ACQUIRING IT.

"Strength and beauty are in his sanctuary."—PSALM xcvi. 6.

STRENGTH and beauty are the two essential elements of a noble manhood and of a beautiful womanhood. They are combined in man and woman in different proportions. Man has more of strength, woman more of beauty. But all true manhood has its beauty, and all genuine womanhood its strength. Rough, naked strength has no comeliness, and weakness no beauty. But combined in due proportion and modified by each other, they become the charm of character and the cause of that attraction which draws human beings together and makes them a delight to each other.

These two primary qualities of all human excellence, strength and beauty, are in the Lord's sanctuary. His sanctuary is in man's will and understanding, and derivatively in his affections and thoughts. The will and the understanding are the grand temple in which the Lord dwells; the affections and thoughts the chapels of various form and use in which the precious gifts of strength and beauty are received from Him and appropriated by man.

When the sanctuary is pure, free from evil lusts and false principles, life from the Lord is received in its own perfect forms, in all its purity, sweetness, and harmony,

147

and then it becomes "the beauty of holiness," in which we are to praise and worship the Lord. This beauty of holiness becomes "the dew of youth," an influence which gives the freshness, the innocence, and the beauty of youth to all the faculties of the mind, and to the forms of that body which we are to inhabit forever. Zion, which is called by the Lord Himself "the perfection of beauty," represents in general the same principles in man as "sanctuary." Zion is man's heart, Jerusalem his understanding ; and it is this Zion, the perfection of beauty, which the Lord exhorts to awake, to shake herself from the dust, and to put on her beautiful garments. Here, then, we have the source of human beauty revealed to us, and the way of access to it pointed out. Its well-spring is in the heart, in the affections. It takes on its forms and colors in the understanding, and comes out in substantial reality in bodily forms and actions. Beauty in its highest qualities is represented as attainable, and we are exhorted to make it our own, to put it on as a garment, to pray that "the beauty of the LORD our God" may be upon us.

The beauty of the Lord, the supreme and infinite type of all beauty, has its origin in His Divine love, and its form and qualities in the Divine wisdom. Man was created in the image and likeness of God. He was made to be a sharer of the supreme beauty. The Lord is in the constant effort to endow us with this beauty, and we are clothed with it in the degree that we become partakers of those Divine qualities which are the essence and cause of beauty.

Regard beauty, of which we propose to speak at the

present time, in any sense you please, in its lowest and most sensuous, or its highest and most interior qualities ; beauty of form, or color, or motion,—in all cases it is the expression of some affection or interior grace. All beauty is spiritual in its origin. The beauty of a material object consists in its meaning, in what it says to us of something more excellent than itself. The beauty of a flower, of a tree, of a winding stream, or of a landscape consists in what it suggests to us of something higher than itself, because it is the form of that higher quality. The beauty of the material world is an effect which expresses the excellence of its spiritual cause.

This must be so from the very nature of the relation between cause and effect. Every cause seeks to reproduce and express itself, in all its qualities, in lower forms. Innocence, purity, and loveliness of character must tend to express themselves in lovely forms. When we reflect that the material universe is the embodiment of the Divine love and wisdom in material substances, we can see why it is that there is so much beauty in the world. Every material object and living thing has a beauty of some kind. Even the weeds that cumber the fields, the thorn and the thistle, which men regard as a curse for sin, the insect which stings and poisons us, the degraded reptile, and the wild beast which tears and devours, have some beauty of form or structure or color or motion. Perverted forms as they are of the Divine loveliness, they still bear some trace of its impress.

If we find traces of the beauty of the Lord in the lowest things, we may expect to find it more fully embodied in the highest, and our expectations will not be disappointed. We shall find it in its perfection in the human face and form. Here also we can see how the outward beauty is the effect and expression of inward and spiritual beauty. This would follow as a necessary result from the fact that the material body is cast into the mould of the spirit. The spirit has fashioned it. The spirit is the potter, and the body is clay in its hands, which it is constantly acting upon to mould into its own likeness. This is true of the material body in the first years of our existence, and of the spiritual body in every stage of our being. There are, in general, two kinds of human beauty: beauty in its essence or cause, and beauty in its expression. All beauty has its origin in love and its expression in truth. A pure and innocent affection in the will, united with genuine truth in the understanding, cannot fail of producing beautiful effects.

We must not forget that love and truth are not abstractions. They are the most potent forces that act upon the spiritual or the material body. We are penetrated by them ; we live and move and have our being in them. The material body is constantly subject to their action, has its life from them. There is a force constantly present in water, and in all matter, which forms it into spheres when the matter assumes a fluid state and is left free to move. So there is in the very nature and activities of the Divine love and the Divine truth, from which we receive all our life, a tendency to the human form and an active influence to make that form as noble and beautiful as possible. Thus those very forces and principles which are the essence and cause of all beauty are constantly acting upon us to make our faces and forms and motions the complete correspondents and embodiments of their nature. Thus the Divine forces which give us life tend to mould us into every form of beauty, in the same way and according to the same immutable law by which the Divine forces in nature tend to make material forms beautiful. All that we have to do to become more and more beautiful is to co-operate with these forces, to let them have free play through us, and to supply them with the right kind of materials for their workmanship.

The first thing we are to do is to exercise pure, innocent, heavenly affections. Without this it is impossible to become more beautiful than we are, or to retain what we may have received from hereditary influences. The beauty of youth, of mere surface and complexion, will fade like a flower. There must be some inherent, vital, and unfailing source which supplies natural wastes with finer and more substantial substances, and replenishes them with perennial freshness and moulds them into a lovelier beauty. The quality and degree of our beauty and nobleness of form will be determined by the quality and degree of our spiritual affections. There is no possibility of failure in this respect. They are orderly results of normal causes. Every affection you cherish leaves its impress upon you. It tends to fashion the external form into its likeness, and there is no escape from its effect.

This is a truth of common observation and experience. We see it in its accumulated and large results, in the faces and forms of every man and woman we meet. Every disposition habitually indulged forms its image in the features of the face, in the motions of the body, and in every fibre and muscle of its form. Its first effect is upon the brain, and through that upon every part of the whole organization.   The face is the index of the mind, because the mind forms it and makes it the theatre on which it enacts all its passions.   Every face is a history, and in its small compass are recorded the sins and sorrows, the joys and fears, the malignities, the lusts, the cunning, the ferocity, the hope and trust, the struggles with evil passions, the integrity, the innocence and peace of many generations.   We can only read some of the most prominent and boldest characters.   But the history of all the influences, large and small, which have combined to form the character of your ancestry from its beginning is embodied in your own person.   We talk of fleeting influences.   There are no fleeting influences. Every influence is eternal.   The Lord does not write human history in fading colors and on perishable leaves. You think you can be false or cunning, that you can indulge in malignities and lusts, and no one will know it, and that you can escape all lasting effects of it.   How much, how terribly much, you are mistaken !   You cannot sulk in the corner ; you cannot indulge in an unkind thought ; you cannot say a sharp word ; you cannot indulge in a revengeful feeling ; no, you cannot think a false thought, or do an evil deed, and escape the record of its shame in the book of your own life.   The Lord has made the mind self-registering.   Every falsity leaves a shadow upon it, every evil a stain.

I know the influence of one evil once indulged may be small ; its consequences may seem as fleeting as the act itself.   But it is not so.   The brutality and ferocity and stolidity and meanness, the low cunning and worldly shrewdness, the stony selfishness and cruel malignities, the pride and vanities and contempt which we see in the forms and faces of men and women are the recorded results of the indulgence of evils which were momentary and casual in their inception.

My young friends, will you not remember this when you are tempted to think falsely, to feel wickedly, or to act sinfully? The wicked feeling has its sharp graver in its cunning hands, and while you indulge the feeling it is etching its ugly lines in your face and twisting your features into its own form. The impure thought is photographing itself upon the delicate but tenacious forms of your whole nature, and leaving its foul stains indelibly impressed upon you. If every time you told or looked a falsehood, or indulged a hate, the name of the evil should come out in distinct and black lines upon your forehead and repeat itself in ugly characters in your whole face, with what horror you would shun it! It is so written, in very faint lines at first, it may be, but every repetition of the evil increases their distinctness. The angels can read the whole history in the hand; they can tell the quality of the mind by the tone of the voice.

According to the same law, every good affection and true thought registers itself in its own proper characters. Every heavenly affection leaves its impress upon you and, to the extent of its influence, moulds you into its own image. Every element of the noblest and purest beauty is contained in the principles of goodness and truth. As these principles are brought into act and become substantiated in the form and features, they change them into their own likeness. And they do it by imperceptible but

constantly acting influences.   When you think kindly of
others and your heart goes out to them in desires for
their good, the beauty of kindness is winning its way
through the labyrinth of many organic forms, leaving its
smile and its impress upon them all as it passes, until it
comes out in open expression upon the face.

Some faces are like landscapes in a day of broken
clouds.   Sometimes the shadows lie dark and heavy
upon them.   When the features are in repose you can
see the history of former generations which has been
stereotyped upon them ; the weariness of protracted
labor, shadows of disappointed hopes, and the sadness
of many sorrows.   But when the light of an awakened
heavenly affection breaks through their parting folds the
face becomes illuminated, transfigured with the glory of
the inward light.   You can look away into its serene
deeps and see in every feature a beauty born of heavenly
influences.

Patience in duty and trust in the Lord contain important elements of beauty, which they impart to the face
and to the whole form.   They give quietness and composure to the features and to the actions.   Through the
face, as through a transparent veil, you can look down
into the serene depths of being, where no storms can
reach, where all is stable and in repose, and see the foundations on which the natural life rests and the perennial
springs from which its thoughts and affections flow.
Every time you repress an impatient desire, every time
you restrain an impatient word or act, every time you
take up the burden of duty cheerfully, every time you
meet the conflicts and the vicissitudes of life in patient

confidence in the infinite goodness which makes all things work together for good for those who trust in the Lord, you make some progress in bringing your whole form into the image of that repose and quietude which impart a charm to every feature and every action.

But the supreme beauty which charms all hearts is innocence, purity. This is the charm of the beauty of infancy and childhood. It is not beauty of form; it is not grace of motion. It is the purity and sweetness of heaven which shine through a little child. The material body is, as it were, transparent. It is like the charm of flowers, which is not so much in their forms as in their delicacy of texture and purity of color and sweetness of fragrance. They awaken the perception that they are offering up themselves for our delight.

Innocence combines all the Christian graces,—unselfishness, trust, repose, unconscious action, which is always beautiful, gentleness, devotion to others, and devout adoration of the Lord; that worship of the heart which surrenders itself to the Divine will, to be guided by its wisdom and to be moulded into its likeness. Innocence is not weakness or ignorance. It is wisdom and power itself. It is power without noise. It is the power which makes the grass grow, and planets fly through the silent spaces with ceaseless motion. It is the wisdom which uses the mightiest forces for human help and culture. It is supreme order, which is always beautiful. Feebleness is not beauty. Strength and beauty must go hand in hand, as they always do when the strength is used for beneficent purposes.

While you are in the effort to keep the great commandment of love to the Lord, and just to the extent that you keep it, you will be gaining the heavenly beauty. You open your heart to the Lord, and to the living springs of all grace and comeliness. You put yourself into His hands who has the perfect ideal of nobleness and beauty, and perfect skill to fashion every feature and form according to it. The Divine truth, which is the Holy Spirit, contains in its substance and in all its forces and forms and influence a tendency to ultimate itself in the perfection of beauty. As you open your affections to the influence of these Divine forces they will flow in and do their work. They will efface the lines of deformity which sin has engraved ; they will harmonize discordant proportions ; ·they will round into fulness imperfect forms ; they will reduce to order conflicting motions, and bring the whole person into unity.

Every effort you make to learn the truths which constitute the Divine wisdom, and to incorporate them into your nature, will have its effect. While you are reflecting upon them they are imbuing your understanding with their sweet and lovely spirit, softening its hardness, quickening its perceptions, harmonizing its activities. The soft and lambent light of truth is flowing down with more fulness and clearness into the eyes, and a power which attracts and makes the heart glad begins to beam forth from them. As you go on with the work and receive more largely of this informing life and beautifying spirit, it softens the hardness and smooths the roughness of the voice, and imbues it with those qualities which touch the sympathies and win the heart ; it penetrates every feature, remoulds the face after the heavenly pattern, rounds the limbs, gives nobleness and comely dignity to the whole form, and sways every motion to harmony born of an inward grace, and expressing it. As the life of the Divine love becomes fuller and purer the whole person will become the very form of heavenly love; it will become the embodiment of Zion, the perfection of beauty.

This is no fancy. Your own observation can teach you that it is not. You know how fierce passions inflame and distort the face, and how heavenly affections fill it with a serene light and a most winning loveliness. You have seen faces that were not regular and cleanly cut in particular features, but which had an inward beauty that charmed every beholder. All that is necessary to render any form of the face fixed and permanent is to cherish the affections which express themselves in that form.

It may be replied that, if this principle is true, the good must be the most beautiful. Yet some of the worst men and women have been famous for their beauty. There is a kind of external beauty, regularity of features, symmetry of form, delicacy of complexion, which is due to inheritance and to causes not within one's self; but if the soul is deformed with evil this superficial beauty is but a veil which ill conceals the ugliness within. Without the beauty of expression which shines forth from the soul the most that the body can attain is the lifeless beauty of the statue or the painted mask.

Again, while it is true that the material body is so intimately allied to the spiritual that it becomes changed by it, making the face the index of the mind, the physical form may respond but slowly to the changes of the spirit ; so much so that a face that is outwardly fair may conceal an infernal character ; and again a plain and unattractive face may clothe a heavenly spirit.   Our spiritual bodies, the bodies in which we are to live and by which we are to be identified forever, are the exact forms of our affections. They change easily, and become the perfect exponent and image of the affections we habitually cherish.   The purer and more interior the affection, and the more fully it becomes united with genuine truths, the more beautiful we shall become.   It is, therefore, in the power of every one to become as beautiful and noble in form as he chooses ; and the way to do it is to cultivate those heavenly affections which mould the face and limbs and every part of the body into forms corresponding to their quality.

Such is the nature of the affections that there is no assignable limit to their strength and excellence, beyond which they cannot pass.   You see what a prospect this holds out for our attainment in personal beauty and nobleness of form.   You can see that what Swedenborg says of the beauty of the angels must be true, because it follows from causes which we see in operation here.   He says their beauty surpasses the power of words to describe or of any human art to portray.   Their faces are so glorious and lovely, and shine with such a heavenly light, that they penetrate the hearts of those who behold them, with enchanting power.   They are the very forms of loveliness.   They are purity and innocence itself.   The eyes of the angels are aflame with heavenly love ; their faces are all aglow with its warmth ; their features are moulded into its nobleness and rounded into its harmonies; its dignity is enthroned in their foreheads; its sweetness is folded in their lips, and its gracefulness sways every motion. The voice is so modulated by heavenly affections that it is felt to be the sweetness and power of love itself speaking. The whole form is the embodiment of a benign power, and radiant with the very life of heaven.

'All the faculties are in the freshness and vigor and resplendent comeliness of their spring-time; they grow as the lily and blossom as the rose. All these elements of loveliness continue to unfold into more excellent forms. It is not the glorious beauty of a fading flower. It continnes to increase; it glows with a serener light; it becomes the more complete and varied embodiment of a holier joy, a purer love, and a sweeter peace. Its perfections must continue to increase to eternity.

All the qualities and forms of beauty are in heavenly love, as all germs are in their seed. You have only to cherish and cultivate them, which is to exercise them in love towards the Lord and towards man. You have only to live the life of them, and you will grow into their appropriate forms, with more certainty than the seed grows into the loveliness of the lily, or the acorn into the grandeur of the oak.

Why is not this an excellence and a glory worthy of our thought and effort? If physical beauty, which fades and perishes so soon, lay within as easy reach as heavenly beauty, which is fresh, perennial, and which will continue to increase in perfection forever, we should all strive for it; multitudes would think no price too great to pay for it.

We are becoming forms of heavenly beauty or of infernal deformity every day. Whether we seek it or not, every affection we exercise has its influence in moulding our form ; every truth we learn enters into its composition ; every thought we think and every good deed we do is the graver's tool which gives a new line of beauty, or the painter's brush which adds a lovelier tint. Yes, every gentle act leaves its gentleness in the hand that performs it ; every noble deed leaves the imprint of its nobility ; every heavenly purpose carried into effect communicates its fragrance and beauty as a Divine benediction to the soul. Strength and beauty are in His sanctuary.

THE ORIGIN OF EVIL.

" The serpent beguiled me, and I did eat."—GENESIS iii. 13.

THE problem to which I invite your attention has excited the interest and baffled the ingenuity and wisdom of the best men and the most profound thinkers in past generations. From the point of view of the Christian Church, its solution has been impossible without involving the Divine character and purposes in many contradictions and absurdities. I believe that the doctrines of the New Church give us the principles necessary to its solution, and teach us how to use them to attain the result. I can hope, however, to do but little more than to state the fundamental conditions of the problem, and point out the direction in which we must look for its solution.

First, it is essential to have a precise and clear idea of what evil essentially is, for, if we have no exact knowledge of the problem, we certainly cannot solve it. We shall be working with materials which we do not understand to produce an unknown result. Is evil a distinct substance, form, or power in itself, acting in opposition to good and tending to pervert and destroy it? If so, it must either be self-existent and eternal, or it must have been created. If it was created, it must have been created by the Lord, and then He must be the author of both evil and good. This is the opinion held by many, and the logic by which they are brought to this conclusion seems clear and irrefragable, if you admit the definition and the premises.

But we cannot admit that there are two self-existent and independent forces or substances or creators, for that would be the admission that there are two Gods. Nor, on the other hand, can we admit that the Lord created evil, for that would be acting contrary to Himself. A Being of infinite love and wisdom seeks to accomplish certain ends, and for that purpose He creates the universe and peoples it with intelligent human beings. Can we suppose that at the same time and running all along parallel with it He creates a discordant power, that tends to oppose and thwart His purposes of infinite love ; that He mars His own work and defeats His own ends ? Such a supposition is absurd. It is impossible in the nature of things. Infinite wisdom could not act in that way ; it would be infinite folly. Imagine a benevolent and wise man earnestly seeking to accomplish some purpose of good, but at the same time voluntarily and knowingly doing something that would defeat his purpose. A wise man could not do it. It would be folly. Much less could a Being of infinite wisdom do anything to hinder or defeat the ends of His wisdom. Every rational mind must conclude, therefore, that the Lord did not create evil. The question arises, then, If evil is not self-existent and the Lord did not create it, wherein did it originate? It could not create itself, it did not always exist, and the Lord did not create it, and yet we have the most mournful and incontestable evidence that it does exist. This is the question to which we must address ourselves.

It is an axiom or a self-evident proposition, that a Being of infinite love could propose no end for His activities but the best and highest good of others, for any other end would show that He was not infinitely good. It would imply that there were some limitations or exceptions to His love. Again, a Being of infinite wisdom could not fail to devise the best possible means to carry into effect His purposes. The least failure in this would show beyond question that He was not infinitely wise: There is some limit to His wisdom. The ends of the Lord, then, must be the largest good of all, and the Divine methods must be the best possible ; they must be perfect.

Everything that tends to oppose the Divine ends, or that in any way or degree tends to thwart them, must be evil. There must be a Divine order and method that are infinitely perfect, and every form and force of which must tend to good. Everything that tends to disturb that order and method must be evil and false. Now let us see, if we can, how such disturbance and disorder could originate and not come from the Lord. In doing this we must commence with things that are known and familiar, and advance step by step from the known to the unknown.

Let us take some article of human invention and construction, a watch, for example. Let us suppose a man has invented and made a perfect watch ; that is, it is made of the best materials that exist, and every part of it is constructed in a perfect manner. It keeps perfect time, and will continue to do so forever, unless the order of its movements should be interrupted or obstructed, or the form of some of its parts should be changed.   Now, every one knows that the watch will lose its perfection.   It will cease to keep accurate time.   It will lose its goodness.   Disturbance and evil will be introduced.   How does the evil originate?   It was not some self-existent, independent power which acted in opposition to the order and motions of the watch.   The maker certainly did not cause the difficulty, for by the supposition he made it perfect in all its forms and materials.   How, then, does it come? From the inherent and essential qualities of matter.   Its parts will wear by friction, and thus the perfect form and finish of the wheels and pivots is destroyed.   The particles worn away accumulate as dust and dirt, the oil evaporates by heat, the surfaces become dry and rough, and the action of the wheels is impeded.   The evil, then, did not originate with the maker of the watch.   He did all that he could to prevent it.   It did not exist previous to the construction of the watch, but it grew out of its action, out of those very qualities which were essential to the existence of the watch.

But some one may say, "Suppose the substances of which the watch is composed were so hard that they would not wear and so smooth that there would be no friction?"   If they had been, the watch would have been impossible, for the substances could not have been cut and cast into the necessary forms.   We cannot avoid the conclusion, therefore, that, given the possibility of the watch, you must also grant the inevitable consequence that it will generate those evils which will destroy it. This principle will apply to everything that man makes. The evil grows out of the essential properties of matter.

If we rise from the works of man to man himself, we find the same elements in the problem, only more complicated. Let us take man as a physical being first, and inquire how physical evils originate.

The organization and mechanism of the material body have always excited the admiration and wonder of those who have examined its structure. That a series of organic forms so indefinite in number, so complicated in their relations, so various in form and use, embracing solids, fluids, and aeriform substances so exact in their forms and so delicate in their structure that the smallest mote impedes and irritates them, and the puncture of the finest needle would arrest the action of the whole organism ; only less than infinite in their motions and uses and relations to one another and to the material world, and so perfectly adjusted to the spiritual body within that they both act as one,—that such an amazing number of organic forms and series of forms should act together in such perfect harmony in such a diversity of conditions is a miracle of wisdom whose depths no finite mind can fathom. When this microcosm, this universe in miniature, is in perfect order, as it came from the hands of its Creator, every organ performs its own work perfectly, and every activity unites with every other and flows towards one end with perfect precision, in perfect harmony. So miraculous are these combinations, and so prompt and certain in their operation, that you cannot touch the body in any point with the finest needle without the knowledge of the fact being instantly communicated to every part of the corporeal kingdom. To effect this communication myriads of myriads of organic forms are excited to action, and they all act together as one organ. And when they act in such perfect unity the effect of every action is a physical delight, and the whole body is good,—in a state of perfect health.

Physical evil is the interruption of this order ; a weakness or defect in some of these innumerable organic forms by which their action is accelerated, impeded, or destroyed. How does it originate? How is it introduced into this perfect kingdom? And in what does it essentially consist? It is not some self-existent force that wars upon the organization, weakens it, makes breaches into the citadel of life, and finally overcomes and destroys it. The Lord did not plant disorder in the body side by side with order. He moulded it into a perfect order and pronounced it good. He did not make it a kingdom divided against itself. Whence, then, came the evil? Did it not inevitably originate in the body's own action? The body has laws and processes of growth, change, and decay. It is a flowing stream, and if the current is arrested or the springs are not fed, it becomes inflamed or wastes away. It reaches its maximum of beauty and power, and then it begins to decline, to wither and fade. It wears out by its own action, like any machine. And this wear is necessarily attended with weakness, obstruction, and physical evil in some form.

But let us take an example in which severe pain and loss of physical structure are the results. The body is so formed that it cannot bear too great a degree of heat without pain and loss of structure. A little child, attracted by the beauty and brilliancy of flame, thrusts its hand into it and is burnt. Evil is introduced into the·

body. It is filled with pain. Its organization in some of its parts is destroyed. Whence did the evil originate? In the fire, do you say? But the fire is good. Man could not live without heat. The earth could not have been formed and the ceaseless activities of the creation kept in play without it. It is the motive power in the universe, the most useful and the best thing in it. How, then, can evil originate from it? There is no evil in it; it is wholly good. Do you say it originated in the child? The child was attracted by the beauty of the flame, in accordance with a universal, most necessary, and benevolent gift of the Lord to man. All our powers are called into play by the attraction of beauty in form and color. The child was in search of good, according to the laws of its being. The evil, then, was not in the child. Whence, then, did it come? From too much heat. From a want of proper adjustment between the relations of the physical structure to the heat. The proper balance, equilibrium, between the two was lost, and hence there was a disturbance in the action of the vital powers.

We may apply the same principle to the gratification of the appetites and every sense. The child will thrust a poison into its mouth as readily as the most wholesome food, if it is pleasant to the taste. He cannot avoid all possibility of violating the laws of his physical being without perfect knowledge, and he cannot gain that without experience. And there are some physical evils from which the most perfect knowledge would not protect him, such as the pain resulting from too great heat and cold, and from unavoidable accidents. For it is not possible to conceive that man could ever have passed through the world without suffering some pain, even if he had never sinned.

If the question is asked why the Lord did not form the material body so that it would not wear out or become deranged or be sensible of pain, the answer is, He could not. He made the best body possible, and out of the best materials. This follows from our axiom, from the very nature of infinite wisdom. Infinite wisdom cannot fail to do the best in every particular, for if it did it would not be infinite wisdom. We can see also, from the very nature of the case, that it would be impossible to create an organic form so delicately and exquisitely sensitive to external impressions as the material body, which would not be liable to pain as well as pleasure. If the organization of the material body must be so perfectly adjusted to all outward relations and to the spirit within that it must act in perfect harmony with both to produce pleasurable sensations, it follows necessarily that any derangement of form or action must produce pain. If the eye, for example, must be so delicately organized that it can be moved to activity by the waves of ether, a grosser substance must cause it pain. A body without nerves would be incapable of pain, and equally incapable of pleasure. There is no way of attaining the end without the liability to obstruction. There is no way of attaining physical good without the liability to physical evil. The very delicacy and perfection of the organization necessary to obtain physical good increases the liability to disorder and physical evil. Physical evil, then, does not originate outside the organization, but within it, from the necessary limitations and imperfections of matter. The

Lord does not create it. He did not create the nerves to communicate pain, but pleasure ; but He could not so form them that they would be the inlets of good, and not, under changed conditions, of evil. On the side of nature the Lord is under the same kind of limitations that man is. In constructing a musical instrument the maker is limited in one direction by his materials. He may make one that is in perfect tune, but from the imperfection of the wood and iron it will become discordant. The Lord would be limited in the same direction. The giant can exert no more force with a straw than a little child.

Here, then, we have numerous examples where discordant action and even destruction grow out of perfect forms and relations, from two causes or limitations. First, from the use of instruments which, by their very nature, lose their perfection of form by their action. And, secondly, from the loss of that equilibrium and perfect adjustment which is essential to the attainment of the good which the Lord has provided for man, and which He is in the constant effort to give him. The Lord did not make man's organization so delicate, and all its relations so nice, that it might easily become deranged, but because there was no other way of giving him the good.

Let us now take another step, to the moral and spiritual plane of life. As a spiritual being, man is a form organized of spiritual substances, as his material body is a form organized of material substances. He was created in the image and likeness of God, and was therefore formed to receive life from Him in perfect forms. His will and understanding, his thoughts and affections, which are organic forms, were made to act in perfect harmony with the inflowing life from the Lord, and when they so act every motion is a joy. As the material body stands between the soul and the outward world, and is the connecting link between them, receiving life from the soul and being acted upon by nature, so man himself is a conjoining medium between the Lord and the outward world. He receives life from the Lord, and as it flows through him into outward act and finds reaction from the material world, he is filled with delight when every form in this wonderful series of connecting links acts in perfect harmony. This was man's state originally, and then he was good. He was in harmony with the Lord, with nature and man. He stood in perfect equilibrium between the forces that pressed upon him, and, consequently, in perfect freedom to turn either way, to the Lord above or the earth beneath. And it was essential to this perfection that he should maintain this equilibrium. Now, the question is, How could he disturb this order? The Lord could not have purposely introduced any disturbing element. There was no self-existent, independent cause outside of man to do it ; and as he was perfect in his own form and activities, whence could evil find entrance?

There were two qualities or conditions of human life that rendered evil possible, or what is the same thing, that rendered it possible for this perfect harmony to be disturbed and this perfect order to be destroyed.

The first was human freedom, this very equilibrium of which I have spoken ; and the second was the absolute necessity that the sensuous plane of life should come into conscious and vigorous existence before the moral and spiritual life, and, consequently, the necessity of judging of things as they appeared to the senses, before the rational degree of the mind was formed.

Freedom of will is the essential human element in man, and freedom implies the ability to choose our course of action and to act according to our choice ; and it also implies that from our point of view there must be some degree of good in either course. If there were no apparent good except in one direction, there would really be no choice. Freedom implies the ability to love one thing or another ; to serve God or Mammon ; to go in the way that the Lord says is right, or in the way that seems to us to be right. Consequently in man's freedom lies the possibility of evil.

Now, if any one asks why the Lord did not so form man that he could only do right, the answer is, that he would not have been a man if He had. The essential element of his humanity would have been left out of his composition. He might have been an animal, a being subject to his instincts, and with no power to transgress them. But he would not have been a man. To ask why the Lord did not create man without the specific and essential elements of humanity, is to ask why He did not make man without making a man, or by making something else, which is an absurdity that answers itself. That very excellence, then, which elevates man above all other created beings, and allies him in a peculiar manner to his Creator, contains within it, or more strictly, *is*, a liability to fall.

Granting, then, that one of the essential elements of freedom is the ability to turn from order to disorder, from good

to evil, it may be further said that the possibility of evil
does not imply its necessity. Very true. The chances,
therefore, were at least equal for man's remaining as he
was created, in the integrity of his being. But he did
not. Why did the scale preponderate towards the evil?
I answer, The weight that turned the balance in favor of
evil was the other necessary element in human life, the
sensuous nature. Man's consciousness must be opened
into this world, and sensuous delights must lie very close
to him and exert a great power over him, before the
reason and the higher faculties of the will are sufficiently
developed to guide and control him. His first knowledge must be that of the senses or of the appearances
of things, and there necessarily grows out of this the
tendency to put too much confidence in their testimony.
They constantly act upon the mind, as gravity acts upon
the body ; they draw us towards the earth, towards natural and sensuous delights. Now observe, these sensuous
delights are just as necessary to human life as the
highest spiritual delights. If we were not drawn by the
pleasures of taste or impelled by hunger to take food,
who would eat? Would the body get regular and sufficient supplies of substances to meet its wastes? But we
are in danger of being drawn on by this delight to indulge
it at the expense of higher and nobler faculties, especially
before we have experience and judgment for our guide.
Children and men fall from this cause every day.

Again, we are compelled to form our first conclusions
and judgments from things as they appear to us, or as
they are to the senses, or to our own experience. Now,
all our life comes from God. It is a perpetual gift to us,

but it seems to originate spontaneously within us. It seems to be our own. Our senses say to us that it is our own, and there is an inclination to listen to them, to believe them, and to claim it as our own, and, therefore, to make ourselves as gods. For that which has underived, independent life is God, and when we think that we live of ourselves, we love ourselves and believe in ourselves and forget the Lord. We are inclined to love that which ministers to our delights; we begin to love to receive good rather than to give good. And this must invert the whole order of our lives; it must incline us to look down to the earth rather than up to the Lord. The senses and sensuous delights allure us and tend to mislead us; they tend to destroy the perfect equilibrium of all our faculties between this world and the spiritual world, between ourselves and the Lord. They act on one end of the scale beam with a continual tendency to turn it in their favor.

These sensuous delights are the serpent that tempted Eve, and they are the serpent that has tempted every son and daughter of Eve to this day. The disposition to judge for ourselves what is good, is the tree of the knowledge of good and evil. The Lord knew the danger of eating of this tree, and warned man against it. He gave him every help which it was possible to give. If man had been willing to obey the Lord instead of his sensuous nature, if he had been willing to act from the real truth, in obedience, rather than from appearances, he would not have fallen.

Some will wonder why the Lord created the serpent, and why He put the tree of the knowledge of good and evil in man's garden; why He gave the principles which they represent a place among the human faculties. The . answer is, because they are essential parts of man's mind. The serpent must be there ; man must be drawn to external things by his delights. The tree must be there ; he must have the ability as of himself to judge of good and evil in order to call all his faculties into play and to make him fully a man. But the senses magnify the good of natural things, and we are overborne by them, and thus the equilibrium is destroyed, and the true, orderly flow of life is obstructed. Man begins to love himself better than the Lord, and the world better than his neighbor. The lower faculties become strong by exercise, and the higher close and dwindle into feebleness by disuse, until man's distinctly spiritual nature dies, and he loses sight of God, of heaven, and of heavenly delights, and only his lower faculties are alive.

The Lord in creating man gave him no faculty that was not essential to his perfection. Every faculty was good. But by the very nature of these faculties they were liable to abuse, to be exercised at the expense of higher faculties. Thus the equilibrium was destroyed and disorder ensued.

All the examples and illustrations which I have given from human employments, from man as a physical, intellectual, and spiritual being, confirm this conclusion. Evil had no existence previous to the creation. It is not some self-existent, independent being or force that is making war upon good, and endeavoring in all possible ways to defeat and destroy it. The Lord did not create evil, nor, on the other hand, could He prevent it, because the possibility of abuse inheres in those very qualities of freedom and rationality which make man to be man.

Mechanical evils have their origin in the destructibility of matter, a quality essential to its usefulness. Physical evils are made possible by the very delicacy and sensitiveness which adapt the body to be man's faithful servant. Moral evil becomes possible when the Lord bestows upon man His crowning gifts of human freedom and rationality, the faculties which if rightly used bring man into the image and likeness of his Maker.

Knowing how evil comes, we know how to guard against it. Having learned that the senses cannot be trusted, we should not trust them. Knowing that natural delights, though good in themselves, clamor for gratification, and if not controlled by reason will destroy us, we must keep them in subjection. There is only one Being whom we can absolutely trust; He is the Lord. Let us trust Him. Let us love the Lord and hate evil.

SIN AND ITS PUNISHMENT.

" The soul that sinneth, it shall die."—EZEKIEL xviii. 20.

BY common consent man is a sinner. The Lord declares it, and man confesses it. Man has broken the Divine commandments, and he now stands before the Lord guilty, rebellious, and justly exposed to the penalty of a violated law. It is, therefore, a matter of the most momentous importance to him to know his exact relations to the law and to the Lord. How does his sin affect his own being? What change does it make in the disposition of the Lord towards him? What is the punishment for sin, and how is it administered? What are the conditions of pardon, and how can man comply with them? These questions have been answered many times. Hundreds of volumes have been written to state and explain them, and yet, to the minds of most people the whole subject is involved in many difficulties, and the most dangerous errors are widely prevalent concerning it. We are, each one of us, a party in this question. It vitally touches our spiritual and eternal interests. It is not merely a question of temporal wealth and worldly prosperity; the riches of the soul are brought into peril of loss; the title to our inheritance of the blessings and honor and glory of heaven is at stake. Let us, then, endeavor to understand the subject as it really is, as

176

reason enlightened by revelation sees it, as the Lord Himself has presented it to us in His Holy Word.

There are four points of inquiry which contain the essential elements of the whole subject. These questions are, first, What is sin? in what does man's offence really consist? secondly, What is the penalty? thirdly, How is it inflicted? and, fourthly, What are the only conditions of escape from it?

A clear and rational comprehension of the principles involved in these questions will enable us to see the whole subject in its true light. I invite your attention, therefore, to what the doctrines of the New Church teach us concerning these principles which involve our eternal interests.

First, What is sin? The common and the true answer is, It is a violation of a Divine law. But this answer, though true, may not convey a true idea, or at least may give us a very imperfect idea of the real nature of sin. We must have a true conception of the nature of a Divine law before we can see what the necessary results of its violation are. If the law is an arbitrary prohibition or requirement, having no necessary, essential ground in the nature of man or the Lord, but is imposed upon man because the Lord had a right to do it, or for the sake of testing his obedience, the punishment is as arbitrary as the law. There is no necessary connection between them. The punishment is not the direct effect of the sin, but of the Lord's displeasure. But if the Divine laws are the principles of man's life; if man before he fell was the personal embodiment of them, as the plant is the embodiment of the laws of vegetable life, or the material body

m

of animal life, then the punishment of their violation follows as a necessary effect.   As the plant withers and dies when the conditions of its life and growth are not complied with ; as the material body becomes feeble and is filled with pain when its laws are broken, so disease and pain and death must inevitably follow disobedience to the laws of the soul.   This point, then, must be settled before we can answer the question we propose for our consideration, and upon its answer will depend the answer to all the other questions.

The prevalent theology is based upon the theory that the law of the Lord, like the civil laws of nations, is in a certain sense arbitrary,—that is, it has no necessary, inherent ground in the nature of man and his relations to his Creator.   The Lord, by His absolute ownership of man, had a right to impose upon him any test of his obedience, or to demand any amount of homage and service He chose, and to attach any penalty He pleased. He therefore gave him such laws and imposed such penalties as in His wisdom and good pleasure He saw best, as an arbitrary sovereign.   In this respect, according to common opinion, human and Divine laws are similar. They may both be enacted for the good of the people, and such penalties for disobedience or non-performance of duty may be imposed as the highest wisdom and the most benevolent intentions may dictate ; but still .they are totally unlike physical laws in their operation.   We call physical laws natural because they are embodied in nature.   But civil laws are in a certain sense arbitrary. They may be the expression of the nature and relations of societies and peoples, or they may not.   They may be enacted and repealed. Men may violate them and escape the penalty, or they may suffer the penalty under false accusation when they are innocent. But a natural law cannot be evaded. Punishment grows out of its violation, and only the guilty can suffer. A natural law can never be repealed or annulled. It may be overborne for a time by a superior force, but its action is never suspended.

If the Divine laws are arbitrary in the same sense that any law of human enactment may be,—that is, if they are not the outward expression of inward principles actually embodied in man's spiritual nature,—the punishment may be remitted at the good pleasure of the Lord, or it may not. And this is the general opinion of the Christian world.

But there is abundant testimony in the Sacred Scriptures that the laws of the Lord are not in any sense arbitrary. "If thou wilt enter into life, keep the commandments." "Thy law is the truth." "I am the way, the truth, and the life" are Divine declarations. All the promises of pardon and eternal life are based upon obedience to the commandments ; for to keep the commandments is to love the Lord and to believe in Him. "He that hath my commandments and keepeth them, he it is that loveth me." Reason also would teach us that Divine laws must be the embodiments of infinite wisdom. Natural laws are the Divine methods of operation in the material world, and they are inconceivably more perfect in their action than the wisest human laws. Must we not believe that the same, if not a much greater, perfection exists in the Lord's spiritual laws? Is it not evident that the moral law existed before it was written on tables of stone? Was it not always wrong to steal and lie and murder? Was man under no obligations to love the Lord and his neighbor before the two great commandments were given? These laws are written in man's spiritual nature. He can no more attain heavenly happiness without living according to them than the tree can attain blossoms and fruit without acting according to the laws of vegetable life, or than man can obtain the blessings of health without obedience to the laws of physical life. They were given in a formal and apparently arbitrary manner because man had forgotten them, and because it was essential that he should know and obey them as the laws of God.

Spiritual laws, then, are of the same nature as natural laws ; they operate in the same way ; they are enacted in man's spiritual nature ; they are the principles of his being which govern all his activities and relations to the Lord and to other beings. When I say to my child, You must not put your hand into the fire, and if you do you will be punished with terrible pain, I merely state a law which exists whether I state it or not. I only give information of a truth which existed before, though I give it in the form of a command. So it is with all the Divine commandments. They are formal statements of the laws of man's spiritual nature.

But it may be said, The commandments are Divine laws. Why does a man violate the laws of his own life by disobedience to them? Because man was created in the image and likeness of the Lord. The laws of the Divine life are finited in him, and he cannot break the least commandment without doing violence to his own nature.

Now we are prepared to answer our first question, What is sin? It is a violation of the laws of our own life. The Lord created us for a definite purpose, and with faculties specifically formed and adjusted to the attainment of that purpose. He established a definite and perfect order and system of means ; and when we step out of that order we turn aside from the true and only path that leads to life. We do the same thing in principle that we do when we disobey a physical law. There are physical, social, civil, and moral, as well as spiritual, sins. All natural, as well as spiritual, laws are Divine, because the Lord instituted them. They are His laws. They are His methods of attaining His ends. The planet obeys His law while it keeps to its own orbit ; the plant obeys His law while it grows and brings forth fruit after its kind ; the animal obeys His law while it follows its own instincts ; and if it were possible for a plant or animal to depart from its order, it would sin against the Lord as well as do violence to the laws of its own life. So when man obeys the Divine laws he obeys the laws of his own being, and when he breaks them he breaks the laws of his own life. Sin, therefore, consists essentially in acting contrary to the laws of spiritual life, as they originate in the Lord and are embodied in man.

All the forms and relations and methods of operation of man's spiritual faculties were created and adapted in the most perfect manner by infinite wisdom for the attainment of a specific end, and that end was the reception of life from the Lord, with its blessedness. Man sins by

16

departing from that order.   He thinks he knows what is good for him better than the Lord does.   It seems to him that the true way to attain life is to love himself and the world, rather than the Lord and the neighbor.   He loves the fruit of the tree of knowledge of good and evil better than that which grows upon the tree of life.   Thus he inverts the true order of his life and disturbs the harmonies of all his spiritual faculties, abandons the methods of infinite wisdom, and violates its laws.   This is sin.

We are now prepared to answer the second question, What is the penalty ?   It must be death.   It could be nothing else.   For if the Lord has established a certain method and chain of instrumentalities for the attainment of life, and has adjusted them to that end with infinite wisdom, to depart from that order must be to fail of the end.   Death follows as a necessary consequence and according to a universal law, as it does in the physical body or in a plant.   But the penalty of sin is not the death of the body ; it is the death of the soul.   " The soul that sinneth, it shall die."   This body dies by the violation of physical and natural laws ; the soul dies by the violation of spiritual laws ; for the body is subject to physical laws and the soul is subject to spiritual laws.   There is no evidence in the Bible, there are no grounds in reason or in the analogies of nature, for the belief that the material body would have been immortal if man had never sinned. The decay and dissolution of the body is not the death of the man any more than the falling of the leaf or the rejection of the husk and chaff is the death of the plant. Man is not a material being, and therefore no material changes can create or destroy him.

But spiritual death is not the disorganization and dispersion of the spiritual substances which compose man's spiritual form. It is rather such a derangement and inversion of his spiritual organism that it is no longer receptive of spiritual life from the Lord. The lower plane of his mind, the natural and sensual degree, has become so deranged and disproportionately developed that the higher planes cannot be formed. Man is a barren fig-tree, which bears leaves only. His faculties are so ajar and discordant in their activities that their movements cause pain instead of pleasure. Like an instrument out of tune, they produce discords rather than harmonies; or like a defective chronometer, they do not move in the order and exact measure of the heavenly principles with which they were made to accord, and consequently the man who trusts to them is led astray. Life is not bare existence; death is not the extinction of being. Life truly considered is the attainment of the ends of our being, the development of the spiritual and heavenly degrees of the mind, and the reception of life from the Lord, in those degrees, in ever-increasing fulness. Death obstructs, withers, blasts them. Death is failure in the true ends of life. It prevents the orderly development of the higher degrees of man's spiritual nature, and brings discord, disease, and pain into all those that remain. "The soul that sinneth, it shall die." The penalty of sin is spiritual death; sin is the cause and death the inevitable effect.

Our next inquiry is, How is this penalty inflicted? Is it imposed like a fine? or measured out like the penalties of human laws? Is it arbitrarily imposed, as so many years of imprisonment or a certain amount of disabilities for so much sin? Is it imposed or remitted at the good pleasure of the Lord, as an emperor having absolute power determines the punishment for offences against his government, and inflicts or remits it according to his will? The Lord answers the question, "The wickedness of the wicked shall be upon him." "In his trespass that he hath trespassed, and in his sin that he hath sinned, in them shall he die." Death follows sin as an inevitable consequence. Sin is death. Man is not punished for sinning as the thief is sent to the penitentiary for stealing. But he is punished in sinning. As spiritual laws are not arbitrarily imposed, so their violation cannot be arbitrarily punished. The Lord does not bruise a man's flesh and break his bones because he falls. The physical injury follows as a consequence of the disobedience of physical law. The Lord does not measure out in an arbitrary way so much pain for so much physical sin, so many twinges of gout or pangs of dyspepsia for so much idleness and luxury. He does not send a fever upon one, a consumption on another, a dropsy or paralysis upon another, as a punishment for the violation of certain physiological laws; they follow as legitimate effects from natural causes. He did not organize the body for pain, but for pleasure; but if man will not obey the laws of his organization, the end is missed, and pain comes as a consequence. So the Lord did not organize the spiritual body that it might be tormented with fears, regrets, disappointments, hatreds, revenges, and remorse, but for the reception of gratitude, love, joy, peace, blessedness, and all heavenly delights. But if man will not obey the laws of his spiritual organization, if he will not follow the methods which infinite wisdom has provided as the only way of attaining these spiritual blessings, he must fail of receiving them. If he will sin, he must reap the fruits of sinning. There is no escape from the consequences. If there had been no written law, if the Lord had never said a word about sin or its punishment, the consequences would have been the same. In a word, all Divine laws, spiritual, moral, civil, physical, and material, are self-executing. There is no difference in principle in their operation. The reward and the punishment inhere in the law, and when we act according to it the blessing necessarily follows, and when we break it the curse follows. Life is the effect of obedience, and death of sin.

Our final inquiry is, What are the only conditions of escape from the penalties of sin? The Lord answers the question, "But if the wicked will turn from all his sins that he hath committed, and keep all my statutes, and do that which is lawful and right, he shall surely live, he shall not die." His release from the penalty, then, is effected by his release from sin. The effect ceases with the cause which produced it. When a man begins to live he ceases to die. The penalty goes with the sin. They are inseparably bound together, like pain and disease. With a return to health, feebleness and pain disappear. Put an instrument in perfect tune and its discords cease. Darkness disappears when the sun rises ; frost vanishes in the presence of heat. So death ceases in the presence of life. This result follows of necessity, if the relation between sin and its penalties is that of cause and effect. The logic, as you will see, is complete, and there is no escape from it, if you admit that spiritual and natural laws are similar in their operation. If the Lord follows an immutable order and method in the administration of His spiritual kingdom, as universal nature attests that He does in His natural kingdom, "The soul that sinneth, it shall die." There are no exceptions, no remedies, no offers of pardon, no conditions of escape except a return to life. This is not the prevalent opinion, and it is worthy of our most careful consideration.

It is an almost universal belief in the Christian Church that the Lord punishes in an arbitrary manner, and that He can remit the penalty of sin from mere mercy, and admit whomsoever He chooses into heaven ; and that He is only prevented from exercising universal clemency by some considerations of justice and consistency. The common idea is that the Divine pardon is similar to that exercised by kings and magistrates in this world. A man has broken some law or committed some offence against the king or ruler, and from mercy or favor, or through the intercession of friends, he is pardoned,—that is, the penalty is remitted ; the man is restored to favor, and occupies the same position which he did before the offence was committed. So it is commonly believed that by the intercession of the Saviour, and the exercise of faith by man, the Lord will remit the penalty of sin and take him to heaven. The whole scheme of salvation, according to the prevalent theology, is based upon this idea, and must stand or fall with it.

This error seems to have arisen from confounding sin with its penalty, while they are as distinct as pain and disease, as sound and the instrument which produces it, or, universally, as cause and effect. The Lord is always, by all the means known to His infinite wisdom, in the unceasing effort to pardon our sins. But He never remits the penalty. "The soul that sinneth, it shall die," is the immutable and irrevocable sentence pronounced against sin, and the law is in as full force now as it ever was. There is no more pardon for violating a spiritual or moral law than there is for breaking a natural law. Every violation of every law, physical, moral, or spiritual, always has been, is now, and ever will be punished. If you throw yourself into the fire or water, or eat arsenic, or fall from an immense height, we know that the Lord will not interpose in answer to any prayer to save you from burning or drowning, from the effects of poison, or from broken bones. He will not arrest His own order and violate His own laws for the sake of saving man from the consequences of disobedience. And yet this is what we are commonly taught the Lord does in His spiritual kingdom, and it is generally believed that our salvation depends upon such interposition. But that is contrary to every principle of the Divine government.

There can be no greater absurdity than that a Being of infinite wisdom should impose an arbitrary law upon His children, which He knew they would break, pronounce an arbitrary punishment, and when they broke the law, as He foresaw they would, set about contriving a plan by which He could save them from His own sentence. With all our weakness and folly, a human parent would hardly do that. What would you say of a legislator or of a king who should promulgate a law which he knew would be broken, and then devise a method of

averting the very penalties he had affixed to it? Would
you not say that the law ought not to have been enacted,
or that the penalty was not wisely decreed? Why do to-
day what you must seek to undo to-morrow or ruin your
friends?

Because there is so much said in the Bible about the
Lord's mercy and His willingness to forgive sin, because
He came down to earth and suffered and died and rose
again to save man from sin, it is inferred that He seeks to
set aside His own law and prevent the execution of its
penalty. But He declares that He did not come to destroy the law or the prophets, but to fulfil; that heaven
and earth shall pass away, but not one jot or tittle shall
pass from the law until all are fulfilled. He did not come,
therefore, to repeal His own laws, to release man from his
obligations to keep them, or to save him from the penalty
of breaking them.

Two great errors widely prevail upon this subject : first,
that the Lord came into the world to save man from the
punishment of sin ; and, secondly, that the punishment of
sin remains after the sin is committed, until some compensation is made for it, or some special act of release is obtained. The Lord did not come to save man from the
punishment of sin apart from the sin itself. This would
be a violation of His own laws and order. The Lord
never remits the penalty of sin so long as the sin remains.
No penalty ever was remitted or ever will be while the
sin remains. He no more forgives us for being diseased
spiritually than He does for being diseased naturally. If
I break any of the commandments, the Lord will no more
forgive me than He will forgive me for breaking my

bones. The two cases are perfectly analogous. The punishment follows as the inevitable effect of its cause, the sin, and it must remain as long as the producing cause remains. If we can settle it in our minds as a great and universal law of the Lord's operation, from which He never deviates, that no penalty is ever remitted and that no sin goes unpunished, we have taken one great step towards the solution of one of the most difficult problems of human life.

The question now occurs, If the Lord never remits the penalty of sin, how are we to escape punishment? Must we suffer forever? No. The penalty ceases with the sin. It would be just as impossible for the punishment to remain after man had ceased to be a sinner as it would be for the cold of winter to remain during the heat of summer, or the pains of a disease to fill the body after the disease was removed and the body restored to perfect health. The executors of human laws can punish after the deed is committed and for it, but the Lord never does. The penalty and the sin are so bound together that they cannot be separated.

But if I broke my bones yesterday, shall I not suffer for it to-day? No, you suffer to-day because they are still broken. The evil is not yet removed. If they were restored to perfect soundness, you would not suffer in the least. You suffer so long as the cause which produces the pain remains, and no longer. Sin is not limited to the overt act, and does not essentially consist in it. The sin consists in that evil state or motive which causes us to commit evil deeds. There is the same distinction between sin and sinful deeds that there is between a tree and

its fruits, or between disease and its symptoms ; between
the flushed face, the rapid pulse, the burning thirst, and
the wild delirium, and the fever which causes them.   The
sin may remain and burn and consume and be the continual cause of sinful acts.   We are not punished for
doing this or that sinful act.   The Lord does not recount
our evil deeds, or keep a record of our good ones.   He
does not keep an account of debt and credit with us.
We suffer because our natures are not in harmony with
the Divine order ; not because they were discordant yesterday, but because they are discordant now.

Strictly speaking, therefore, we never suffer spiritually
for a past evil.   When the sinful state is gone, the pain
that originated in it goes with it.   The most fatal misconceptions of the Divine character have arisen from the
erroneous belief that the consequences of sin remain after
the sin itself is removed.   And many of the difficulties
which good men have found in reconciling the Divine
benevolence with the punishment of the wicked have
their origin in this falsity.   It is a terrible injustice to the
Lord to suppose that we shall be eternally punished for a
sinful act, or any number of sinful acts committed in this
life.   It follows as a necessary consequence of the law
which we have been considering that we shall never be
punished in the spiritual world for what we do in this
world.   We shall be punished only for what we do there.
When a man passes into the spiritual world through the
gate of death the Lord does not say to him, You were a
great sinner while you lived upon the earth, and now I
am going to punish you for it forever.   If the wicked go
away into everlasting punishment, it will be because they

will go their way in everlasting opposition to the Lord's way, which is the only way in which happiness can be found. The Lord sends His angels to every one, saint as well as sinner, and invites them all to heaven, to the enjoyments of eternal life. He places all in the most favorable conditions to disclose their true characters. If they can conform to the order of heaven in will and in understanding, in thought and in act, they will enjoy the blessings of such conjunction with heaven and the Lord. He will not bring up old scores against them. If one will turn from his sins, '' all his transgressions that he hath committed, they shall not be mentioned unto him : in his righteousness that he hath done he shall live.'' But if he still continues to love himself supremely, and to break the Divine commandments, which, as we have seen, are the laws of his own being and the only ways in which life and happiness can be obtained, he must suffer the consequences. The Lord cannot prevent it. '' The wickedness of the wicked shall be upon him.''

We are brought to the inevitable conclusion, therefore, that there is no hope for the sinner but in being cleansed from his sin. So long as he is a sinner he is not in harmony with the Divine order. His will cannot receive the Divine love and his understanding the Divine truth in their true forms and order. He is an instrument out of tune, and his activities can only be discords ; he is a corrupt tree which cannot bring forth good fruit ; his spiritual body is diseased, and all its activities are death rather than life, and he will remain spiritually dead until he turns from all his sins, which cause that death. When he keeps the Lord's statutes and does that which is lawful and right, he will surely live ; he will not die.   These are the conditions, and the only conditions, on which we can be saved.

My whole effort has been directed to one end, and that is to show that there is nothing arbitrary or fluctuating in the punishment of sin.   Man is not punished for sinning, but in sinning ; sin and suffering are intimately connected, and by no possibility can they be separated.   The Divine laws are not modelled after human laws.   They are all self-executing.   They are never annulled or repealed or modified.

This truth is very broad and comprehensive in its applications, and will reverse many of the opinions and much of the reasoning upon the Lord's relations to man. It relieves the subject of human salvation from all its mysteries and complicated technicalities, and makes it as plain and simple as the curing of any natural disease, and much more certain, when the prescribed remedies are applied.   For we have a Spiritual Physician who understands the disease perfectly, and who never fails to cure all who apply to Him and follow His prescriptions.   We must direct our attention to the sin, to the disease, and not to the pain it causes.   We must learn the Lord's commandments, that we may know what the laws of life are, and then we must obey them.   We must shun what they forbid.   We must do it now, to-day, every day. The Lord will assist every effort we make.   He came into this world by assuming a human nature, that He might remove every obstacle that prevents His access to us, that He might apply the remedy directly to the disease, and so bring His life down to us, even in the grave of our sins, that He might become our resurrection and life. He is present with us now by the influences of His Holy Spirit, and assists every struggle for release from sin, and favors every aspiration after a heavenly life. Infinite love, wisdom, and power are on our side, and we have only to remove the obstructions to their application to our own life to be sure of escaping every torment of sin and of enjoying every heavenly blessing we are capable of receiving. Therefore, "cast away from you all your transgressions, whereby ye have transgressed; and make you a new heart and a new spirit: for why will ye die, O house of Israel? For I have no pleasure in the death of him that dieth, saith the Lord GOD. Wherefore turn yourselves, and live ye."

THE DIVINE MERCY IN SUFFERING AND EVIL.

" But the very hairs of your head are all numbered."—MAT-
THEW X. 30.
*" He maketh his sun to rise on the evil and on the good, and
sendeth rain on the just and on the unjust."*—MATTHEW V. 45.

IN the first of these passages the Lord declares the uni-
versality of His providential care ; and in the second,
that His care extends to the evil as well as to the good, to
the just as well as to the unjust. By the sun and rain are
meant His love and wisdom. He here assures us, therefore, that He exercises the same love towards the evil
that He does towards the good, and that He employs
His Divine wisdom just as fully for the benefit of the unjust as He does for the good of the just.

This is not the common opinion, and it is not apparently in accordance with many passages of the Word, in
which the Lord declares His hostility to the wicked.
But there is no real contradiction between Divine declarations. Some express the real truth ; others the apparent
truth. Persons who oppose us in any course we are pur-
suing seem to be our enemies. Our children often think
we are hostile to them because we do not grant all their
requests, or because we oppose them in what seems to
them to be good. The real truth is that the Lord's
providence is over all men, at all times, in all states, in
temptation and sorrow as well as in prosperity and joy,

194

and is continually exercised for their good. It does not seem so to us, because the Lord knows that often what we think to be for our good is hurtful to us. Opposition to that seeming good, but real evil, is, therefore, a favor to us. The Lord regards every human being with infinite love, and He deals with every human being with infinite wisdom. He does all for every one, in every part of His universe, that infinite wisdom and infinite power can do ; for the evil as well as the good, for the ignorant heathen as well as the most intelligent Christian, for the sick as fully as for the strong, for the lowest spirit in hell as well as for the highest angel in heaven. But what He can do for each one depends upon his state, upon what he really needs. Therefore the Divine life is received by no two in the same manner.

This principle is clearly exhibited in human life. What we can do for another, supposing we have the power, depends upon what he needs. If he is rich, we cannot help him by giving him money. If he is well, medicine will do him no good. If he has an abundance of provisions, it will not help him to give him bread. If he is wiser than we, our advice is of no service. But if he is poor, or sick, or ignorant, we may help him in those particulars. If he is perverse, we may help him to overcome his perversity. If he is starving for natural or spiritual food, we can feed him.

But what the Lord can do for us is not only limited by our necessities, but by our willingness to be helped. In all the Lord's dealings with man we must recognize the immutable truth of man's freedom, and that the Lord always respects his freedom. It is not the Lord's power, nor the Lord's disposition, nor the abundance or scarcity of means, nor the capacity of man's nature that is the limit of the good the Lord can do for him. It is man's freedom. How much good can he be led, in freedom, to receive? Man's freedom in this respect is like a vessel. It is the capacity of a vessel and not the ocean that limits the amount we can put into it. We often wonder and sometimes complain because the Lord does not give us a more abundant and richer good. When we see the apparently vast inequalities in human life, and the immense amount of suffering and sorrow, we are surprised that the Lord does not interpose in behalf of the destitute and the afflicted, more fully equalize human blessings, and bestow His bounty with a more liberal hand. But there is no withholding of His blessing. He gives to every being the largest measure of the highest good he can be induced to receive. We do not wonder that the sun does not clothe a white and burning bank of sand or a stagnant pool of water with wheat and vines. The heat and light of the sun fall upon all places of the same aspect alike, and enter and vivify what there is to receive them. So it is with the Divine love. Let us, then, settle it as an immutable truth that the Lord always gives us all the good He can lead us in freedom to receive.

It is my own fault if I suffer. The Lord did not send this affliction upon me. I brought it upon myself. He tried to prevent it, but could not without doing me a greater injury than the one I have received. And He is even now trying to bring out of this suffering all the good He can.

But that we may see this truth in a clearer light let us consider more particularly the manner in which the Lord sends His blessings to us and leads us to good.

The Lord never provides evil or punishment or suffering for any one. But He permits them, and He permits them for our good. The Lord has arranged everything in the universe for the happiness of man, and He has organized man himself to receive delight from everything. So long, therefore, as man lives in the order of the Divine providence he receives nothing but good. For example, the Lord has arranged a certain order for man's physical life, concerning food, raiment, sleep, and exercise. This order is perfect. It is from the Lord's will. If man lives according to it he receives only good. It is the same with his moral, intellectual, and spiritual life. But if man violates this order he takes himself out from its harmonies, and so far cuts himself off from the will of the Lord. The Lord can no more reach him in that way. He separates himself from good and comes under another law, the law of truth which condemns him. The order which was provided to bring the soul good and only good now acts against it and condemns it, because the soul does not move with it. You have seen a complicated piece of machinery driven by a powerful engine. Every part of the machine was arranged according to a certain order, to accomplish a certain end. Suppose this order and every part of the machine to be perfect. Every wheel and spring and lever plays in harmony, and the end, which is the good sought, is accomplished. But if some wheel gets out of place or some spring breaks, the order is destroyed. The whole force that propelled the machine now serves to break it up and destroy it. The force of the engine that acted only for good now crushes, now acts for evil. So when man violates the order of infinite wisdom embodied in his soul, that order acts against him, and man suffers according to the extent of the violation. Now, the Lord did not provide this suffering ; it is not from His will, but He permits it, and He permits it for man's good in the state in which he then is.

But when we say He permits evil we must not understand the permission in the sense that He concurs in it, or that He led man into it, or sent it upon him in any sense. All the laws of the Divine order are good, and when man by disobedience departs from the Divine order it is he who casts himself into punishments and torments.

The case is the same as with the parent and child. A wise parent wills only the good of his child, and shows him how to attain the good. But if the child will not obey in all things ; if he desires to do things which the parent knows are not for his good, he may still permit him to have his own way if he believes that forcible restraint would do the child more harm than to follow his own inclinations. He knows, perhaps, that he will never be satisfied until he has tasted the bitter fruits of his own choice. Such cases come within the experience of all parents. Now, the parent does not provide the false and evil course for his child. He does not provide the sufferings which are caused by it. He does not will it, but he permits it, because to restrain the child by force would be a greater evil.

In the same way the Lord permits us to disobey His

laws. He tells us the consequences ; but we do not believe Him, and we cannot be made to believe Him until we have tried it for ourselves. He permits us to plunge into evils and falsities, and to bring their inevitable punishments upon ourselves, because the evil is not so great as would result from forcibly restraining us. Thus He permits it for a relatively greater good, or because it is the least evil under the circumstances.

But the Lord does not leave us in our sins. He uses the suffering as a warning to go no farther astray. Every pain we suffer is a voice of warning, a cry that we are in danger. When I put my hand too near the fire the smarting cries out to me, " You are violating a law of your physical life !'' When I labor too long and too severely, the weariness and pain declare in unmistakable language that I am in danger of overtaxing my strength. When I violate a moral or spiritual law, conscience lifts her voice and inflicts her pangs. The Lord permits these things for our good, but He did not provide them for the smart and pain. The Lord did not provide fire to burn us, but to warm us, to cook our food, and to serve a great variety of useful purposes. The Lord did not weave a fine texture of nerves throughout the whole human body for the purpose of filling it with pain. He formed them to be the medium of communicating a delight from everything we touch. He did not create the conscience to sting and madden us, but to be a light to guide us and an approving voice to comfort and sustain us in the right. He did not make the head to ache and the whole human body to be racked with pains, to be eaten up with ulcers, and withered with palsies. He formed it to be the beautiful home of the soul while it tarries in the world, the free and happy instrument with which it communicates with the material universe and gains the materials for the development of its own form and life. And yet He permits the body to become a most foul, repulsive, and hideous thing.

But it is important to a true knowledge of the Divine character for us to keep in mind that the Lord does not permit those things for the sake of punishment. He permits the punishment for the sake of preventing evil and of leading men back to good. All those passages in the Word which represent the Lord as hating the evil, burning with fury towards them, and inflicting upon them the most terrible punishments, express not genuine, but apparent truths. They state things as they appear to man, not as they are when viewed from the Lord. You will observe, however, that this view gives no license to man to commit evil. On the contrary, it shows that evil and suffering are inseparably connected. The Lord Himself cannot prevent the suffering. "The soul that sinneth, it shall die." But it shows the Divine character to be very different from that which is often attributed to the Lord. It shows how suffering and sin in the world are perfectly consistent with His infinite love and wisdom.

There is another reason why the Lord permits man to act out his evils in freedom, and that is that he may see them in their infernal deformity and put them away. Man must exercise the same freedom in putting away his evils that he does in committing them, for all his real actions are voluntary. The natural man is full of evils, which must be put away before he can be regenerated.

But an evil cannot be resisted until it is seen, and it cannot be seen until it appears. We ought not to commit evil, however, that it may appear. We ought to see it in its first motions in our thoughts, and there repress and shun it. But most persons, will not examine themselves with candor, by the light of Divine truth. We are loath to confess even to ourselves that we are sinners ; and many persons will not do it until their evils come out into act, and in all their frightful deformity boldly confront them. And even then they shut their eyes against them until they are compelled, by seeing their fatal consequences, to avoid them. Thus the Lord's providence is over us at all times, and He makes the best use of our evils for our good. What He cannot prevent without a greater injury to us He permits, and permits that He may make the commission itself of the evil an aid in removing it. He is merciful even where it is impossible to remove the evil, as is the case with all who are evil at heart, after they have passed into the spiritual world. The punishments they inflict upon one another are permitted for the purpose of repressing their evils from fear, and thus preventing those who commit the sin from sinking into still greater evils, and thus incurring a severer punishment. Thus the Lord is ever seeking our good, and never fails to do the best for us that infinite wisdom can effect. He does not cease to love us and work for us when we are in evil. He does not leave us to ourselves when we wander from Him, but, like the good shepherd, He leaves the ninety and nine that are safe and goes after the one that is lost.

We must not infer, however, that it is no matter what

we do, if whatever happens is best for us.   We must remember that it is best under the circumstances, taking
all things into consideration.   For example, suppose you
are disappointed in the attainment of some good upon
which you had set your heart, or you are afflicted by
some terrible bereavement.   The Lord is doing the best
He can for you.   The evils you suffer are to prevent
greater evils.   Still, it is not as well for you as it would
have been if you had lived a better and more orderly life.
You are sick, perhaps, and suffer much pain.   Your
sickness is not sent upon you by the Lord.   It has come
from the violation of some physical law, and, though
your suffering is best under the circumstances, your condition might have been better if you had not disobeyed
the laws of your physical life.   It is best for the wicked in
the spiritual world to be restrained from greater sin and
greater misery by punishment ; but it would have been
far better for them if they had repented and shunned
their evils as sins against God in this world ; for then
they would be angels in heaven, and they would be en-
tering into the enjoyment of all heavenly delights.

There is also one important principle of compensation
for our natural sufferings which no huite mind can ever
fully estimate.   A natural evil may be permitted and used
by the Divine Providence to effect a spiritual good.   Man
has a twofold nature, and suffering and disappointment in
one degree or plane of his mind may be overruled for his
greater good in another.   We see some persons who seem
to be always in affliction.   Nothing that they touch seems
to prosper.   They never succeed in business ; if they run
for office they are sure to be defeated ; if they engage in

an enterprise they fail ; they always meet with what we call accidents, and everything seems to go wrong. Now, out of this apparent misfortune there may be educed a much greater spiritual and eternal good than could have been gained by the greatest temporal prosperity. What, therefore, seems to us misfortune may really be the greatest good fortune. The man who suffers these things may get more real good out of them than his neighbor, who succeeds in everything he puts his hand to, can get from his prosperity. A natural loss may contribute to a great spiritual gain. In this way there are compensations for natural evils, whose value we can never estimate, and which may immeasurably outweigh the ills. One thing is certain : the Lord permits them for a good end, and with our co-operation He will bring good out of them, all the good that is possible to infinite wisdom and power.

What a cheerful view does this truth give us of life ! With what a merciful and loving tenderness does it invest our Heavenly Father ! How the disappointed hopes, the ignorance, the failures, the bereavements, the sufferings and sorrows of poor, erring humanity, change their repulsive aspect ! How is all that we have called unfortunate, and mourned over in our own lives, brightened and changed into new forms of beauty and good by it ! Let us try to bring home the blessed truth to our own souls as an undoubted reality. Our very hairs are numbered. The Lord does not turn away His face from us because we turn our faces from Him. If we are spiritually naked and hungry, sick and in prison, He will no more leave us than a devoted parent would leave a beloved child when he was sick and in affliction. If possible, the Lord then regards us with more tenderness than at other times; and, though He cannot communicate to us any good but what He can lead us voluntarily to receive, He watches over us every moment of our lives, and seizes upon the slightest opportunity, and makes the most of every possible occasion to soften the hardness of our nature, to bend our wills towards a true order, to lead us back into harmony with Him. Why are we so slow and reluctant to believe in His mercy and loving-kindness? Why are we so prone to doubt His care for us, and to make our natural prosperity the measure of His good-will towards us? When we suffer, why will we accuse the Lord of unkindness or want of care, when the only reason the Lord does not give us a greater measure of good is our unwillingness to receive it? Why do we not commit our way unto Him, and trust Him, and let Him lead us in the paths of righteousness, beside the still waters, and restore our souls to their true order, harmony, and peace? Oh, you who go trembling with many a fear, whose souls are chafed and worried and stung with many an anxious care, whose hearts are heavy with many a burden of grief, why will you not accept the blessed invitation, "Come unto me, all ye that labor and are heavy laden, . . . for I am meek and lowly in heart; and ye shall find rest unto your souls"? Come, the Lord will take you by the hand. He will help you at every step. He will strengthen your weakness of will and act. He will lead you as gently as love itself. He will reward every right effort. Come up from the corruption of the grave and the coldness and darkness of death into the light and order and peace of heaven. Come, all things are ready. Come, and begin to live.

THE ATONEMENT: WHO MADE IT, WHY IT WAS NECESSARY, HOW IT WAS EFFECTED.

" For he said, Surely they are my people, children that will not lie: so he was their Saviour.

" In all their affliction he was afflicted, and the Angel of his presence saved them: in his love and in his pity he redeemed them; and he bare them, and carried them all the days of old."
—ISAIAH lxiii. 8, 9.

THE subject to which I invite your attention is justly regarded by the whole Christian world as vital to man's salvation. Our eternal happiness or misery rests upon it. We all know that we are sinners ; that we have rebelled against the government of the King of kings and Lord of lords. We are under condemnation. We confess it by our fears. We are already suffering the penalties of our disobedience. We feel it in the weariness of servitude, in the weakness and pain of disease, in cares, anxieties, disappointments, in yearning for a freedom we do not possess, in aspirations for a good we cannot gain, and in the sharp thrusts of conscience for violated law. The whole earth is a prison whose walls are not stone or iron, but ignorance and error and evil ; and multitudes fear that they will be released from this prison-house only to be plunged into a more terrible one. Whether you believe the Bible or not, whether you accept the common doctrine of sin and punishment or not, you know that

you suffer ; you know that your affections, your understandings, and your lives are not in the harmonies of
Divine order.   You know that you are weak and blind,
that your heart is full of fears and questions about your
relations to the Lord and your chances for future happiness.

The subject we are to consider is, How the differences
between us and the Lord are to be harmonized ; how His
claim upon us is to be adjusted.   If it is a punishment
which must be inflicted, who is to bear it ?   If it is a debt
which must be paid, who will pay it ?   If it is a case of
spiritual disease, weakness, and death, which have come
upon man as a consequence of violating the laws of spiritual life, how is he to be restored to spiritual soundness
and health, so that his whole nature shall act in harmony
with the Divine nature ?   Put the question as you will, it
touches every vital interest and immortal hope of man.
It is the essential question between man and the Lord,
the root principle on which all other questions depend.

There have been many opinions and theories upon this
subject, some of which have become obsolete.   But there
is still a great variety of opinion, and will continue to be
until men understand how we are related to the Lord,
until we regard the subject from central and immutable
principles.   This is the only point of view from which it
can be understood.   This is, therefore, the first question
to which I ask your attention.   How do we stand related
to the Lord ?   The answer is so important to our understanding of the present subject that we shall consider it
with care, at the risk of restating some principles already
familiar.

According to the doctrines of the New Church, the primary and essential relation between man and the Lord, which gives character to all other relations, is that of the recipient of life to the Source and Giver of life. Every human being is the direct recipient of life from the Lord, at every moment of his existence, just as truly and absolutely as the first man was at the first moment of his existence. The Lord now breathes into our nostrils the breath of all the life we have, in every particular and degree of our existence. "In him we live, and move, and have our being," is a plain and exact statement of the truth. "Without me ye can do nothing." The amount and quality of our life is measured by the degree of reception. This is the essential relation which we sustain to the Lord. It is described in many ways, but this is the essence of them all.

It is necessary to recall another point. While every particle of life is constantly given, the current which comes to us from within flows by such secret channels that we are wholly unconscious of it, and consequently we are in as much freedom to act as we should be if it were underived and absolutely our own. Though we are only recipients of life, we are as free to act as the Lord Himself. Though we are as dependent upon the inflowing power for every movement of mind and body as a machine is for the movement of its wheels and springs, yet we are not machines. We have power to act in one way or in a different one. We can close our minds to the truth as we can our eyes to the light. We can receive or reject, act according to the commandments or contrary to them. But we possess this power only because the Lord constantly gives it to us.

The Lord created man to receive life from Him in its true forms and harmonies. He made him in His own image and likeness that man might receive and possess in a derivative and finite form all those qualities which exist in the Lord in their infinite perfections. So long as man received life from the Lord in its true order and in its unperverted forms, his whole nature was in perfect accord with the Divine nature ; all his activities flowed in the currents of the Divine harmonies. Man's life was in perfect unison with the Lord's life. Man and the Lord were at one with each other. They were like two instruments in perfect tune. This is the normal, orderly relation of man to the Lord.

Now, if I have succeeded in conveying the idea I intend, it will be seen that man's relation to the Lord is not essentially a legal one. It is not the relation of a citizen to the state or of a debtor to a creditor. It is not in any sense an arbitrary or factitious one. It is more like the relation of a plant to the sun, or of the body to the soul. It is a relation which inheres in and grows out of the essential nature of the beings related. Arbitrary human relations may be used, for the want of better means, to express those which inhere in the essential nature of man and of the Lord. We may call God a King, a supreme Ruler, an almighty Sovereign, who acts according to His own pleasure, but we must take these words in their highest and not in their lowest sense. We must think of a king or sovereign from infinite love and wisdom, and from our highest conceptions of love and wisdom, and not measure the Divine character by an earthly despot. The Lord is our Father ; but we must not bring Him down to the level of human parents ; we must exalt every fatherly quality to the highest possibilities of our conception. These natural relations are steps to assist our minds to rise up towards the Lord and gain some true conceptions of Him, and not weights to hold us down to the earth. Whatever corresponding human relations we use to express our relations to the Lord, we must always take them in their highest sense. They are at the best but fiugers which point in the direction in which we are to look and go.

Such being our relations to the Lord, we cannot conceive that He would subject man to the control of any arbitrary law, or that He would attach any arbitrary penalty to the violation of any law. The Lord is related to man as a spiritual being in the same way that He is related to him as a physical being. Every one can see the absurdity of attempting to subject man's physical nature to any arbitrary laws. Would it not be equally absurd to impose any arbitrary rules for the government of his spiritual nature ? It is contrary to reason, contrary to all known methods of Divine working. It is leaving methods which accord with the constitution and nature of things for those which have no necessary relation to them ; it is abandoning law and following caprice.

It cannot be denied, however, that there are many statements in the Sacred Scriptures which seem to favor the idea that the Lord does govern in an arbitrary way, and exacts obedience because He has the right to demand it and the power to enforce it. But it can easily be shown that the commandments and prohibitions are only arbitrary in form, to adapt them to the condition of men. A law of life may be stated as a principle, as a warning, as a command.   The consequences of its violation may be pointed out or not, according to circumstances and the conditions of those who are the subjects of the law, while the law itself is inherent and essential.   This principle is so necessary to a correct understanding of our relations to the Lord, that it is worthy of illustration.

An engineer who understands his business perfectly is called upon to build a bridge across the chasm below the Niagara Falls.   He knows the force of gravity, he is acquainted with the strength of the materials he is to use, he knows what form is most conducive to strength, and what relations the parts should sustain to one another, and to what strain the structure will be subjected, and he gives his orders accordingly.   Put stone here, iron there. He gives specific directions about the form of the parts and the way they are to be joined together.   His directions are issued in an arbitrary form, as though his will were law and he were a despot.   But there is nothing arbitrary in his directions.   They are based on immutable law, to which he must conform or his structure will prove a failure and become the cause of sorrow and suffering and death.   So all the precepts, prohibitions, statutes, and commandments contained in the Bible, in whatever form given, are based upon the immutable laws of the Divine wisdom, upon the essential principles of man's nature, according to which his life unfolds and he attains the end of his being.

The true relation between the Lord and man is often expressed in specific terms.   He is the light of the world ; He is the life of men.   " In him we live, and move, and have our being;" "I am the vine," He says to His disciples, "ye are the branches." In this last expression we have a perfect example of our relation to the Lord. We are related to Him as the branch to the vine. There is nothing arbitrary about it. The branch grows out of the vine, and partakes of its nature. It gets all its life from it. And the amount of the life it receives depends upon its connection with it. If that connection is interrupted or broken, or if the organism of the branch is in any way deranged, it cannot bear fruit.

If we suppose that the branch has the power of closing its doors against the life of the vine, which comes to it in the currents of its juices, or of so changing their nature that they produce poison instead of grapes, we shall have a perfect illustration of how man as a sinner is related to the Lord.

By sinning, which is violating the laws of his life, man has interrupted the inflow of life from the Lord into his soul, in its full and normal currents, and so perverted what does reach him that it is changed into the poison of evil, and he does not bear the fruits of heavenly joy and peace.

The question is, How is the branch to be restored to its union with the vine? How is the recipient of life to become readjusted to the source of life, so that all its channels shall be opened and filled with life? They cannot open themselves; they cannot be forced open by any violence; one branch cannot help another in this extremity. It is not a question of punishment for having broken a law. That does not enter into the consideration of the subject. It is a question of reunion of the branch with the vine. It might be bruised to a jelly, or ground to powder and cast into the fire ; that would not tend to its reunion with the vine. On the contrary, it would make reunion impossible. It is not a question of debt. Suppose it was. The branch is indebted to the vine for the grapes it ought to have borne. Destroying it will not pay the debt. And if the debt were paid, it would not have the slightest influence in restoring the union between the branch and the vine. Suppose the penalty for man's sins were paid by the suffering of another person ; it would not restore man to conjunction with the Lord ; it would not have the slightest tendency to do it. The gulf between him and the Source of life would remain as great as it was before. The breach has not been healed, because it was not an arbitrary but a real one. The healing is not a vicarious work. If the laws which man had broken were arbitrary, they might be annulled or the penalty remitted at the good pleasure of the legislator, or for any considerations he might designate. But as they are laws of man's life, the very principles on which his existence is based, they cannot be annulled without destroying him. No being Divine or human can keep the laws of life for him, or suffer for their violation for him.

As we have seen, spiritual laws are of the same nature as physical laws, and we know perfectly well that one person cannot keep these for another. It is a law enacted by the Lord Himself and written in every member of the material body, that man must be constantly supplied with a proper amount of wholesome food. The penalty of continued disobedience is death. Can one person keep this law for another? Can one man eat for another? Can the best friend on earth or in heaven save another from starvation by eating for him? Every child knows that would be impossible. A law of life which inheres in the essential nature of man cannot be vicariously kept, nor can disobedience to it be atoned by vicarious punishment. A debt can be paid by another, because the relation of debtor and creditor is not a vital one. It has no organic connection with man. An arbitrary law may be broken and no one suffer for it; but a vital law cannot, and the one who breaks it must suffer.

According to the same principle, a moral quality cannot be transferred from one person to another. Neither goodness nor wickedness are transferable commodities. "The soul that sinneth, it shall die. The righteousness of the righteous shall be upon him, and the wickedness of the wicked shall be upon him." Vicarious virtue, or vicarious guilt, or vicarious reward or punishment, is not possible. It is contrary to the nature of God, and the nature of man. It is just as impossible in the spiritual plane of man's being as it is in the physical.

Now we have cleared away the obstructions and have gained the right point of view to understand Who made the atonement, Why it was necessary, and How it was made.

Who made the Atonement? The Lord's answer is that He made it. He is the only being who could make it. And He affirms and reaffirms in the most emphatic manner that He is the only Redeemer and Saviour. Put out of your thought, if you can, every idea which disturbs or weakens the distinct conception that God is one in essence and person. Think that there is only one Being who is God. Call that Being by whatever name you please, but keep before your mind's eye only one Person, one Being. Call Him Jehovah, God, Lord, Father, Son, Jesus Christ ; but think of one Being, one Divine Person. That Being created man. He is the source from which man constantly derives his life. He alone can give life and restore man to such union with Him that he can receive it in larger measures and higher forms.

It may help us to get this distinct idea of the unity of God to hear what He says about Himself. "Surely God is in thee ; and there is none else, there is no God. Verily thou art a God that hidest thyself, O God of Israel, the Saviour." (Isa. xlv. 14, 15.) "Have not I Jehovah? and there is no God else beside me ; a just God and a Saviour ; there is none beside me." (Isa. xlv. 21.) "I, even I, am Jehovah ; and beside me there is no saviour." (Isa. xliii. 11.) "I am Jehovah thy God, . . . and thou shalt know no God but me : for there is no saviour beside me." (Hosea xiii. 4.) "As for our redeemer, Jehovah of hosts is his name." (Isa. xlvii. 4.) "Jehovah, my strength, and my redeemer." (Ps. xix. 14.) "Thus saith Jehovah, thy redeemer, . . . I am Jehovah that maketh all things ; that stretcheth forth the heavens alone ; that spreadeth abroad the earth by myself." (Isa. xliv. 24.) There are many other passages to the same effect.

If words have any meaning, these mean that Jehovah is the Redeemer and Saviour, and that there is no other being who is in any way a party or sharer in the work. Jesus Christ was not another being. He was Jehovah, clothed with a human mind and a human nature. He was not changed into that nature. He did not divest Himself of any power or attribute by His descent into this world in a personal form. He was the same omnipotent, omniscient, omnipresent Being ; He did not cease to be the Alpha, the beginning, the first, when He became the Omega, the ending, the last. He simply invested Himself with the means of revealing Himself immediately to men, and of bringing Himself into direct personal contact with His children in every plane and degree of the creation. As earthly sovereigns sometimes disguise themselves as peasants and common citizens, assuming their manners and their language, that they may gain the means of relieving their ills and improving their condition, so Jehovah assumed not only the outward garb, but the material and spiritual organization of His children, their mind, their habits of thought and feeling, every form and quality which constitutes their natures. In this way He assumed their weaknesses, their evil tendencies ; He could be tempted at all points as they were ; He could live their life ; He could feel the force of all their struggles and trials and sufferings, come into a personal experience of every illusion and every sorrow, feel the sharpness of every pang, and the despair and agony of every lost hope. He could stand where dying man stood and bring Himself into close and conscious relations with him in every phase of his being. He was not thereby changed into a weak and dying human being, as a king is not changed into a peasant by assuming his manners and dress.

Now we have before our minds, in distinct and personal form, one Divine Being, one God, the only God, adapting Himself to all human conditions, from the highest to the lowest. The thought is not divided. It goes straight to one glorious Person. The affections are not distracted. They rest on one Being, who is love and wisdom itself. There is no remote, indistinct, awful embodiment of inflexible justice demanding the exact punishment stipulated in the bond. We see a Father with a heart of infinite tenderness and love, Himself coming to the rescue of His lost and dying children, that He may bring them into such relations with Himself as the source of life that He can heal all their diseases, rectify all their perversities, and restore them to union with Himself.

This is a work worthy of infinite love and wisdom. The idea that my Creator, my Father, my God did not stand aloof in stern and solitary grandeur, but came to me, His lost and perishing child, took upon Himself my nature, my mind, my affections, my flesh and blood even, and with infinite compassion and tenderness opened my eyes to see Him, unstopped my ears to hear the sweet words of comfort and hope, the winning call to follow Him to heaven and eternal rest,—this idea satisfies my reason and hlls my heart. I can understand that infinite love could do this. It satisfies every instinct and conception of the parental nature. I can do something for my children, feeble and imperfect as my love is. I can work for them, I can suffer for them, I can bear with them, I could plunge into the water or the fire to rescue them ; and I can understand how infinite love could take upon itself our nature, polluted as it is by sin, and exposed to temptation and pain, to save us.

But I cannot understand how love or justice or mercy could punish the innocent instead of the guilty. I can see neither love nor mercy nor justice in that. I could not punish one of my children for the disobedience of the others. Every principle of justice in my nature revolts against it. It seems to me the greatest injustice, while no suffering is saved by it. The punishment is simply transferred from the guilty to the innocent, from the many, and poured with terrible concentration upon one. Such a transfer satisfies neither love nor justice. Nothing is gained by it. Every principle of right is violated. It also necessitates two distinct Divine beings to carry a vicarious scheme of salvation into effect ; all our relations to the one only Lord are thrown into confusion, and we are brought into no more intimate union with Him than we were before. All that is claimed for the vicarious scheme is the transference of a penalty from the guilty to the innocent. But if my Creator, my Heavenly Father, the constant source of my life, touched with infinite pity, came after me, His lost and dying child, found me, took me by the hand, tried to gain recognition and lead me back to life, I can understand that. It meets every demand of my nature.

But if it was not to suffer a penalty, and if it was to restore man to union with Himself, the question still remains, Why was it necessary to take upon Himself man's nature? The question has already been answered by inference if not directly ; but it demands a fuller and more direct reply.

To see the reason clearly we must go back to our original point of view ; we must keep in mind that the

real relations between man and the Lord are those of the recipient of life to the Giver of life, of the branch to the vine. The interior degrees of man's being were nearly dead. He had lost all true knowledge of God. He had almost lost the knowledge of His existence. He had made the Word of God of none effect by his traditions ; he had so perverted every form of his spiritual organism that he called evil good and truth falsity. Communication with the pure and good in the spiritual world was interrupted and nearly closed, and man was surrounded within and without by beings like himself   Every child was born with the perverted spiritual as well as physical nature of its parents ; it breathed an atmosphere poisoned with every evil. Man in his relations to the Lord was like a tree stripped of its leaves and bruised and marred, and so excluded from the light and heat of the sun that its influences could reach it only in feeble and reflected forms. All the avenues between man and the Lord, the source of his life, were so closed and perverted that he was dying. He had lost all consciousness of the higher qualities of goodness and truth. The Lord could not get access to him from within. He could not reach him through others. There was only one way. He must come Himself. But He could not come to man without bridging the gulf between the infinite and the finite, between the Divine and the human. Man was in a merely sensuous condition ; the Lord could not come to him except where he was. He must confront him face to face. He must do as Elisha did to the Shunammite's son. He must stretch Himself upon man. He must put
His mo l   ;   :   )on man's

eyes, and His hands upon man's hands. He must bring His life in direct contact with man's organism, and in forms that would take effect. Here was a real difficulty to be overcome. It was not a legal or technical difficulty ; it was not any fiction of justice. It was a question of reaching man where he lay dying, and of breathing new life into him. There was no other medium of communicating life than a spiritual and material organism which should touch the Divine on one side and the material on the other, and so connect them link by link until the chain was complete and the Divine power could be brought to bear upon man. Then when he should touch this Divine human presence virtue would go out of the Lord to heal him, as it did to the woman who touched the hem of His garment and was made whole.

The human nature of our Lord is called by many names, according to the offiee it performs. It is called the Son of God and the Son of man, because it was begotten of God and born of man. It is called the right hand and arm of power because by means of it the Lord could bring His Divine power to bear upon man to save and bless him. It is called the door because it opens the way of access of the Lord to man and of man to the Lord, swinging either way. It is called the mediator between God and man because it is the medium by which the Divine life is transmitted to man, and the way by which man ascends to the Father. "No man cometh unto the Father but by me." It is called Jesus, Saviour, because it is the means by which man is saved. It is called Christ because it is anointed to subdue man's enemies and to rule in the power of the Divine truth. It was what all these names describe, and much more ; but there was one thing it was not. It was not a being or person separate and distinct from the one God. It was the necessary means of closing the breach between the recipients of life and the source of life ; the means by which God came to man.

I have one more question to answer, and I am done. How did this assumption of man's nature by Jehovah effect an atonement between Him and man? The answer to this question will depend upon what is meant by atonement. If by atonement is meant a satisfaction of Divine justice, made by suffering a penalty which is equivalent to that which man would have suffered if it had fallen upon his unsheltered head, then I grant it did not accomplish that. If Jesus Christ is a distinct person from Jehovah, and He assumed this nature for the purpose of paying a debt to Jehovah which man could not pay, then I do not see how Jehovah, who is the source of life, is brought into any nearer relations with man, who is merely a form recipient of life. I do not see how it connects them in any way. If by atonement is meant the settlement of legal difficulties between man and his Maker, I grant that the doctrine which I have stated does not explain it, because it has no relation to it ; it does not look to it in any respect ; it does not recognize any such difficulties. If you mean the removal of any vengeful or unkind feelings from the heart of Jehovah towards man, effecting a willingness in the Divine mind to acquit man of the punishment due to his sins, in consideration of the sufferings of another, then I confess that the doctrine that Jehovah Himself assumed a human nature from pure love to man, for the purpose of reconciling man to Himself and bringing him within the reach of His Divine arms, that He might raise him up and draw him closer to His infinite heart, does not account for any such effect. None of these purposes look to any real union between man and the Lord. They only look to the payment of a debt or the satisfaction of some legal claims of the Lord upon man. Supposing such a result to be reached, it leaves man intellectually and morally just where it finds him. No new and higher knowledge of God is communicated to him, no discords in his nature are silenced, no evils are removed, no sins are remitted ; only the penalty is paid. No new and higher life is breathed into his soul, reviving and quickening and purifying and enlarging it. No new bond of union is formed between man and the Lord, no old one is strengthened. Man has gone into voluntary bankruptcy, and all claims against him have been cancelled because a Friend has paid them. He remains as naked and destitute as ever.

But if the work of atonement consists in the removal of obstacles to the inflowing of Divine life into men, which really exist, and a reawakening of his spiritual consciousness ; if new channels are opened between the Lord and man, through which the river of life can flow into his parched and withered heart ; if new and clearer knowledge of the Lord is communicated to him, new help is given to him to overcome his evils ; if his spiritual blindness is cured, his ears opened to hear the Word of the Lord ; if the lame begin to leap as a hart, and the tongue of the dumb to sing, and man is lifted out of the dust and darkness of a merely sensual life ; if all the activities of his nature are brought into harmony with the Divine nature, and his whole being is quickened with a new and higher life, and he is drawn into closer union with the Lord,—if such blessed results are meant by atonement, then we can see that this bridging of the gulf between the Source of life and the recipients of life is the direct, orderly and specific means of accomplishing it. It involves no distinction of persons in God, and no conflicting elements in His character ; it leads us into no legal absurdities. This is a doctrine which is in harmony with reason and a sense of justice, and it brings the Lord, the only Lord, our Father, Redeemer, and Saviour, so near to us, and presents Him so distinct and glorious as the embodiment of infinite love and wisdom, that our hearts must be hard indeed if we cannot love Him, and are not powerfully impelled to study His commandments that we may learn the ways which lead to closer union with Him and diligently walk in them. This is a real at-one-ment. There is no fiction about this. It is the restoration of man to conjunction with the Lord. It is the renewal of the covenant between man and the Lord. It is the provision of the means by which man can gain the remission of his sins and the Divine prayer can be fulfilled, " That they all may be one ; as thou, Father, art in me, and I in thee, that they also may be one in us : that the world may believe that thou hast sent me."

I must say one word in conclusion about the practical value of true knowledge upon this subject. If our salvation depends upon our character, upon our intimate and vital conjunction with the Lord, who is the source of

being cleansed from sin itself

and not upon the remission of a penalty ; upon the re-creation of our spiritual faculties and such a change in our whole spiritual nature that it is brought back into harmony with the Divine nature and restored to its original excellence ; and if in this work, as in every other, we are to co-operate, you can see how dangerous it would be to rely upon the hope that some one else has suffered for us, paid the debt for us, borne the penalty for us, and transferred His merits to our account. Any doctrine or theory which turns away our attention from our inherent and essential relations to the Lord, and obscures the truth that there are no obstacles to our salvation but false and evil principles in us, and that there is no way of salvation but shunning evils as sins against God and living according to the commandments, is misleading, and will end in absolute failure. The Lord did not come to suffer in our stead, to pay a penalty for us, to be good for us. He came to help us to resist evil, and thereby escape its penalties. He came to help us to live according to the laws of life, that we might enjoy the peace and blessedness which results from so living.

THE FIRST AND SECOND DEATH.

"And I say unto you my friends, Be not afraid of them that kill the body, and after that have no more that they can do.

"But I will forewarn you whom ye shall fear: Fear him, which after he hath killed hath power to cast into hell; yea, I say unto you, Fear him."—LUKE xii. 4, 5.

THERE is no subject, it would seem, which would interest man so much as that great change in his existence which is called death, and yet there are few questions concerning which so little is known and so many errors prevail. The most common opinions concerning it are that it is a mystery, a terror and an agony ; that it was sent upon man as a punishment for disobedience, and that it is a standing monument of the Divine displeasure. Consequently, men almost universally shrink from it with horror, and to many it is the one dark cloud and terrible dread of life. Poets and orators and Christian teachers hold it up as the most awful calamity, and it is the severest punishment known to human laws.

But much of the mystery and terror that invests it is due to entire misconceptions of its origin and nature, and these misconceptions seem to have their origin in confounding the two deaths and attributing to one the qualities that belong to the other. Men have attributed to natural death the pains and sufferings that belong only to spiritual death. Indeed, most men overlook the second

224

death entirely, and, if they think of the subject at all, think only of natural death.

A careful examination of the Sacred Scriptures and enlightened reason will show us that natural death, by which we understand the separation of the soul from the body, was not sent upon man as a punishment for sin, but is an orderly step in the progress of his life. It was not this death that came into the world by sin. If man had never sinned he would still have cast off his material body and passed on into the spiritual world.

We need go no further than the first intimations of death which we have in the Sacred Scriptures to learn that it was not natural death that came by sin. The warning given to Adam and Eve was, "In the day that thou eatest thereof thou shalt surely die." (Gen. ii. 17.) But they did not die a natural death in that day. Either that was not the death referred to, therefore, or the warning was a false one. And this we cannot for a moment suppose. So when Moses said to the Israelites, "See, I have set before thee this day life and good, and death and evil" (Deut. xxx. 15), he cannot mean natural life and death, for if they had obeyed every one of his commandments they would not have lived forever in this world. The Lord also commanded Jeremiah to say to the Jews, "Thus saith the Lord: Behold, I set before you the way of life, and the way of death." (Jer. xxi. 8.) In the Psalms also it is said, "Thou hast delivered my soul from death." (Ps. lvi. 13 ; cxvi. 8.) The apostles also often speak of death in this sense. But what our Lord said to Martha is conclusive upon the subject, "Whosoever liveth and believeth in me shall never die." (John xi. 26.) By this He could not mean natural death, for multitudes which no man can number have lived and believed in Him, and their bodies have returned to the dust from which they were formed. When the apostle says that death came by sin, and that death has passed upon all, for that all have sinned (Rom. v. 12), he evidently means the death of the soul. There is no evidence in the Bible that natural death was caused by sin. It is a mere human inference. It is no doubt true that much of the sickness and pain that generally precedes and attends our departure from this world is more or less remotely caused by sin, because evil desires and false principles lead to the violation of physical laws, to intemperance in eating and drinking, to anxieties and excitements and disorders of life. The average duration of human life in this world has without doubt also been much shortened by evil, for we know that the average duration of life increases as civilization advances and men become more observant of the laws of life. But there is no evidence that man would live forever in this world even if he lived a perfect life. Immortality in this world is certainly not taught in the Bible, and there are many rational considerations and inferences from the Sacred Scriptures that show conclusively that it is not according to the purposes of the Divine wisdom that man should live here forever.

So far as our knowledge extends, the existence of every living thing organized of matter is limited. It has laws of birth, growth, and decay. There is no exception. Every plant in the vegetable kingdom, for example, attains its growth and does not pass beyond a certain limit. It may remain stationary there for years, for centuries, and yet the moment it stands still it begins to decline, and eventually it will fall and perish. The same is true of the animal kingdom. There are no exceptions to the law. Now, it is worthy of notice that animals and vegetables have not sinned ; they live according to the true order of their creation. Man, as to his physical nature, is an animal, and the laws of his generation, development, and life are the same. There have been, and no doubt are still, multitudes of human beings who have lived in perfect health. And yet they grow old and die. Nor do they die of any disease ; when the body has done its work it shrivels and falls from the soul as the husk from the corn.

But again, so far as human observation extends, the development of organized beings and things proceeds by distinct steps, the prior acting as an instrument for the creation of the succeeding, and being left behind it in the ascent. In the vegetable kingdom, when the germ expands, the outer covering which contained it is thrown aside ; the blossom fades and perishes when the fruit is born and begins a distinct existence ; and again, the husk and chaff and rough covering which have served as a body and vessel and protection for the fine, fluent substances of the seed during its formation wither and die when the seed is ripe. The same order and method prevails in the animal kingdom. This is beautifully exemplified in insects. There are three distinct steps in insect life. A caterpillar is hatched from an egg, then it becomes a chrysalis enclosed in a hard covering, and apparently almost lifeless, and then a moth or butterfly.

During these metamorphoses, or changes of form, it never goes back and resumes its former state. The moth does not become a worm and the worm an egg. But it continually advances until it completes the cycle of its life, preparation being made in each state for the succeeding one.

Have these analogies and this method of the Divine wisdom, which is universal so far as we know, no significance? So far as our observation extends, we find creation and life proceeding according to the same order and method in man as in all other creatures. Can we suppose that the order is reversed the moment we reach the limits of our own observation?

Man is a spiritual being. He has a spiritual body, for the apostle Paul declares, "There is a spiritual body." Man has a nature of a degree distinctly higher than the animal, than any other created being. And is it not according to all the analogies of the Divine method of creating that man should attain his highest state by successive changes of state? continually throwing off and leaving behind those materials and instruments which have been used as means for its attainment? If there is any force in reasoning from universal methods, I do not see how we can come to any other conclusion than that natural death is a step forward in life, if man has a distinctly spiritual nature, a spiritual body.

But if the laws of analogy did not point with sure indications to the great truth that natural death is only a step forward in life, we might infer it from the infinite nature of the Divine love and wisdom. Suppose it had been the original intention of the Creator that man should live immortal upon this earth, there must soon have been a limit to the number of human beings He could create; for while man lives upon the earth clothed in a material body he must be fed with products from the earth, and even in the most perfect order of things the limits of its power to sustain human life must be reached; and when that limit is reached the whole order and nature of man must be changed. Society must to a great extent become stationary. No new elements could be constantly added to it; no new varieties of character be constantly adding to its perfection. Conceive for a moment the earth to be crowded with a population to the full extent of its capacity to support life, and the same beings to dwell upon it forever, with no infancy, no childhood, no old age, nothing to call forth our sympathy, nothing to awaken fresh and lively hopes,—would not such a state be more like the dead level of a stagnant pool than the running stream of an ever-varying life? Would not some of the elements which seem most important and even essential to human happiness be wanting?

But suppose the earth to be filled with happy people. Could the comparatively few human beings the earth could sustain satisfy the infinite love of the Lord? There is something of the infinite even in the material world. We see it in the variety which everywhere exists; no two things or beings are alike. We see it in the tendency of every plant and animal to reproduction and multiplication. Can we for a moment suppose that man, who stands at the head of the Creator's works, should be the only exception to this law? that while plants and animals are produced in endless variety in a circle of suc-

cessive generations, man, who was created in the image
and likeness of God, should soon reach the limit of his
numbers, and beyond that limit could know no increase
through the coming eternity? How much grander the
idea, and worthier of infinite love, and more in accordance with all we know of the Divine methods, that an
endless succession of generations should be born upon
the earth and transplanted into the heavens! Thus
human life upon the earth, instead of being the completed work of the Lord, is only its beginning. Earth is
the nursery and seminary of heaven, where human souls
capable of receiving the Divine life and reciprocating the
Divine love, capable of loving and being loved, can be
born with endless variety and number.

But again, if man was born to live forever in this
world, what becomes of all the promised blessedness of
heaven? Are we not taught in the Sacred Scriptures,
both by positive precept and inevitable inference, that
heaven is a better and more perfect world than this?
What becomes of the happiness which eye hath not seen,
nor ear heard, nor heart conceived? Is heaven, the
abode of the angels and the Lord, a mere refuge from
this world? and does its principal excellence consist in
the contrasts it furnishes to this life? Would there have
been no mansions in heaven for us if there had been no
sin upon earth? Would there have been no songs of joy
there by human voices if there had been no wail of sorrow here? Even upon the supposition that the angels
are a race of beings distinct from men, would heaven be
as perfect, would the angels be as happy in their bright
abodes, without a constant accession of human beings

from the earth to instruct and love? If you insist that man was born to be immortal in this world, but that the happiness of heaven exceeds anything possible to this life, as the prevalent theology does, you admit that man has been a gainer by sin; he has escaped from a world of material limitations and imperfections and gained entrance to one where all the conditions of his existence are perfect, where he can associate with angelic beings and enjoy a fulness and perfection of happiness impossible to this. If you admit that heaven would not be as perfect without a continual influx of life from this world, you admit that both angels and men are gainers by natural death.

Whatever view we take of the subject, then, I see but one escape from the inevitable conclusion that natural death has in itself no real terrors; that it is an orderly step in man's successive creation, and a part of the great original purpose of the Divine love and wisdom, according to which there is to be an endless succession of human souls created upon the earth, who, after passing through various stages here, are to find their final home in the spiritual world. I say I see but one escape from this conclusion, and that is in the admission that the spiritual world is not so real and perfect a world as this. And that admission involves so many and great absurdities, such an entire inversion of all the methods of the Divine order; is so contrary to the whole tenor of the Word and subversive of the precious promises and immortal hopes it holds out to us, that it seems impossible that any rational mind could entertain it for a moment. If the spiritual world is not the vain dream of an idle fancy;

if the Lord and the angels and the promises of heavenly blessedness are not fallacious hopes, then that change in our organization, that disrobing of the spirit by its resurrection from the material body, that escape from the imprisonment and bonds of the flesh, which men call death, has no real terror, and, instead of shrinking from it with horror, we ought to welcome it as our deliverer from bondage, as an introduction into life.

And without doubt we should regard death in this light if we had not invested it with terrors which belong to an entirely different subject, and lost all true idea of the nature and reality of the world to which it introduces us. Before man had so far receded from that world by a life of evil as almost to forget its existence, death had no terrors. It was the gate of entrance into a new life. He lay down to sleep with the delightful hope and perfect confidence that he would wake in a new world. Death was going home; it was the conscious entrance into a higher state of being. It was the happy reunion with loved ones who had gone before. It was a step which brought him nearer to the Fountain of all life and the Author of all human blessedness. How could it be regarded with fear? How could the soul shrink from it with horror? Suppose the chrysalis, imprisoned in that hard covering we may call its body, buried in the earth and limited to a bare existence, could have a perception of the change that is soon to take place in its state. It is soon to burst the gates of its present life and emerge into a new world of light and beauty. Instead of being buried in the dark earth, it is to soar aloft through the air, to bask in the light and warmth of the summer sun, to sport in joyous flights in happy bands, to feed upon the honeyed dews and the distilled sweets of flowers. Do you think it would look forward to such a change with dread? But the change from the chrysalis almost devoid of life, shut up in the dark, to the gay and beautiful insect is not so great as the change that takes place in man in his resurrection from the material body. This change, then, which men call death, this putting off of the material body, is not, cannot be, an interruption of the Divine plan, a thwarting of the Divine purposes of good towards His human children. It must be the fulfilment of those purposes. All Scripture properly understood, all right reason, teaches us that it must be so. To deny it is to plunge into inexplicable absurdities.

But there is a death which we ought to fear, and from which we shall do well to shrink with horror, and that is spiritual death, sometimes called the "second death." This death does not consist in a cessation of existence, nor in the departure from this world to the spiritual world, but in the inversion and destruction of the true order of man's nature.

Man is said to be alive, in the Word, when he receives life from the Lord according to the original order and constitution of his nature. The Jews were promised life if they would obey the laws of the Lord. The whole Word is full of the same promises. "If thou wilt enter into life," said our Saviour, "keep the commandments." He came that men might have life. This was spiritual and not natural life. And the reason why life is promised on the condition of keeping the commandments, and often as a reward for keeping them, is be-

20*

cause the commandments are the laws of life. The rewards are not arbitrarily given, but follow as a consequence, as the physician may promise health on the condition of our obeying the laws of physical life.

Man was created by infinite wisdom according to a certain order. By observing this order he would attain his life, a life ever increasing in fulness and degree. Any deviation from that order would be attended with some loss of life. It would prevent man from receiving life from the Lord in its fulness and perfection. The moment man violated a law of his spiritual nature he suffered some loss of spiritual capacity. Man began to die. This was the warning the Lord gave Adam and Eve, "In the day that thou eatest thereof, thou shalt surely die." And the warning was not an idle one. They did die in the day, not the natural day of twenty-four hours, but in the state and according to the degree that they ate of the forbidden fruit, which was evil. And this is a universal law in all orders and degrees of the creation. When the laws of vegetable life are broken, the plant begins to die. When the laws of animal life, of man's physical life, are violated, the animal and the body begin to die. Death follows as an inevitable consequence. It is not arbitrarily inflicted. As the soul is immortal, spiritual death is not the cessation of existence, but the loss of the soul's ability to receive life from the Lord in true order. The substances which compose the soul cannot be dissipated as the material elements which compose plants, animals, and the material body can. Man as a spiritual being must continue to exist, but in a state of spiritual death.

There are two principal characteristics of this death worthy of our notice.

First, it is a loss of life. Man was created by the Lord with the power of perpetual and indefinite advancement in his capacity to know and love and be happy. The more we learn, the more we are capable of learning. The more we love, the more we are capable of loving. The more we enjoy, the more we are capable of enjoying. So that the feeblest child upon the earth may ultimately pass beyond the present state of the highest angel. But spiritual death arrests this development. It closes up the higher degrees of man's mind against Divine influences, and shuts out the light and life of heaven. His whole nature becomes stunted and dwarfed. He stops in the grand and endless career of life at the beginning, and loses all the glory and blessedness of the eternal future. And no finite mind can estimate that loss. Men are often inconsolable at the loss of property or office, on account of hinderance in some earthly career, but that is a mere nothing compared with his loss who dies at the beginning of life. How sad it is to see a blind child ! By the death of his eyes how much he has lost ! He must wander in darkness through the earth, comparatively helpless, for ten, twenty, fifty years, unconscious of its beauty of form and color, of the significance of expressive faces and gestures, of the changing glories of the seasons, of day and night, and the ever-shifting play of things by which the web of human life is woven. How great, how irreparable, how sad the loss ! And yet what is that compared with the loss of one's spiritual sight? Nothing,—absolutely nothing ! One is the loss for a few years of the sight of earthly things, the other the loss to eternity of the inexpressible beauty and glory of heaven. This is but one of the senses.

Suppose you had held in your hand the first grain of wheat that was created. You planted it, and in time it just pushed its head above the ground, and there its progress is arrested. It remains a green blade, but becomes nothing more. What a loss to humanity! Thousands of millions of acres, waving with golden harvests, the staff of life for thousands of generations, broken. It surpasses the power of the finite mind to conceive the loss to humanity, and yet that is nothing compared with what every soul will lose whose progress is arrested in the first beginning of life by spiritual death. "What shall it profit a man, if he shall gain the whole world, and lose his own soul?"

You observe that I say nothing so far about pain and punishment, but speak merely of loss of attainment, of what man does not gain, of the endless and only less than infinite blessings the Lord intended for him which he fails to receive. And if he were to stop there, like the grain of wheat arrested in its growth, and suffer no pain, suffer nothing but the loss, can you conceive anything more terrible? What a blasting of hopes! What bankruptcy! What eternal ruin! Who would not fear a death which closes the gates of such hopes against us and bars us from the possession of such endless and ineffable joys?

But this is not all. By that inversion of life which we call spiritual death the soul comes into such a state of disorder and discord with the Fountain of life and with all outward things that it is filled with perpetual pain. It is not my purpose to describe the woes and agonies of the second death. We all know something of what they are, for there is not a sorrow or pain that afflicts human hearts that is not the effect of the second death. Count up your own sorrows, the pain from blasted hopes, the pangs of regret, the stings of remorse, the chafings from conflicting interests, the smarts of jealousy and shame, and the great shadow of fear that lies like a cloud upon all hearts ; measure the sum of human suffering in the hearts around you, and they will declare the awful consequences of this death in a language more forcible and eloquent than the painter's colors or the writer's words. Add to these, if you can, the future consequences of this death, the night that has no hope of a coming morning, the cup of misery that can never be drained, the feverish and tormenting desires that can never be appeased. Is there not reason in the Divine words, " And I say unto you, my friends, Be not afraid of them that kill the body, and after that have no more that they can do. But I will forewarn you whom ye shall fear : Fear him, who after he hath killed hath power to cast into hell. Yea, I say unto you, Fear him" !

Is there not every reason to fear this death ? Human language is totally inadequate to express its horrors. Human imagination cannot adequately conceive its awful terrors. You may fear it ; you ought to fear it ; teach your children to fear it ; warn your friends and neighbors to fear it. It is the most terrible thing in the universe.

And yet men do not fear it. They play and dance with it ; they crown it with roses, and sink willingly into

its embrace.   Gentle and timid women, who would scream at a harmless insect and fall into a swoon at the sight of blood, will gayly and boldly toy with death ; will greet it with gay laughter and song, and cherish it with
· its hideous deformities and the sting of its endless pain in the secret shrine of their hearts.   And men who call themselves ruined if they lose money, who are ashamed of goodness and have not sufficient courage to say, I have done wrong, are bold enough to do the wrong.

I know of no illusion of evil so cunning and destructive to human souls as that which conceals the horrors of real death with deceptive and vain delights, and invests a mere step in life with all the horrors of death.   How we mourn when a beloved one is translated !   We look at the body which is cast off, and our eyes are blinded with tears.   But who weeps over the dead souls that fill our houses and throng our streets?   The stir and bustle and noisy activity that everywhere meet the eye and fall upon the ear are not the sounds of life.   The shout and song that come from festive halls are not the sounds of living souls, but too often the wild, mad revelry of death. And the earth, this beautiful and glorious earth, created to be the birthplace of immortal souls and the sweet cradle of infancy, the nursery of heaven, has become a vast sepulchre, a dwelling for the dead, a grave in which human souls are buried.

We die spiritually before we do naturally.   The death of the body only lifts the veil and reveals to us in clear light the death of the soul that already exists, and permits us to pass on to its full consequences.   When the body has performed its use, it fades like the blossom, it withers and falls like the husk, and reveals the life or death that exists within. It does not cause it ; it does not add to it or subtract from it, any more than the removal of the chaff adds to or subtracts from the wheat.

Let us not, then, confound these two things so entirely distinct and different, and live in constant dread of that death which is but an orderly step in life and a provision of infinite mercy, while we forget the real danger of our souls.

HEAVEN.

"In my Father's house are many mansions: if it were not so, I would have told you. I go to prepare a place for you.

"And if I go and prepare a place for you, I will come again, and receive you unto myself; that where I am, there ye may be also."—JOHN xiv. 2, 3.

I INVITE your attention to what the doctrines of the New Church, as contained in the writings of Emanuel Swedenborg, teach us concerning heaven. Swedenborg presents the subject in his work on "Heaven and Hell" from two points of view : from the nature of the Lord and from the nature of man, and we must take the same position and view it in the same light if we desire to get any clear idea of his disclosures concerning it.

The Lord is essentially a being of infinite love and wisdom. His end or motive in creating the universe and man must have been the formation of a heaven of intelligent beings whom He could bless with the largest measures of the highest happiness it is possible for a finite being to receive. Infinite love could do no less than this. Infinite wisdom also could not fail to provide the best possible means in every form, quality, and method for attaining the ends of infinite love. If you assume that the Lord could have had any other end in the creation than the greatest good of the greatest number, your supposition denies His infinite love. It falls short of the highest purpose which even a finite mind can conceive ;

how, then, can it be infinite? If you assume that the Lord has not devised the best possible methods to carry His purpose into effect, you do not accord to Him infinite wisdom and power. He could have done better than He has, and that would be infinite folly and failure. The Lord's nature demands that He shall provide a state of endless and boundless blessedness.

We must come to the same conclusion if we view the subject from the nature of man. There is not a principle or power or form in man's soul, mind, or body, when unperverted, which does not look to the same end. If you examine the material body in its relations to the material universe, you find that every bone, muscle, tendon, nerve,—every organic form in its least and largest parts, was designed directly or indirectly to be an inlet of delight ; to contribute in some way to man's happiness in this world. If you examine the material universe you find that everything, from the rock to the sun, was designed to contribute to human well-being ; to sustain, to protect, to delight, and to bless man. If you view the human body in its relations to the human soul, you discover that it is designed with an exquisite skill to clothe the soul and to serve as its instrument in gaining ideas, in developing its affections, and in forming the basis for an immortal career in another world. If you look at the nature of man himself, his love for knowledge and delight in obtaining it, his power of loving and the blessedness which flows from the exercise of that power ; when you consider that his capacities to know, love, and enjoy are so great that nothing can satisfy him, so immeasurable that it is impossible for a finite mind to conceive of any assignable limit beyond which he may not pass, what other conclusion is possible than that the Lord created man and specifically formed him in every organ, quality, and principle to be a recipient of endless and ever-increasing happiness? To deny it is to attribute to Him the monstrous mistake and folly of creating human beings with capacities and wants for which He provided no means of supply, thus compelling His children to go on their endless way with a burning thirst which He has provided no living waters to assuage, and consuming hunger which there is no bread to satisfy. That would be terrible beyond conception. Annihilation is better than that. There is, therefore, no rational escape from the conclusion that the Lord, man, and nature all point in one direction, to a state of complete and perfect human happiness.

Our next question, therefore, is, How is this happiness obtained? What makes heaven? Observation, experience, reason, and the Lord Himself in the Sacred Scriptures, give one answer to this question. Heaven essentially is a state or condition of the soul, of the will and understanding, of the affections and thoughts. "The kingdom of God is within you." There is where heaven begins. It must be there or it cannot be anywhere else. Every faculty of man's nature, as we know, was made to be an inlet of delight, and when all his faculties of will and understanding preserve the perfection into which they were created, and act in the form and order designed by infinite wisdom, the result must be happiness and heaven according to the measure and degree of their capacity.

The internal condition or state is the first essential. Without that no external conditions or possessions would be of any value. No one can be admitted into the heaven of light, with its splendors and beauty of color and form, until the eye, which is the kingdom of light in the body, has been formed in him ; no one can be admitted into the kingdom of harmony with all its concord of sweet sounds, until the organ of hearing has been formed within him. The same principle holds in regard to every sense and every delight. It is, so far as we know or can conceive, a universal principle, a method of attaining His ends which the Lord always adopts. We see it also in all our works. When men seek to use the power of steam or falling water to do their work, they must construct engines and wheels adapted to the nature of the element they use. When they desire to get harmony from the idle wind they make an organ. They can get it in no other way. The sun cannot create harvests of corn and fruit for man until there is some germ or vegetable form for its heat and light to flow into and awake to activity. So it is with the soul. It must be so constituted, and must be in such a state, that it is capable of exercising heavenly affection, or it can never attain heavenly delights. A stone cannot see though the light floods it ; it cannot feel though the heat penetrates it ; it cannot hear though the winds play all their melodies over it. It cannot enter the heaven of beauty, of harmony, of delight, because they cannot enter it. The principles which constitute their kingdom are not embodied in it. These are illustrations of the method which the Lord in His infinite wisdom has provided for the attainment of His ends. And the method is universal. It is grounded in the very nature of things. We cannot enter heaven merely by going to any place, or by admission to the society of the angels. That would be of no use to us whatever if we could not receive the life and exercise the affections of the angels. What is the use to the blind man of increasing the light? To enter heaven we must be in a heavenly state.

What, then, is the heavenly state? It consists essentially in love to the Lord and man. Negatively, it is freedom from sin, from impurity, and from falsity. Positively, it is the harmonious action of all the faculties of the soul in the order established for them by infinite wisdom. It is for man as a spiritual being what the perfect action of eye and ear are for him as a natural being. By his senses, when they are sound, man is admitted into all natural delight. When his spiritual faculties are sound and in true order, he is admitted by them into all heavenly and spiritual delights.

This state is called by various names. It is being reconciled to God. It is making our peace with Him. It is being one with Him, so that He can dwell in us, and we in Him. It is believing on Him, loving Him, and living according to His commandments. It is a life according to the order embodied in the human soul by infinite wisdom to carry it on to the end designed for it by infinite love,—that is, to a state of complete and ever-increasing happiness.

We all, no doubt, agree that one of the essential elements of heaven is a heavenly state of the affections and thoughts. But if we stop here we have told only half of the truth. No perfection of internal spiritual state would secure our happiness unless there were something without us to call our affections and various spiritual faculties into activity. Heavenly happiness is not possible without a substantial world in which the heavenly inhabitants dwell. If there were no light the most perfect eye would be of no more use to man than a ball of glass or an empty socket. This is true of all the senses. A material body perfectly organized in every part, without an external world adapted to it, capable of flowing into it and exciting its forms to activity, would be entirely destitute of sensation. Organization is only one of the factors of sensation. It is just as impossible to produce harmony from an organ in a perfect vacuum as it is to produce sensation by organization alone. I am certain you will give your assent to this.

The same law applies to the spirit. You cannot think without some object to think about. You cannot know without something to know. You cannot love without some being or thing objective or distinct from yourself to love. The various faculties of the soul, like the germ of a plant, remain inactive until called into play by some power or object without or distinct from themselves.

So, we hold, it must be with the soul in the spiritual world. The spirit itself must be an organic human form or it could not preserve its identity ; it could not be in any state of goodness and truth, or in any other state. State or condition is not an abstraction. It is the form and quality of something. The state of your health is not some abstract condition apart from your body. If you had no body you would have no health, and you would be nobody. If the spirit had no form and no organization, it could not be happy or miserable. To talk of its being admitted into ·heaven would be absurd, for there would be nothing to admit. To say that it hears, sees, feels, can talk and sing, would be contrary to the nature of things.

No one can see without eyes ; and no one can see with eyes unless there is light and some form from which the light is reflected. The spiritual world, therefore, must be a real and substantial world. It must comprise those forms and objects which compose a world. Its inhabitants must be distinct from one another. That world must have a sun, or there can be no light. It must have an atmosphere, or there can be no speech, no song, no sound, no action of any kind. There must be the two factors, a heavenly state and a heavenly world, to produce happiness. Happiness is inconceivable without both. If we deny substance and form to man as a spirit and to the spiritual world, instead of securing conditions more favorable to human happiness, we have no conditions at all. The true way and the only way, therefore, of obtaining a correct idea of heavenly happiness and the means essential to securing it, is not to deny to man as a spirit and to the spiritual world all the properties, forms, and relations of this world and this life, but to carry out his state and relations in this world to more perfect conditions in the other.

As a man is a spirit in the human form, he has, after laying aside the material body, all the organs, external and internal, proper to a human being. He has eyes organized of spiritual substances, and he can see spiritual objects. He has ears, and he can hear spiritual sounds and be affected by spiritual harmonies. He can taste and feel, and enjoy the fragrance of pleasant odors. When the spiritual body is raised up or withdrawn from the material body, a man retains every sense he ever had. Indeed, his power of sensation always belonged to the spiritual body, even before it was withdrawn from the material body. The material body was only the instrument the spiritual senses used to gain a knowledge of material things, as we use optical instruments to assist the vision of the naked eye. There was no more change wrought in the spiritual senses by discarding the material organs than there is wrought in the eye by removing the glasses we use to assist our imperfect vision. The spiritual faculties remain the same in themselves, but they come into more favorable conditions for delightful exercise. Freed from their material covering, they are more delicate and sensitive to every contact and relation. Their power of sensation is indefinitely increased.

At the same time the whole human form becomes a more perfect expression of the beautiful heavenly character. Consider the law by which this is attained. Any affection by continued exercise fixes itself in the features and becomes embodied in the whole form. Care ploughs its furrows in the face, sorrow casts its shadows over it, joy irradiates it, lust brutalizes it, cunning and fear leave their impress upon it, contentment and peace give to it a sweet and serene repose. This relation between outward form and inward state is more fully realized when man is freed from the incumbrance of the inert material body. He becomes the form of his ruling affection.

His love to the Lord and man becomes effigied in his face and in his whole form. He becomes an embodied affection. His face is moulded into its image. His wisdom glows in his eyes, irradiates his face, is moulded in his limbs, sways all his motions into graceful action, gives symmetry to his whole form, flows in harmony from his lips, gives sweetness to his voice, and speaks in every action. Instead of losing his human form and lapsing into a vital principle or a formless vapor, and thus losing his identity as a man, he comes into a more excellent human form ; he becomes more distinctly himself.

The human form contains all the elements of beauty and grandeur. This human beauty is not lost in heaven. On the contrary, it is indefinitely enhanced in every essential quality. Infants and children grow up in heaven to the stature and the perfection of adult life. The aged find a fountain of youth in heavenly affections. The material body only grows old, and men and women in the spiritual world soon return to the full vigor of their best days, and continue to grow towards the perfections of immortal youth.

While those who enter heaven continue to advance by lovely paths towards immortal youth, they do not become merged into an indiscriminate mass. On the contrary, every one becomes more distinctly himself. A man becomes more distinctly masculine. A woman becomes more distinctly a woman, and the embodiment of every feminine grace and loveliness,—of a grace and loveliness peculiar to herself. The varieties of heavenly beauty increase with the number of heavenly inhabitants. Every man and every woman is the embodiment and form of

some variety of goodness. In man the masculine qualities predominate, in woman the feminine. The lines
between them become more distinct in heaven than they
can be on earth, and they grow more distinct to eternity.
Every one becomes more distinctly individualized. Thus
the unity of heaven is not the harmony of sameness, but
of distinct and infinite variety.

All qualities of human beauty are combined in the
forms and natures of the heavenly inhabitants,—dignity,
grace, sweetness, purity, harmony of proportion, elegance
of form, and loveliness of expression. Swedenborg has
given us some pictures of those who have passed from
earth to heaven. He had a rich vocabulary and he was
a master of expression, but he generally ends by saying
that their beauty is such that no words can express it, no
painter can represent it. It is the holiest love, the purest
and sweetest charity, in living, glowing, perfect form ; so
living and speaking that it penetrates the hearts of the
beholders.

This perfection of form is the effect and expression of
internal states of progress in knowledge, of growth in
goodness. Truth is infinite. No finite man can sound
its depths or exhaust its riches. The wisest men in this
life only learn a few facts and gain a knowledge of some
general principles. But the more we know, the more we
shall see that there is to be known. The horizon of
truth enlarges as we rise. When we pass into the other
life we pass from darkness into light. The intellectual
faculties are freed from the limitations of time and space
and the imperfections of the material body, and from the
hinderance imposed by artificial language and methods.

Thus, while all the faculties gain an immense increase in power the facilities for acquiring knowledge keep even pace with them. Truth is not learned by rote, and only understood after long and painful reflection. Knowledge is gained by intuition. The understanding is illuminated by Divine truth, and revels in its light as in its own native sphere. It is continually surprised and delighted with new discoveries of the wisdom and goodness of the Lord. It penetrates deeper into causes, and rises higher into purer light.

The affections also enlarge with the intellect, and keep even pace with it. This is another source of happiness. There is no divorce between the head and the heart. The will and the understanding, so long put asunder by evil and falsity, are reunited in heavenly marriage, and become one. All that the heart loves, the head sees and the hands gain. There is no conflict between the desires and knowledge. Attainment always equals expectation.

Such a life is so remote from our observation or experience in this world that it is difficult for us to form any just conception of it. But what more could we hope for than the attainment of such a state? To be free from all struggle between our desires and our knowledge of duty ; to be delivered from every weight and shadow of the past ; to see clearly, to love freely, to attain fully, and to be conscious of rapidly advancing to new heights of wisdom and larger measures of love, and to know that this growth, with its delight, will continue with accelerating velocity forever! Can you ask more than that? Can you conceive anything better than that?

The happiness of heaven is also greatly increased by

the excellence of heavenly society. Intelligent beings cannot come together and live within the influence of one another without forming society. Society is the sum total of the knowledge, influence, power, and character of the individuals who compose it. If the men and women who compose it are selfish, ignorant, brutish, lustful, fierce, and revengeful, the society they form will be infernal. It is of no consequence where they are. Place them in paradise, and they would soon change it into a hell. Its clear and sparkling water would become a standing pool, breeding miasma and death. If the good and evil are mixed, as we find them in this world, there will be the conflict of elements which rages everywhere around us. If men and women who are intelligent, pure, unselfish, animated solely by love to the Lord and to one another, live together, the result will be a heavenly society. Place them in the foulest dens, and the filth and vile odors and decay and darkness would disappear, the stagnant pools would vanish, and sweetness, order, purity, comfortable dwellings, and peaceful activity would soon take their place. Put such a company on a desert island, and they would soon make it a paradise. What, then, must be the nature of a society formed of angelic men and women? I say angelic men and women rather than spirits or angels, because I want to keep the truth distinctly before you that the inhabitants of heaven are not shadows or ghosts or vital principles or a hybrid, half bird, half woman, but real, substantial human beings in human form, with human affections and capacities for human happiness. Stretch your imagination to its utmost ; combine all you can conceive of intelligence and wisdom, of dignity softened with grace, of strength wedded to gentleness and flowing into acts of kindness and tender regard for others ; the dignity of a great nature united with the docility and innocence of childhood. Imagine the men to equal, nay, to surpass in all masculine perfections the highest ideal of the greatest minds. Imagine the women to equal the men ; to be the embodiments of womanly wisdom and sagacity, of strength put to gentle uses, of quiet dignity veiled with modesty, of gentleness and purity exalted and glorified by the free play of heavenly affections, and the whole form the living image of angelic loveliness. Could beings of such natures associate with one another and not form a heaven? Could human souls fired with such heavenly affections and armed with such amazing power fail to find each other?

Now, according to Swedenborg, heaven is composed of such societies. It is not a huge mass of formless spirits, nor is the position of any one fixed by arbitrary allotment. The societies are as numerous as the general varieties of human affection, and the members who constitute each society are drawn together, under the auspices of the Lord, by reciprocal affinities. Heaven is in the human form, in the same sense that human societies are in the human form. Every society must have a head and heart and lungs, mouth and hands,—that is, it must have members who perform the same office for the society that those organs do for the physical body, and there are large societies which perform these offices for the race. In heaven these societies are more nicely discriminated than they can be on the earth. There societies are formed by those who pass into the heavens from the earth, and every one is drawn to his place by the affinities of his own nature, by the peculiar bias or quality of his affections. Every human being is the embodiment of some special form of affection. The Lord never duplicates anything. No two societies are alike, and no two members of any society are alike. The unitary life of a society grows out of the free play of the harmonious varieties which compose it. There is no sameness and no dead level in heaven. There are those there who have been members of a heavenly society for thousands of years. There are infants who went up from their mothers' arms to-day. There are young men and women, fathers and mothers, whom we have known and loved, who have cast off their earthly garments and have passed on to their homes in the heavens. Each has been drawn to his own society and his own home by the power of love; he has been welcomed with the most ardent affection, and instructed and cared for with angelic wisdom and devotion. Each one has retained that peculiar character which constitutes his identity, and has found his place according to his character. All the societies in heaven are formed according to this universal method of Divine operation.

Heavenly employments are another source of happiness. How are men and women going to spend their eternity? Not in singing. Singing is a very delightful employment, but I think we should all weary of it. They do sing, however, and play on all kinds of instruments, and the music is the perfect expression of some affection, and it awakens in every one who hears it the affection

22

which it expresses.   Every heart responds and vibrates in unison with the harmony.   There are occasions when society answers to society, when myriads of voices and myriads of instruments join in chorus to celebrate some attribute of the Lord's love and wisdom, and the whole heaven flows into sweet and ecstatic song.   But singing is no more the business of human beings in the other world than it is here.

Nor do they spend their time in praying and perpetual worship.   They have their worship and their temples and their ministers.   Some know more of the Divine love and wisdom than others, and it is the delight of every one to communicate his thought and affection to others. And they instruct with a wisdom of which we can form no adequate conception, and they worship with a profound humility and an ardor of devotion unknown to us. But they have other ways of showing their love to the Lord.   Here, again, Swedenborg is consistent with himself.   He tells us that the employments of angelic men and women are vastly more numerous than employments on earth, but most of them are of such a nature that they cannot be described in human language.   Some heavenly employments are revealed by Swedenborg and in the Sacred Scriptures.   Angels are always attendant upon men, and do all in their power to withhold them from evil and lead them to good.   They watch over infancy and childhood, and breathe into the pliant natures of the young something of the purity and beauty of their own souls.   They always attend upon the dying, and minister to every want of the soul new-born into the spiritual world.   They instruct infants who die, and children, and the ignorant but well disposed of all ages and nations, in the truth, and by all means known to angelic natures they lead them into a heavenly life. Being animated solely by love to the Lord and man, it is their highest delight to do good to others; to communicate their knowledge, their affection, and their aid in every possible way.

There are also governments and administrations and ministries of many kinds in heaven. They are far more numerous there than they are upon the earth.

Heavenly beings also have their recreations and festivals, their private and public social circles. Kindred souls commune with each other and reveal their inmost natures; friends meet with friends and enjoy the quiet flow of affection. For those who take pleasure therein there are always subjects of profound study. Truth is infinite. The more we know the more we shall discover there is to be known. Some will learn faster than others, and will take delight in communicating their knowledge. And as they learn more of the wisdom and power and infinite goodness of the Lord, they are filled with a more glowing love and a deeper peace.

That their employments are more various than ours, and of a nature impossible to describe in human language, is consonant with reason and with our own observation of the progress of human employments in this world. How impossible it would have been a few centuries ago to describe the various employments of men at the present time! They were not known. There were no words to describe them. It must be that in a state of life so remote from this as that in which angels dwell there must be employments and relations impossible for us to express or conceive.

One thing, however, we must not forget : there is no labor in heaven. There are employments, activities ; there is service, help, use ; but there are no repulsive tasks, no exhausting toil, no weary limbs, no aching head, no distracted mind. Every one does that which he can do best, and which he delights to do. His heart, his head, his whole life is in his use. His love, wisdom, and power increase with exercise. He loves more, can do more, and enjoys more in every step he takes than he did in the one which preceded it. And so every man and woman who enters heaven will go on forever.

The essence of all this heavenly happiness is the love to the Lord and the neighbor which fills every angel's heart. Every one loves others more than himself. There can be no heaven where there is no love to the Lord and man.

In going from this world to heaven we go from the unreal to the real ; we go from obscurity into light, from shadow to substance, from sameness to variety, from deformity to beauty, from the artificial to the essential, from confusion to order, from discord to harmony, from poverty to wealth, from restraint to freedom, from disappointment, labor, weariness, disease, pain, fear ; from tears and sorrow to fruition, to joy, peace, and blessedness ; from a foreign land we go to friends, to kindred, to home, to the Lord.

CHILDREN IN HEAVEN.

"All thy children shall be taught of the LORD; and great shall be the peace of thy children."—ISAIAH liv. 13.

AMONG the many wonderful things revealed to men concerning the spiritual world, none are more interesting to a parent than those which relate to the condition of infants and children in that life. There are but few parents who must not feel a personal interest in this subject, for there are not many who have not been called upon to surrender one dear object of affection to the Great Shepherd of souls. As the poet has beautifully sung,—

> "There is no flock, however watched and tended,
>   But one dead lamb is there;
> There is no fireside, howso'er defended,
>   But has one vacant chair."

A third part of the human race die in infancy and childhood. A third part of heaven, therefore, must consist of those who have left the earth in the morning of life. For all infants and children, of whatever parents, whether Christian or heathen, go to heaven and become angels.

I say become angels, for they enter the spiritual world as they leave this. They have the same form, the same infantile and childish nature; they are as ignorant and helpless. The only change that has taken place is their withdrawal from the material body and consequent open introduction into the spiritual world.   They need the watchful care and instruction of others as much as if they had remained in this world.   But the Lord does not leave them orphaned and helpless ; He makes provision for their wants.   They are all "taught of the LORD," not directly, but mediately.

Infants are committed to the care of those angels who love them with a purer, wiser, and more ardent affection even than their own mothers.   It may be difficult for a mother to believe that any one can love her child as well as she does.   But there is much that is selfish, worldly, and weak in parental affection.   It does not always lead us to consult the best good of the child.   Parents themselves are ignorant, and do not know how to guide their children right.   They are in evil and falsities, and do not know what is the highest good.   They are deceived by the fallacies of time and sense, and they sacrifice the children's spiritual and eternal good for some temporal gratification.   But it is not so with the angels.   Their love is not mixed with any alloy of self   They look only to the real good of those infant angels who are committed to their care.   Their love is not a weak and erring natural affection, but a pure, strong, and unchanging love, gentler and tenderer than ever warmed the heart of any mother on earth ; a love that never falters, never wearies, that broods over and cherishes in its warmth, and gently calls into action all the latent powers of the children, as the warm breath of spring wooes from the seed the tender bud and beautiful blossoms of the plant.   Not only is every want supplied more fully and tenderly than any

mother on earth could supply it, but every possible provision is made for the children's comfort and happiness.
They are ministered to by a perfect love, that has wisdom
and skill and power to carry into effect all its desires.

Nor do children in heaven seem to themselves to be
among strangers. Many a mother's heart has been
grieved at the thought that her child should be removed
from the bosom of the family and placed among strangers.
She cannot but think that her little one will miss her and
pine for her, even though it dwells with the angels. But
it is not so. The child does not go among strangers.
The angels to whose care it is now openly committed
have always been watching over it. It has always been
in their society. It was by their ministry that it first
awoke to conscious life ; it was their sweet influence that
excited the first smile ; it was their life that flowed into
the mother's heart and formed its image in the mother's
face, and created the attraction between the child's and
the mother's life. Thus the child sees faces that are
already familiar. The longings of its heart are satisfied.
It feels at home ; it lacks nothing ; no want of its nature
is unsupplied.

Infants and children are not committed to the angels in
general. Each one is a special trust to some one angel.
Each child is committed to some one angel who is the
best fitted of all who dwell in the heavens to take charge
of it. Children differ in genius and character, and so do
the angels. And that one of all who dwell in the heavens,
who is best suited to the peculiar disposition, and best
able to touch the secret springs of character in each child,
is selected to take care of it. Infants are committed to

the care of the celestial angels, who are the very forms and embodiments of innocence and love. They take them to their own bosoms, tender and glowing with heavenly affections, and educate them, develop their powers in heavenly order and harmony until they arrive at a state when their wants demand a different culture. They are then transferred to others, and thus their wants are always supplied.

As infants go into the spiritual world as infants, and children as children, they need instruction. They gain no knowledge by this change of worlds. They do, however, gain more favorable conditions for acquiring it. They are freed from the clog and weight of the material body. They have a spiritual body, still in the same child-like form, but it is not enveloped in a material body. It, therefore, moves with greater freedom and develops more rapidly. It does not become wearied so soon, and is freed from the weakness and disease of our material natures.

The child is now in a world where all things are more real, substantial, and perfect to every sense. The senses are far more acute and subtile in their powers ; everything is in a clearer light and appears in a more distinct form, and all the forces that flow into the soul are more powerful, and move it to a more intense and vigorous life. Every faculty has a freer play and a wider range and a truer direction. So great is the change that it is difficult, if not impossible, for human language to describe it. Its most fitting representative is the change in the state of the earth from winter to summer. The young soul throws off all its torpor and coldness ; all its faculties are called into play, and unfold like the plant when the earth is warm and tremulous with the inflowing life of a summer sun.

Children in the spiritual world are much more easily instructed than in this world, because they have formed no bad habits and imbibed no false principles which oppose the truth. We see that these obstacles are very great, but they are much greater than we suppose. Instruction here is very often the blind leading the blind. False principles are actually inculcated ; corrupt and destructive ends are directly sought ; evil habits are confirmed, the understanding perverted, and the heart corrupted. And when the good seed is sown it falls on stony ground or in the hard-trodden paths of natural, worldly life, where it cannot take root. The greater part of our education has no reference to our spiritual nature. In the opinion of the world, a man may be highly educated and refined ; he may be learned in all the sciences and classics, and yet be totally blind to the first principles of spiritual truth. He may even deny that there is a spiritual world and that he has a soul. The most of our education consists of instruction in natural things, and it is directed to worldly ends. And these selfish and worldly influences, which are opposed to a true spiritual life, begin to operate upon us in infancy, and follow us all along in our education, so that, when we come to teach or to learn spiritual things, we find the ground preoccupied. We have to contend against these false principles and habits. We have much to unlearn, which is far more difficult than to learn. But this is not the case with our children who have been removed to the spiritual world.   They are not taught anything which they have to unlearn.   Every step is an advance towards a higher state.   They are not enticed away by evil examples, but all influences conspire to help them on, to unfold their natures in heavenly order.

Children in heaven are not educated alone, but with other children of a similar genius and state.   Children are social.   They are never so happy as when they can mingle freely with those of a similar disposition.   In the spiritual world all the innocent and sportive principles of their nature have free play.

But this is not all.   The methods of instruction, the skill of the teachers, and the truths taught are as much superior as the state of their minds to receive instruction and the conditions in which they are placed.   They are taught nothing but the truth, and truth which relates to life.   They are taught that the Lord is their Father, and that they receive every good from Him.   They are also taught the nature of charity, or mutual love, and its duties. They are taught how to live the life of heaven, and are continually initiated into the practice of what they learn. They do not commit the truth to memory, but to life. They have no hard lessons to learn for future practice. But they learn to-day the lessons they need to live to-day.   Instruction is spiritual food and drink.   As we cannot eat for a distant future, so the children in heaven cannot be instructed for the future.   They receive their food day by day.   It is also exactly adapted to their wants and apprehension.   Their life is unfolded in true order.   There is no forcing of the mind.   Progress in knowledge is more like the growth of a plant.   The blossom is not sought before the leaf, nor the fruit before the blossom. The angels have the most exquisite perception of the state of those they instruct, and they touch with the utmost delicacy and skill the secret springs of the will and understanding.

The lives of these heavenly children are also unfolded from within. Freed from the restraints and heavy encumbrance of the body, every organ in their tender spiritual forms is free to move in harmony with the inflowing of life from the Lord, which comes to them from within. Here we learn facts and store them up in the memory, and then compare and arrange them, and thus by slow and laborious processes acquire some knowledge. But in the spiritual world it is not so. There outward things exactly correspond and represent the states of thought and affection within, because they are formed from them. Thus children in heaven see their own life as in a mirror in all things around them.

They are led to knowledge by their delights. All their activities flow from love, and instruction is given to gratify that love, to answer its questions, to satisfy its wants. We can gain some idea of this state, for we see something similar to it, though in a much lower form, in the insatiable curiosity of children in this life. Suppose that curiosity to be increased many degrees, and to be excited only by those things, or those subjects, which are true and good, and suppose it to be in our power to satisfy it, to answer all its questions so fully, to explain and illustrate all it sought to know so clearly that every step would be clear and definite, and firmly planted in the path of life, and every desire satisfied. And suppose this to be done without any weariness to the young soul, without blunting the keen edge of its curiosity, but rather sharpening it and giving it more strength for higher knowledge, would not that be the perfection of instruction? This is the state of all children in the spiritual world. Their intellectual faculties are excited to action by their affections, and thus they are constantly led, and not driven. Their faculties are all called into harmonious exercise, and their exercise is play, yet with all the good and substantial results of the most patient and laborious effort.

Instruction can be given there also by methods altogether beyond the power of any earthly teacher. It is found here that maps, charts, diagrams, and apparatus for visible illustration are most efficient aids in the communication of scientific truth. With a planetarium we place before the eyes of the pupil the relative size and motions of the heavenly bodies ; we spread out the earth before him, and in various ways represent the customs and character of the people, and the nature and forms of vegetable and animal life. But we are limited on all sides by the imperfection of the materials we must use and by our own power to use them. In the spiritual world there are not these limitations. All its substances yield to the plastic forces of the affections and thoughts more readily than the most fluent materials to the hand of man. Every affection is represented to the life in forms that actually correspond. Thus instruction is not so much verbal as pictorial and representative. They have not merely pictures of visible objects that exist in other places, but representations of affections and thoughts or principles and processes of spiritual life.

Suppose, for example, that an angel wished to teach a company of young children the nature of innocence. Instead of a verbal description, which they must commit to memory, and which then might not be understood, they would be surrounded by all those forms which represent innocence, as by lambs and kids and the young of various animals and birds, and beautiful infants, all sporting together in perfect peace, harmony, and delight. The whole atmosphere would seem to be alive with beautiful forms, and the earth itself filled with living objects which represented to the life innocence in its various kinds, degrees, and relations. Everything that appeared would be the actual correspondent of some form of innocence. Innocence itself would pass before the children like a panorama in a thousand true and beautiful forms, and they would perceive the meaning of all these things.

Thus the children's natures are unfolded in heaven in true order and symmetry. The affections and the intellect go hand in hand. To love is to know, and knowledge is the form of love, and both are embodied in use, in life ; and thus the whole nature, from centre to circumference, is filled with ever-increasing delight.

Swedenborg says it was granted to him to see little children most charmingly attired, having garlands of flowers resplendent with beautiful and heavenly colors twined about their breasts and tender arms. "And once," he says, "to see them, with those who have charge of them, in company with maidens, in a paradisal garden most beautifully adorned, not so much with trees as with arbors and covered walks of laurel, and with paths leading inward. And when the little children entered, dressed as I have described, the flowers over the entrance shone forth most joyously. From this it may be manifest,'' he adds, ''what delights they have, and also that by these pleasant and delightful things they are introduced into the goods of innocence and charity, which are thus continually instilled into them by the Lord.''

What a beautiful sight must such a company of children be in the spiritual world ! Surrounded by all things of a loveliness and beauty corresponding to their own beautiful natures ; without a weakness or a pain or a single cloud of sorrow to overshadow their sunny hearts, rosy with perfect health, elastic, graceful, and vigorous in the harmonious development of every organ and power ; innocent, lovely, and loving in all their intercourse, their faces shining with heavenly affections and delights, their voices soft and sweet with celestial harmonies, and their whole forms glowing with the Divine life and becoming the actual embodiment of it ; no clouds above them, no inharmonious and unsightly objects around them, no fear of coming evil, no regrets, no tears, and not a jar in the harmony of their natures ; clothed in heavenly garments of a beauty corresponding to their intelligence, they are beauty, joy, innocence, peace, purity, not only personified, but actually embodied in form.

Would you who have children in these heavenly nurseries call them back into this world, imprison them in the material body, shut them up in our dark dwellings, expose them to the contagion of corrupt examples, and subject them to our imperfect guidance and instruction ? Much as you desire to have them bodily and visibly with you, you could not do it. No. It is well with them.

THE MINISTRY OF ANGELS TO INFANCY.

" Take heed that ye despise not one of these little ones ; for I say unto you, That in heaven their angels do always behold the face of my Father which is in heaven."—MATTHEW xviii. 10.

THE relations we sustain to angels and departed spirits are frequently referred to in the Sacred Scriptures. Their presence with men and their influence in human affairs is described as intimate and powerful. Many instances are given in the Old and in the New Testament of the appearance of angels to men and of the services they rendered to them. They gave them instruction on occasions of great difficulty and danger. They came as messengers from the Lord to make known His will and to announce the coming of great events. They protected men from impending danger ; they delivered them from bondage and led them into the promised land ; they showed their deep interest in human affairs on many occasions and in many ways during the whole of human history as recorded in the Sacred Scriptures.

But the prevailing belief in the Christian world has been and still is, that these are exceptional instances ; that the homes of the angels are remote from this world, and that they come to us only in some great exigency to bring an important message, or render a service that requires supernatural wisdom and power, and that when that service is rendered they leave us, put off the human form which they assumed for the occasion, and return to their bright homes in heaven.

But the Sacred Scriptures reveal a different and much more comforting doctrine. They declare that the Lord gives His angels charge over us to keep us in all our ways. In full accordance with what the Lord reveals to us in His Word, the doctrines of the New Church teach us that angels and spirits, who are regenerated men and women and children born upon the earth, are always with us ; that they are far more closely connected with us than our most intimate friends who are still with us in the flesh, and that they are always on the alert to protect us from danger and to render us any service we will receive at their hands. Being spirits, they cannot manifest themselves to our natural senses, and never did in olden times. The veil of the senses was drawn aside, and the spiritual sight of prophets and apostles was opened to see the angels in their own permanent forms. The coming and going of these heavenly messengers was an appearance due to changes wrought in men. Spirit can only reveal itself consciously to spirit. Innumerable forces are constantly acting upon us and rendering us the most important services, of which we have no direct consciousness. We cannot see them or hear their voice or touch their substance. The force we call gravity is constantly drawing us to the earth, but we cannot see it or touch it, and it utters no sound. One medium reveals itself to the eye in the form of light, but can awake no consciousness in the ear or touch. Another hlls the ear with harmonies, but is powerless to gain any recognition from the eye. We live and move in the midst of an ocean of the most subtile forces which sweep through us and have a most potent influence upon us, which are indeed essential to our existence, but of which we have no sensible knowledge. It is, therefore, perfectly in accordance with the Divine methods of creating human beings and developing their affections and intellectual faculties that the most powerful influences may operate upon us without revealing themselves to the senses.

We cannot communicate any knowledge to our little ones in the first stages of existence by word or deed. We can render them the most important service, but they do not know it. The mother is related to the newborn child much as the angels are. The little one lies unconscious between them. The mother reaches it and ministers to it from the material side, the angels from the spiritual side of its nature. Gradually the natural consciousness is opened. The infant begins to recognize natural objects, to be consciously affected by natural forces. Its natural faculties develop and gain power. It recognizes those who minister to it. The mother's smile awakes an answering smile. The mother's features grow familiar and the faces and voices of friends can be distinguished from those of strangers. But it will be many years before it will recognize the voice and the glorious beauty of its angels who have watched over it with more tenderness and assiduity and a purer affection than the mother's. The veil of flesh must first be removed.

Two classes of beings bend over every cradle, each to render their own special service. The mother gives natural sustenance, protects from natural danger, to win

23*

into power and conscious action the natural faculties ; the angels keep watch and ward to protect the little one from spiritual dangers, to cherish and wake into action by their brooding love the tender germs of spiritual and heavenly affections which they have assiduously planted, and to impress upon them the innocence, the order, the beauty, and the harmony of heaven.   This is a service essential to the child's regeneration.   By this means are formed the germs of the heavenly nature and of all the spiritual faculties.   These germs become the vessels for the reception of life from the Lord.   The angels who plant them, guard them and assiduously cultivate them and use all their heavenly skill and patience and tenderness and power to give them conscious existence and a controlling influence in the conduct of life.   They do not despise or neglect one of these little ones.   The mother may grow weary, but they never tire ; the mother may be selfish and worldly and ignorant and neglect the little ones, but their angels regard them with unselfish and unchanging affection.   They possess a wisdom born of Divine love, and they know how to touch the most hidden and delicate springs of the children's nature ; to bend, to cherish, to mould their tender forms into the Divine image and likeness with a skill beyond our conception. Through their instrumentality the Lord photographs His image upon the purest substances of their being, substances that are exquisitely sensitive to all heavenly impressions and adamant to retain them.   These forms are the Divine patterns after which the whole nature is to be moulded ; they are the heavenly ideals which go ever before us, become our inspiration and our hope, and lead us ever onward and upward towards the Lord. As there are in the germ of every seed the pattern of the plant which grows from it, and some shaping power which infallibly moulds every form of branch, leaf, blossom, and fruit into its own likeness and qualities, so the heavenly principles inseminated by the angels contain within them the promise and potency of every heavenly good. Like the germ of the plant in the seed, they may never be brought into actual and conscious existence. They may be neglected and left to lie dormant. By the development of selfish and worldly affections stumbling-blocks may be put in their way and obstructions to their development may be formed, which render their birth and growth impossible. They may be despised, as they often are from ignorance of their nature or unbelief in their existence. But the fact remains a fact of such momentous importance that we who, nominally at least, believe in the constant presence of these pure and glorious beings who stand ready to co-operate with us in every effort for our children's happiness, ought to give heed to the warning of our Lord contained in our text.

I know with what incredulity men regard the assertion of the constant presence of the angels. To aid our dull and doubting minds, let us consider for a moment the plain and legitimate meaning of our Lord's words.

"Their angels." Whose angels? Theirs, the angels of the little ones. A little boy was sitting in the midst of the disciples as a representative of all the little ones : our Lord referred to his angels. Is this a random or an idle phrase? What can it mean, if children have not angels suited to their genius, who wait upon them and are ready at all times to render them every possible service? Can we give any other meaning to the words? Look at the logical force of the declaration. The Lord had placed a little child in the midst of the disciples and declared it to be the type of true greatness. Then He warned them against offending or placing any hinderance in the way towards heaven of one of these little ones. He declared that it is profitable to cut off the right hand or pluck out the right eye and cast them away if they cause us to offend one of these little ones, or stand in the way of their spiritual growth. Then He gave the warning, "Take heed that ye despise not one of these little ones; for I say unto you, That in heaven their angels do always behold the face of my Father which is in heaven." If the angels who stand nearest the Lord, the purest, the loveliest, and the wisest created beings, are constantly devoted to the service of the little ones, can we despise them? The Lord presents it as a reason why we should not despise them, that their angels do always or through everything behold the face of His Father who is in heaven. Let us consider the force of this reason. But to see its full weight we must understand what is meant by their angels always beholding the face of the Father.

The face is the clearest and fullest index of the mind. It is the theatre on which the fears and hopes, the joys and sorrows, the desires and passions, and all the thoughts and affections act their parts and reveal themselves to others. It is formed by the spirit for this purpose, and every feature has a distinct part to perform in the great drama of life. Its organs are few, and yet singly or in combination they express with miraculous precision the intelligence and ever-changing emotions of the soul. Sorrow casts a shadow over the face like a cloud, joy lights it up like a burst of sunshine, intelligence shines in the eye, love beams from every feature, shame crimsons the cheek, suspicion lurks in the eye, pity trembles in the lips, anger knits the brow, passion inflames every feature. Every shade of intelligence and every degree of feeling shifts the scenes to a corresponding form to suit its purpose. It is the offiee of the face to represent the soul. This is acknowledged by common consent, and is instinctively expressed in human speech. To turn away the face denotes aversion of affection ; to hide or cover the face, concealment of purpose or withholding favor ; to face a difficulty is to meet it firmly and with composure ; to turn the face to one, to lift up the face, is to regard with favor.

From this offiee of the face it is used in the Sacred Scriptures to express the disposition of the Lord towards men. He is said to hide His face,—" Hide not thy face from thy servant," prays the Psalmist ; to turn away His face, to set His face against the wicked, to lift up His face, to cause His face to shine upon His servant. Men are exhorted to seek His face and to come before His face. Many similar expressions are used to express the feelings with which the Lord regards men, His relations to them, His attitude towards them. The face of the Lord stands as the symbol and representative of His love and wisdom, as a man's face is the representative of the love and wisdom and various attributes of his character.

Now we may be able to see what must be the character of the angels to whom are committed the little ones, and all the spiritual principles in the human mind which the little ones represent. The translation of the words which our Lord used does not express the meaning of the original quite clearly. "Behold" should be, look at; and "always" should be, through everything. The passage would then read, "Take heed that ye despise not one of these little ones; for I say unto you, That in heaven their angels through everything look at the face of my Father which is in heaven;" that is, through everything and in everything they see the love and wisdom of the Lord. They are themselves so innocent, so wise, so pure, so filled with the Divine love, and every thought, desire, affection, and purpose is so conformed to the Divine image and likeness that every motion of their souls is in harmony with the Lord. They look to Him and regard Him in everything. They are wise with His wisdom, they are strong with His strength, they are kind with His kindness, they are patient with His patience, they are skilful to touch the secret springs of human life and to evolve heavenly faculties from their first germs with His skill. As in a mirror they see His face in the beginnings of the human soul; they see some reflection of His image in every instrumentality employed for its development, and with some gift of His wisdom know how to use it. They have a keen perception of the bearing of every influence, of the varying changes of every state upon the character. Nor is their ministry an occasional and fitful one. They do not come on special occasions and go when the exigency is passed. They never weary, they are constant in their service; they come as near as possible to every one, and render every service in their power. They regard the highest ends in all their watching and waiting and humble service. They look at the face of the Lord ; they watch its growing or fading image in the soul. They seek with angelic affection and wisdom to bring it out in clearer lines, to develop it into more distinct and substantial form. With what infinite skill and tenderness and patience they do their work ! They engage in it from no mercenary motives ; they are not hired servants. They minister with patient assiduity from love to the Lord and the little ones who have just commenced their endless journey, from a heavenly desire to aid the father and mother in this heavenly service.

Think of it ! Try to bring it home to yourselves as a reality ! Two parties in two worlds separated only by the thin veil of flesh are engaged in the care and nurture of your child. As the mother does her work the angels do theirs. The mother cares for the body, the angels for the soul. The mother seeks to awaken the slumbering natural faculties into conscious and vigorous action ; the angels, to call into existence the germs of the spiritual faculties which in due time will introduce the child into a new world, and give him capacities to receive the Divine life in higher and richer forms. So the wise and faithful mother and the wiser and more faithful angels walk side by side invisible to each other, but regarding the same object, and with affections directed to the same end. Each one is helping the other ; each one is doing a work essential to the natural and spiritual growth of the little, helpless pilgrim just landed upon the shores of life. Is it not a beautiful and comforting thought that every mother has such devoted heavenly servants to co-operate with her? 'When you look at the little one lying helpless in your arms, is it not encouraging to know that it is nurtured and strengthened with forces ministered by unseen but skilful hands without which it would fade and vanish away? Your ears are too dull to hear the music of their speech ; your sight is too dim to see the heavenly beauty of their faces. But when the little one smiles it is not only in answer to your love, but to theirs. The opening faculties which are watched with so much interest and delight are awakened by the angels, who cherish the children in their own bosoms, and give of their own life to them. The little ones have no power in themselves to live and grow. Parents cannot give them this power. It comes from within ; it has its constant origin in the Lord, but in one direction it comes through the angels. It flows from them as a sphere of love which is life.

But the infant is itself a symbol and beautiful exponent of the beginnings of a multitude of distinctly spiritual faculties in every mind, which are inseminated by the Lord as mere possibilities, which have their immutable laws and essential means of growth, which require the skilful, constant watchfulness and the tender nurture of angelic wisdom. Every one who gains eternal life must be born from above. As the perverted natural mind is first developed, these little ones from heaven are born in the midst of enemies ; they are like lambs among wolves ; they are like infants hated, rejected, and left to perish by cruel parents. If there were no help from within, there would be no hope of safety. If there were no truths planted in the natural mind to serve as a basis and means of support, as ground in which heavenly principles can take root ; if no gentle and innocent affections, no holy and heavenly states, were treasured up in the will in the beginning of life, there would be no possibility of regeneration. Birth from above would be as impossible as the growth of a seed whose naked germ was planted in the frozen ground. By calling into action good, innocent, natural affections in our children, we are giving motion to the natural faculties that are in harmony with the spiritual faculties hereafter to be born ; we are giving them the key-note to heavenly harmonies. And as no impression upon any mind is ever obliterated, as no motion is ever effected, no state awakened, which may not be called up again into conscious action however long it may have remained quiescent, there is a possibility that heavenly light may penetrate the natural darkness, that heavenly affections may find some welcome in the hostile natural mind, that heavenly harmonies may awaken the memory of some corresponding affection planted by the angels in infancy, to vibrate in unison with it. In this way and by these means the spiritual gets a foothold in the natural, and extends its power until every false and evil affection is subdued, the enemies are driven out of the holy land of the soul, and the heavenly inhabitants gain peaceful and everlasting possession.

Such is the immeasurable importance of early impressions. Such is the work which the angels to whose care the souls of our children are committed are in the constant effort to accomplish. Is not the thought of this heavenly help encouraging in our efforts to correct the evils which are constantly appearing in our children? Is it not a comfort and a hope when we grow weary, that we have such faithful, wise, and powerful assistants? Will you not find it an additional motive to be faithful to the trust committed to you, and to appreciate more highly the value of every step you take for these little ones? When you see their smiling faces, think of the Lord's words, "Take heed that ye despise not one of these little ones." Why? Because so great is their worth that they are objects of special interest to the angels. They are not alone; you are not alone. Their angels who through everything look at the face of the Lord, are present and ready to work with you in every effort for their spiritual and eternal good.

But these words of warning and hope are not limited in their application to parents; they apply with equal directness and force to every one who is trying to overcome evil and live a heavenly life. There are germs of heavenly principles in every mind that are struggling for existence. They come to our notice only occasionally. They seem to be remote from our life; their voice may be feeble and only faintly heard in the din of worldly affairs; they appear to be of but little importance compared with the natural interests that clamor for our attention. We do not appreciate their importance, and too often despise them. They have many obstacles to overcome; we put many stumbling-blocks in their way. But they are of more precious value than any other possession. They are not only greater than any or all natural possessions, but they are the greatest in the kingdom of heaven.

Our angels dwell in them; they operate upon us by means of them. Their love flows into them, and by them they seek to lead us to heaven.

By means of these little ones they lift us up from sensual and natural things; with gentle but constant attraction they draw us away from the love of self and the world, and seek to turn us to the Lord. They see in all these germs of heavenly life the face of our Heavenly Father, and they seek to bring it out into greater distinctness and into permanent forms. They fight our battles for us; they bring us sustenance when we are famished and faint by the way; they give us strength in our weakness, comfort in our sorrow, and hope in our despair.

Is it not a comfort to know that we have such kind, patient, powerful, wise servants to help us in the most difficult and important work of life, and that they are not far away in some remote region of the universe? They are here to-day. They stand close to us, separated only by the thin veil of flesh. They dwell with us in our homes; they walk with us by the way; they go with us to our business and our pleasure; they watch over us when we sleep, and stand ready to serve us when we wake. The bond of conjunction with us is these germs of heavenly character which it is the mission and joy of the angels to assist in becoming angels like themselves. In view of these considerations, we can see how momentous is the Lord's warning, "Take heed that ye despise not one of these little ones."

In conclusion, there is another application of this truth which it may be useful for us to consider. The church is our spiritual mother. Every society of the church bears this intimate and tender relation to all the children of its members and to every one within the circle of its influence who is awakening to the consciousness that he is a spiritual being. To every society the Lord says, "Take heed that ye despise not one of these little ones; for I say unto you, That in heaven their angels do always behold the face of my Father." It is hard for us to realize that the little children and those who are just being born from above deserve our special and most tender care, and that we should take heed that we despise not one of these little ones. When the Lord sets a little child in the midst of a society He commits it to the care of that family of the church, and asks every member of that family to co-operate with Him and His angels in protecting it from harm, in providing it with spiritual clothing adapted to its condition and food suitable for its nourishment. We are too much inclined to direct our efforts and our care to those who in some way can provide for themselves. But we must not despise the little ones, who need our help more than others. Our instruction should be adapted to their wants; we should make special provision to awaken their interest and call their tender spiritual faculties into play. We should surround them with influences, as far as possible, that will tend to develop their spiritual faculties. We must co-operate with their angels to make them the children of our Heavenly Father, by doing our work on this side of life as thoroughly and wisely as possible. It is the most important work given us to do. It is the most important use to which we can devote our time and money and strength. It should fill our hearts with strength and hope and joy that we have such lovely and faithful and glorious helpers. They are with us in every effort we make for the children. Every affection of love for this use is the effect of their pure breath flowing into our souls, every thought is the gift of their wisdom. They go with us step by step in everything we do to bring the little children to the Lord, that He may take them up in His arms and bless them.

24*

NATURE A DIVINE LANGUAGE.

" All thy works shall praise thee, O LORD."—PSALM CxIV. 10.

EVERY work is stamped with the impress of its maker. The changes which men have wrought in the natural world are the ultimation of their thoughts. Every intelligent being is at all times, and by all modes in his power, striving to project himself from himself, and to fix his spiritual form in the ultimate forms of material life. His body is but the granite and the marble rendered fluent and cast into the mould of his spiritual form, and so perfectly cast that it is the exact form of the real man. There is no part of the body which does not speak. The character is not only indicated by the size and configuration of the head, but it is written on every organ. The foot and the hand speak. The gesture, the gait, the posture, the quality of the voice, the nose, the lips, the chin, the neck and chest are as truly types and expressions of the man as the head, the eye, and the spoken word.

The influence of character extends beyond the body and puts its mark upon the objects of the world about us. Indeed, the body has been formed only as a means to an end. It is the instrument by which the soul strives to subject all material things to its power and to transform them to its own likeness. The Indian dwells in primeval forests, and shares his life with the bear and the

282

wolf, because his nature is dark and solitary, and he finds in all things which surround him types of his own cruel, sombre, and crafty soul. The Arab of to-day is the Ishmaelite of bygone centuries, and he is content with his lot because he finds in the patient camel, the fierce lion, and the burning, desolate, and shifting sands the exponents of his own enduring, ferocious, and unstable nature. But put a new thought into one of these stereotyped sons of the desert or forest, and you will soon see it playing through him and working changes in his external condition. What is it that has so changed the whole face of nature on this continent during the last two centuries? Has not this been done by the instrumentality of new spiritual conditions? The men who succeeded the Indian had ideas of fixed habitation, of the comforts of home, of society and government. They loved the sunlight, variety in food and clothing; they had tastes to gratify of which their rude predecessor knew nothing; they preferred the domestic animals—the cow, the ox, the sheep—to the wolf, bear, and panther; the forest which had stood for centuries bowed before them and passed away, and in its place were found waving wheat-fields and the golden corn. The comfortable home displaced the wigwam, and the school-house, the church, and the legislative hall the council-fires.

But this was only the first step in the transformation. The soul finds her wants to be continually multiplying. Herself not subject to the laws of time and space, she wishes to free her servant the body also from these bonds; and to accomplish this she sets the hand at work and forms the steam-engine and the railroad. But even this is not sufficient, and she compels the lightning to ride express for her and make known her wishes and wants, and by these means she contrives to make herself ubiquitous. Should we enumerate all the improvements of modern times, all the achievements of science, we should find they are but material types of the human soul. She has hard elements to deal with, but she is invincible, and she makes the rock and the ore and the fickle wind and the unstable sea plastic to her hand and obedient to her will. She reproduces herself in lower forms, and makes everything utter her name and character.

Now, if this is true of man, finite and feeble as he is, blind to his own necessities and his noblest capacities, how much more must it be true of Him who is the prototype of all things, and in whose all-embracing power and wisdom the universe is more plastic than the clay in the hands of the potter! If man reproduces and ultimates himself in all his works; if trade, commerce, mechanism, agriculture, literature, music, art, are but so many images of himself, so many tongues by which he utters his wants, his affections, his hopes and loftiest conceptions,— if all man's works praise or condemn him, must it not be much more true that the whole universe is a Divine symbolism of the infinite Creator's perfections? Does not day unto day utter speech and night unto night show knowledge? Do not all His works praise Him? Does not every created thing have some voice to utter in making known His wisdom, power, and love? If man cannot change the forms of material things, make a nail, or a shoe, or an engine, or a book, or a picture, as he surely cannot, without leaving his own mark upon it, can we conceive it possible that God could create the world, and man, and all the complicated relations which they sustain to each other, without transcribing Himself into His works? Such a supposition would be contrary to all the observation and experience of men. It would involve the absurdity of making the Creator act from a power and wisdom which He does not possess.

It is a prevalent opinion that general truths alone are taught in the creation. Just as there is an idea of a general providence, while a particular providence is denied. But it is absurd to suppose that there can be anything general without the particulars which compose it. It is a mathematical axiom that the whole is equal to the sum of all its parts ; but the common idea involves the absurdity that there can be a whole without parts. There can be no general truth without the specific truths which make up the general one, just as there can be no house without the rooms which compose the house. There can be no such natural object as the earth without the various minerals which compose it. There could be no natural body without the head, trunk, limbs, bones, cartilages, muscles, veins, and arteries which compose it. We must conclude, then, that if the wisdom of God is manifested in the universe in a general way, there must be in the various parts of it those particular truths which constitute wisdom, for wisdom is not simple, but wonderfully complex. Infinite wisdom must embrace the knowledge of all things in all their relations, and everything, both as a whole and in all its parts, must be an expression of the Creator's character, a revelation of Himself in the most external plane of life. Thus the term "nature" is exactly significant of the objects to which it is applied, literally meaning that which is born. The natural world is born of the spiritual, and it is a revelation, an embodiment in finite forms of the infinite perfections of the Creator.

All can see that the heavens declare the glory of God ; that in a most general way all the Lord's works have relation to His love and wisdom. But we wish to go farther. We wish to know what the world says about His love and wisdom ; and to learn these specific truths we must question particular objects. The Lord has inscribed His love and wisdom in indefinite variety of form and quality upon all His works, the dew-drop and the leaf and the microscopic insect containing traces of His limitless power and love as truly as a world or man. Each object speaks a different message. Everything in the universe that is in true order expresses some particular of the Lord's love and wisdom.

And, further, if all natural objects are types of the Divine perfections, they are also a mirror in which man can see himself reflected, for man was created in the image and likeness of God ; consequently, what is a representation of the one will, in some sense, be a representation of the other. But I wish only to confirm this truth, that the creation—what we call "nature"—is a Divine language, both as a whole and in all its parts, in which the Lord expresses Himself.

Let us notice some of the qualities and characteristics of this language, and perhaps we cannot do it in a better way than by comparing it with the artificial language of men. We have a very erroneous and superficial idea of the essential nature of language. It is so familiar to us as the vehicle of thought that we are too apt to think of it as thought itself, as something coeval with the existence of man, and in every possible condition of his existence essential to his happiness and improvement. But in this we are deceived by appearances. Language in itself is artificial, mechanical, and dead. It is but the counter by which the real coin is represented. It is the dead fragments broken from the living forms of nature, the dried leaves and flowers that once were fragrant and beautiful with the glow of life. In its origin it is all derived from the natural world, and from the relations its various objects sustain to one another and to man. The very word "language" comes from the name of the organ by the aid of which it is spoken,—the tongue. If we could trace every word to its origin we should find that it had its beginning in the motions, changes, and accidents of external things, and that the terms used to describe these natural relations were gradually transferred to the operations of the spiritual man. The natural relation between words and the thoughts they represent has in most cases been lost, and there is now little but a conventional connection. But the natural world is a thought in material form. The Divine love and wisdom flow into it, while it is fluid and plastic to the spirit, and its simplest and most complex forms are the exact representation of the influent life.

Again, it requires many words to express one idea of thought, and, words being conventional and having no necessary connection with the idea, the proper words are not always suggested, even if they are known. Words dwell in the memory, and even when there they are not always prompt to come at the bidding of the will. There are but few, perhaps none, who have a perfect command of language, and even if one had this gift he could not express himself fully. As a common currency, a kind of small change, verbal language answers very well for the purposes of common life, for business, and the interchange of those affections and thoughts which lie nearest the surface of our nature. But how do we stammer and ejaculate, and even become speechless, under the influence of some overmastering passion ; and how impossible do we find it to express the nicer shades of thought and affection ! The delicate texture of our higher emotions is destroyed, and the true aroma of life vanishes by translation into speech, and, as I have before said, we get, in words, only the dead forms of what was fresh and living in the soul. Who ever expressed himself as fully in words as in actions ? Our affection and thought flow forth in a full and continuous stream into our actions, while in speech we hesitate, and stammer forth only a few fragments of what is full and perfect within. The best book is but a dried mummy compared with the full, rich, living soul that penned it.

The primeval man had no artificial speech. Spoken and written language came with man's degeneracy. In his innocence he was in harmony with nature. Everything which he saw around him was the perfect utterance of his Father's love and wisdom, and the projection of himself. There was a chord within that answered to every key without. There was an inherent, natural, and necessary relation between himself, the outward world, and its Author, and it was not necessary for man to speak or reason. He perceived and knew. He looked through natural forms to the living principles which they represented. Just as when we see the name or form of one dear to us, we do not rest in the name or form, but pass on immediately to the qualities which it suggests.

Such was the language of nature to man in his innocence, and the language has never changed. It is as full and perfect now as it ever was, but we have lost our knowledge of it. It is our mother tongue, but, like erring children, we have wandered into strange lands, among barbarous people, until we have lost the memory of nature's speech, and we have been compelled to resort to the harsh jargon and imperfect utterance of an artificial language.

Artificial language is limited on every side. Having no meaning but what common consent gives it, its shallow depths are soon exhausted. It is so devoid of necessary precision, and so imperfect a vehicle of thought, that it has been wittily said that it was given to man to conceal his thoughts. How different is this from the language of nature ! That is limited only on one side,— by our power to understand it. It has a kind of self-adjusting power by which it adapts itself to every state. The child sees something ; he is delighted with the beauty which lies on the surface, rejoices in the smiles, or is terrified at the frowns of nature. The philosopher sees farther. He strives to look into the causes and relations of things, but the knowledge of the simplest natural object was never yet and never will be exhausted. When one depth is explored another opens, and thus we are led on from deep to deep until men of the highest genius have been compelled to acknowledge that they were only children gathering shells upon the shore, while the vast ocean lay unexplored beneath them.

Again, our language is divided into innumerable dialects, so that a lifetime is not sufficient to learn the speech of all men. But there are no dialects in nature. It is the mother tongue of man. It speaks to him in every age and clime and condition. Even now, when, as I have said, he has lost the particular meaning of natural things, he still feels a mysterious sympathy with them. He is bound by invisible ties to everything around him, and he feels that the same power which throbs in nature vibrates through him. The poets and men of fine organization and delicate, sensitive natures have ever delighted to ascribe to nature a powerful influence over their own hearts. But it is felt by every one. The blue sky filled with the splendors of the sun, or gemmed with innumerable stars, overarches all on the round globe, and fills the mind of the rude savage as well as the Christian with a sense of the power and glory of the Lord. The flower and the dew and the stream and the ever-changing beauty which plays over the face of the world glide into the hearts of all, carrying a balm for the torn and bleeding heart, strength for the weary, hope for the despairing, and a deeper delight to the rejoicing. The lone Indian hears the voice of the Great Spirit in the roaring cataract, and stops to worship.

Finally, words are ever changing in their meaning. New meanings are constantly being added to them, and old ones are becoming obsolete. But nature is the fresh and living thought of the Creator, for it exists only by a vital connection with Him. Thus, in whatever aspect we view it, we see the immense disparity between these two modes of expression. There is the same difference which we find everywhere between the work of the Lord and the work of man. The one is perfect in its kind and degree, rising towards the Infinite and glowing with His influent life ; the other limited on every side, shallow, cold, and dead.

I have attempted to show from various considerations that the natural world must be a Divine language, expressive of the Divine love and wisdom ; that each natural object must have a specific meaning, if there is any meaning in the whole ; that all created things are so related that they utter the same voice with indefinite variety,—all are truths relating to man and to God, and linking the two together ; and that the language is worthy of its Author, infinitely above the language of men in every quality, in extent of meaning, in precision, in fulness, in perspicuity, in power, in adaptation to every state. Truly, ''The heavens declare the glory of God, and the firmament showeth his handiwork. Day unto day uttereth speech, and night unto night showeth knowledge.''

PARABLES.

*" All these things spake Jesus unto the multitude in parables;
and without a parable spake he not unto them:
" That it might be fulfilled which was spoken by the prophet,
saying, I will open my mouth in parables; I will utter things
which have been kept secret from the foundation of the world."*
—MATTHEW xiii. 34, 35.

THE parables form one of the most beautiful and instructive portions of the Sacred Scriptures. Whether
one believes in their Divine character or not, he can
hardly fail to be impressed with the lessons they teach
and the beautiful form in which the lessons are communicated. It may be interesting and instructive to consider
what a parable is, and why our Lord employed parables
so often, when it would seem that a more explicit form
of speech would have been better suited to the occasion.
A clear understanding of the causes which led our Lord
to use this method of communicating Divine truth will
show that in this, as in all other respects, He was guided
by the highest wisdom.

The Lord gives the reasons why He speaks in parables.
One of them is that He may "utter things which have
been kept secret from the foundation of the world." It
is also evident that Divine truth is given in the form of
parables to adapt it to a peculiar state of mind. The
Lord makes a distinction between His disciples and the
multitude in this respect. "Unto you," He said, "it is

given to know the mystery of the kingdom of God ; but unto them that are without, all things are done in parables : that seeing they may see, and not perceive ; and hearing they may hear, and not understand." The ground and force of this reasoning will appear more clearly when we see what a parable is and what relations it sustains to "things which have been kept secret from the foundation of the world," and to "the mystery of the kingdom of God," which it is given to the Lord's disciples to understand.

First, let us consider what a parable is. The original word means to throw or to place one thing beside another, so that they shall be parallel to each other, or correspond or answer to each other. A parable is a similitude taken from natural things to instruct us in the knowledge of spiritual things. The accuracy of the instruction de-pends upon the truth of the relation between nature and spirit. A complete parallelism between natural and spiritual things, in which the natural side of truth runs parallel with the spiritual, answering to it in every point, is a parable. A parable is not a fable, which is a fictitious composition employed to illustrate a natural or a moral truth ; it is not a figure of speech. There is nothing arbitrary in its structure. Spiritual forms and relations are presented in material forms ; and this is done, not merely in a general way, the natural forms, as it were, touching some parts of the spiritual. There is complete parallelism ; there is union at every point. A parable is a picture of a spiritual truth. It is a picture, done in material colors and material forms, which perfectly represents the spiritual counterpart.

To get an adequate idea of a parable we must pass beyond the words used to express it, to the forms and actions themselves. The material actions and forms constitute the parable, and not the words used to express them. Thus the parable of the Prodigal Son, or of the Ten Virgins, is a drama, in which great spiritual laws are acted before us, and presented in a form and manner adapted to our senses.

Parables are much more common and universal in their use than is generally supposed. In a true sense, the whole material universe is a parable. It is the effect of which spiritual forces are the cause, and these forces run parallel to it in every particular. The material world is cast into the mould of spiritual forms. Nature does not form itself. There is no power in the dead and passive mould—in carbon, oxygen, or in any of the primary elements of matter—to organize themselves into a plant. There must be a spiritual force acting into them and casting them into its own forms. Nature is a parable revealing the spiritual and Divine forces from which she lives. Trees and animals are special forms in the universal parable of the creation, which teach us special truths. They are letters in the great book, they are characters in the great drama, not selected and trained, but created for their parts.

The human face is a parable. The soul created it, in the first instance, in its own image, to be the stage on which its actors can represent the comedies and tragedies and daily history of its life. The soul stands behind the scenes and shifts them to express its own states. Every feature is a parable, and represents its part, and expresses the affection or thought whose form it is, more clearly than words can. All painting and sculpture are but copies of these parables which the face and the whole body are expressing. A smile is a parable of some pleasant, gentle affection diffusing itself through the soul, as the morning light spreads itself over the mountains and throws its shining mantle over the hills. In itself it is only a little shifting of the scenery of the face, and yet how much it expresses! The mother can tell, who has seen the first recognition and response to her affection in the smile of her first-born. The husband or the wife can tell, who has watched the face of estranged affection in doubt and fear, and has seen the cold and rigid muscles relax and the light of love run brightening over every feature.

A tear is a parable, and in its crystal sphere lie sorrows deeper than the caves of the ocean, and darker and wilder storms than ever swept in fury over its surface. What histories of disappointed hopes! What tragedies of suffering and slain affections! What wrestlings with adverse fortune! What fears of coming evil! The weariness of waiting, the despair of losing, the agony of death itself are imaged in a tear. It has also a lovelier offiee. The tear of penitence holds treasured in its crystal deeps a life of waywardness and wandering, of evil and sin, turning back to the Father's house. It is hardness of heart melting into submission to Divine truth ; it is sorrow brightening into joy ; it is the first drop from the unsealed fountains of the heart whose bitterness has been healed. A tear! How small it is! Nothing but a little water with a savor of salt in it, and yet it means more than ocean and cloud and storm. It is the parable of a fallen humanity, of a soul estranged from the Lord, of a nature which has become a discord in the Divine harmonies, its fears and its sorrows, its conflicts and its despair. And when the Lord would picture to us the peace and blessedness of heaven, He finds no more fitting way of expressing it than in the beautiful words, "And God shall wipe away all tears from their eyes."

The face is a parable in which are written all thoughts and all affections which are possible to the human soul. The whole body is a parable, but the face is the most clear and beautiful and the richest in meaning. It speaks of the innocence of childhood, of the purity and sweetness of angelhood ; and it can express in living and perfect forms every phase of action and every state of affection of a soul in its descent from heaven to hell, and in its ascent from hell to heaven. The material universe is a parable. How beautiful, how grand, how glorious, how full of meaning it is ! But all its meaning, all its beauty, all its grandeur are gathered into the human face, and are there written in finer lines and lovelier, and with larger and more delicate shades of meaning. Such are parables.

And without a parable the soul does not and cannot speak to another soul dwelling in a material body. How can I express my thought and affection? How can I convey it to another soul? It can only be done by means of the material body and the material world. Speech is not possible in this world without the aid of material symbols. Sound is a parable ; light is a parable, and what a beautiful and glorious one it is ! The written word is only a conventional sign of a material act or form. No, the only access we have to one another in this life is by means of parables.

The Lord, therefore, only made special use of a universal law when He selected and arranged certain material things and natural actions to embody and express Divine truths in a form specially adapted to human conditions. He took some of the most beautiful objects of nature, and the most significant relations of men, and with infinite wisdom arranged them in such forms that they might be to the common speech of nature and of man as the ruby and emerald and diamond to earth and common stones ; and therefore, by way of distinction and pre-eminence, we call these forms of speech which lie so near to nature parables, though they are not exceptional methods of communicating spiritual truth in any other sense than that they are divinely excellent and perfect.

Having thus considered the nature of parables, we are better prepared to understand the Divine purpose in using them. It was to "utter things which have been kept secret from the foundation of the world." By the world here we are not to understand the material universe merely. It is the *cosmos,*—the order and harmony and resulting beauty and use of the Divine truth embodied in spiritual and in material forms. This order and beauty have their foundation in the Divine truth. Wherever you see powerful forces moving in harmony to accomplish beneficent ends, whether in the spiritual or in the material plane of existence, whether in church or state, in domestic or industrial life, or in the activities of nature, creating beauty for the soul or food and clothing for the body, there you see a parable teaching the truths of the Divine wisdom, and revealing the secrets of the Divine love which lie at the foundation of all created intelligences and forms.   It is to reveal these secrets, to admit man more fully and interiorly into the purposes of His love and the methods of His wisdom, that the Lord opened His mouth in parables.

This is a purpose the Lord has always at heart, an end for which He is always working.   It is to let man into His secrets, to take him to His infinite heart, to give Himself to His children, to share His blessings with them, to teach them, to lead them, to live for them, and, if need be, to die for them.   The Lord is love itself, and He wants companionship ; He desires to tell us His secrets ; He longs to unbosom Himself to us, and to show us the hidden and most lovely forms of His wisdom ; and He adapts His speech to our capacities and to our wants. He opens His mouth in parables.

To His disciples it is given to know the mystery of the kingdom.   A disciple of the Lord is a learner of His truth.   So far as we become disciples of spiritual truth, we are introduced into the secrets and understand the mysteries of the Lord's kingdom.   As we learn and live we pass within the veil of nature and see the truth, and become quickened with the love, of which the natural form is the parable and expression.

But to the multitude who stand without, the Lord speaks in parables, that, seeing, they may not perceive. Why should He do this when it is His purpose and the constant effort of His love and wisdom to reveal Himself to men in forms as interior and as full as possible? Because He desires to have us take up into our affections, and appropriate to our lives, and thus make a part of ourselves, the goodness and truth He gives us. He does not desire to make machines of us, mere automatons, to grind out effects as the mill grinds corn. He does not desire to lift us up into a light that would blind us, and to carry us along struggling against forces which would destroy us. He desires the free companionship of love, and not an enforced, unwilling presence. Besides, He knows how much we can bear, and how high we can ascend and live and feel at home, and remain, and He never seeks to raise us above that state by any force. He guards our freedom as the essential human principle in us, whose loss would be the defeat of His purpose in creating us.

The Lord knows that there would be no use, but great harm, in raising us into a state in which we could not be kept. In that case the good and truth would be profaned,—that is, they would become mixed with evils and falses. By the good received man would be drawn towards heaven, and by the evil he would become distracted,—drawn asunder. He could not live in either heaven or hell. He would be like a fish in which lungs had been formed to breathe the air, but whose organism and nature in other respects were adapted to the water. If it should return to the water, it would be suffocated ; if it remained on the land, it could not obtain its food, or enter into any of its delights.

The Lord seeks to make everything He creates homogeneous throughout its whole nature, and to give to all its faculties unity of form and harmony of action. To man He has given capacities to rise through all grades of being, from the lowest to the highest. All His provideuces are arranged to raise man to the highest, and give him the best. But in doing this the Lord seeks to elevate man's whole nature, not to rend and destroy it. He does not, therefore, seek to convert one faculty unless He sees that He can convert them all. He does not seek to raise either the understanding or the affections into a state higher than that which the whole nature can attain, and in which it can permanently remain, while man acts in perfect freedom. For this reason the Lord adapts His truth to man's state, giving it in the form of parables to the multitude, and speaking more plainly to those who can receive higher truth, but always with the purpose of revealing Himself to man, and raising him up to as high a state as possible, and of uttering "things which have been kept secret from the foundation of the world."

When truth is given in a plain, didactic, and positive manner, we must accept or reject it. A square issue is made, and there is no way of evading it. Not to accept is to reject ; and when decidedly rejected we are not likely to give it further thought. The Lord, therefore, presents His Divine truth, as far as possible, in familiar forms. He adapts it to man's low and weak state. He does not force the issue upon us, but seeks to prepare us for it, and to lead us up to it by orderly steps. He veils it, and holds it before us, and embodies it in forms that are attractive to us, that appeal to something in our nature. He bridges the gulf between us and Himself with natural truths, and makes it pleasant with human fancies, that He may win us to act in freedom. He makes the steps short and not too difficult, that we may not be discouraged and sink down in despair. Truth is the way : He has built it with histories and stirring natural events, which attract even the sensuous nature of childhood ; He has beautified it with symbol and parable, and made it charming with song, that every principle in man's nature, even the sensuous, may be appealed to.

The very defects which the dry and severely rational and logical mind thinks it detects in the Sacred Scriptures, their simplicity, their pure naturalness in some parts and wild fancy in others, are among the most beautiful exhibitions of the Divine tenderness and loving consideration for man in his lowest states. The Lord brings Divine and heavenly truth down into the lowest forms, and conceals its blinding splendors by the shadows of earth, tinting them with heavenly beauty, to gain recognition and awaken curiosity and to secure a lodgment for them in the memory, that He may, when time and occasion and changing state permit, give more light and reveal Himself and the grand possibilities of the soul in clearer and higher forms.

Truth in the form of a parable is peculiarly adapted to all the wants and conditions of the natural mind, and to the Lord's purpose of regenerating it. It leaves the mind in freedom. We see the truth, and we do not see it. In a purely natural state represented by the "multitude" we may see nothing but the letter, the casket which contains the jewels. But that is so beautiful that we preserve it for itself. The child and the simple-minded can admire a parable as a pretty picture alone. They do not know that there are the most precious jewels within. They do not care to know. They cannot see them, and if the casket were opened and the diamonds and rubies were put into their hands, they would throw them away; they would be nothing but coarse pebbles to them, because their intrinsic beauty and worth can be seen only in heavenly light and by the eye opened to spiritual vision. But they are there, and when the Lord can cure our natural blindness, we can discover their heavenly value.

We can see something in a parable, all that we have eyes to see. We think we see all the meaning it has. Therefore we reject nothing. A perverted rationality cannot argue against a parable. We might as well argue against the glories of an evening cloud or the loveliness of a flower-garden. Our self-derived intelligence is not aroused. A parable does not ordinarily offend us. We can turn it this way and that, place it in all lights and study it as a picture. It is a picture, and even the multitude can see enough of meaning and beauty to make it worth possession. They see the outward form, even if they do not perceive the inward meaning. They hear the natural sound, though they do not catch the undertone of heavenly harmony. But by these natural means they may be led into a spiritual state in which they can see the other side of the parable, which the natural represents.

And this is what the Lord designs to effect by these natural means. He does not carry us; He leads us.

He gives us power and then encourages us to use it. He does not force the light upon us, but helps us to grow up to it, sharpens our sight to see it.

A parable is Divine truth in natural forms. The natural image is of such a nature and so connected with spiritual and Divine truth that there is no limit to its meaning. While it contracts to the capacity of the smallest minds, it enlarges to the dimensions of the greatest finite intelligence. It does this in whatever way we view it, whether as a picture of one state or of many ; whether we regard it as a whole or in its particulars. Every fact has its significance and an orderly relation to all the other parts. You cannot take anything away from one of our Lord's parables without marring its proportions or dimming its meaning.

As parables are the natural expression of "things which have been kept secret from the foundation of the world," their beauty, fitness, and precision of meaning increase as we pass within, and rise to the spirit to which they correspond. They are like the bud which encloses within it a beautiful blossom, and within that delicious fruit. Infinite things lie enfolded within them, which we shall continue to discover as our eyes are opened. And the truth we see will be the form of some good which we shall enjoy as our affections become purified and enlarged. Thus the letter of the parable will undergo a constant transformation, more heavenly truths blossoming out of it, and more precious fruits ripening in it. Spiritual mysteries will be revealed, and the secret purposes of the Divine love and the secret methods of the Divine wisdom will be brought to light, and by means of them man will be brought nearer to the Lord. Every parable is a ladder like that which Jacob saw. Its foot rests upon the earth, its top reaches unto heaven, and on its bright rounds the angels of Divine truth ascend and descend to man, to instruct and bless him. The whole Bible is such a parable, every particular of which is given to embody and shadow forth some quality of the Divine love and some form of the Divine wisdom. Its histories, though records of deeds actually done by men, are parables shadowing forth the infinite mysteries of the Divine nature. Its plain precepts, its statutes and commandments, its sublime and lovely songs, its wild and glorious prophetic visions, and even its dry genealogies, are parables, the vesture of many colors clothing the splendors of Divine truth, adapting it to human conditions, and revealing to man in every state all the truth he can receive and appropriate. It is a law of the Divine order, founded in the nature of man and the Lord, that without a parable He does not and cannot speak unto us.

THE END OF THE WORLD.

" One generation passeth away, and another generation cometh: but the earth abideth for ever."—ECCLESIASTES i. 4.

THE belief that the material universe is finally to be destroyed has been and still is almost universal in the Christian Church. Some have maintained that matter will be entirely annihilated; others, that it will only be burnt up and reduced to its simple elements, and that out of these elements new heavens and a new earth will be formed, and that the new earth will be the eternal dwelling-place of the righteous. Their bodies are to be raised up from the earth, and their souls brought back and reinstated in them. The Lord is to come down from heaven and dwell with them and be their King. All traces of sin and imperfection will be destroyed in the general conflagration, and the whole earth will become an Eden, the garden of the Lord, and all those glowing prophecies concerning the peace and happiness of the righteous will be fulfilled.

About the time when this great change is to take place there has been much difference of opinion. There can be no reasonable doubt but the apostles expected it in their day, and Christians have been looking for it and predicting it every century since. Many of us can remember the excitement caused by Millerism. Many persons were so sure that they had discovered the year and the day when the end was to come that they had their ascension robes made, and, clad in them, they assembled on the appointed day, expecting that the Lord would come in the clouds of heaven, and that they would be caught up with Him in the air while the earth and the heavens were being consumed.

Learned commentators and diligent students of prophecy postponed the end to 1866. It is quite safe to say now, however, that they were mistaken in the time, if not in the event itself.

There is another important point upon which there is an equally serious conflict of opinion. Some believe that the millennium—that is, a period of a thousand years in which the Lord is to reign personally upon the earth, and righteousness and peace are to prevail universally—will take place before the world is burnt up. Others believe that the world is to be consumed first and that the millennium will take place afterwards, and among those who entertain this opinion are many of the most learned divines in all branches of the church. There is a general assent to the doctrine that the earth, if not the material universe, is to be burnt up, and either annihilated or made over into a new one.

But the doctrines of the New Church teach directly the reverse of this. They declare that this earth and all the earths in the material universe were created to be the birthplace of intelligent spiritual beings, who commence their existence in a material body, and after a time discard it and pass on into the spiritual world, where they are to dwell forever. The earths are the seminaries of the heavens. The material universe was created from the spiritual universe, and bears the same relation to it that the body does to the soul, that the husk does to the corn, or the shell to the fruit. Every human being begins his existence upon some material earth, and sooner or later passes on into the spiritual world. Thus the work of creation is continually going on. New souls are continually being created and passing on to their eternal home. Generation after generation commences existence, passes across the stage of this life and on to eternity, and, as we believe, will continue to do so forever. I invite your attention to the grounds for this belief.

The doctrine is entirely in accordance with Scripture when correctly understood. There are some passages both in the Old and the New Testament which describe remarkable changes as taking place in the earth and the heavens. The sun is said to be darkened, the moon changed into blood, the stars to fall from the heavens, the foundations of the earth to be shaken, the heavens to be rolled together as a scroll, when, in the words of Peter, ''the heavens shall pass away with a great noise, and the elements shall melt with fervent heat ; the earth also, and the works that are therein, shall be burned up.'' '' The earth is utterly broken down,'' cries Isaiah, ''the earth is clean dissolved, the earth is moved exceedingly. The earth shall reel to and fro like a drunkard, and·shall be removed like a cottage ; and the transgression thereof shall be heavy upon it.''

Now, it is simply impossible that all these particulars can be literally true. It is impossible that the stars should fall to the earth. The earth is a mere grain of sand compared with the stars. We can see that the sun might be darkened, but how impossible that the moon should be turned into blood ; or, if possible, what use could there be in it? In one place it is said that the earth shall be burned up, in another that it shall be removed like a cottage ; and again that "every mountain and island shall be moved out of their places." In one place it is said the nations are to be gathered together in the valley of Jehoshaphat. Sometimes this great consummation is represented as having taken place, and again as about to take place in some future time. The disciples asked the Lord, saying, "Tell us, when shall these things be? and what shall be the sign of thy coming, and of the end of the world?" And the Lord answered, "This generation shall not pass, till all these things be fulfilled."

It is impossible to form any definite conclusion from attempts to interpret the Scripture literally. No human ingenuity, no grasp of intellectual power, can reconcile all this imagery and show its bearing upon one natural event. But, furthermore, the word translated "world" in the phrase "the end of the world," does not mean world in the sense of a material earth, and never did. A recent commentator says, "It is very remarkable that the word which means world in Greek is never used where what is supposed to be the end of the world is described." The Greek word *aiōn* means an age or dispensation, or period of the church. In this sense we speak of past ages. We apply it to a special development of life and literature, as when we say the Elizabethan Age. The apostles, without any doubt, used the word *aiōn* in this sense. Our Lord had just foretold the destruction of Jerusalem. He had just told the disciples that there should not be left one stone upon another of the temple that should not be thrown down ; and He had said, "Ye shall not see me henceforth, till ye shall say, Blessed is he that cometh in the name of the Lord." Then they asked Him, "When shall these things be? and what shall be the sign of thy coming, and of the end of the age,—of the Jewish Church or Dispensation?" They supposed He was going to establish a new age or kingdom in the place of the Jewish Church. The question is, therefore, natural and pertinent. But if they meant the earth there seems to be no reason for such a question. There was nothing in the preceding conversation to lead to such a question.

If our Lord's answer also is carefully considered it will be found to have no special application to such a question, and commentators have had the greatest difficulty in reconciling many things in it with the idea that it refers to the end of the material world. Many things apply with great pertinence to the destruction of Jerusalem, but others do not. The apostles, without doubt, found their questions answered to their satisfaction. They believed that the end would come in their day, and we find them frequently referring to it in their epistles. "The time is short." "The day of the Lord is at hand." They frequently speak of being "in the last days," "in the last times," "in the ends of the age." That they did not fully understand what the change would be in all its breadth and detail is evident from their own language. Before our Lord's death and resurrection they supposed the Lord came to establish a political kingdom and restore Israel to their former power and splendor. Their views became more elevated after our Lord's ascension ; they knew that His kingdom was a spiritual kingdom, but still they did not fully comprehend its nature, and probably expected that its establishment would be attended with many signs and portents, with many civil and physical commotions. There are evidences, however, that they did not understand the terms literally which speak of commotions and destruction. At the day of Pentecost, when the apostles were filled with the Holy Spirit and began to speak with other tongues as the Spirit gave them utterance, some, mocking, said, ''These men are full of new wine.'' But Peter said, ''This is that which was spoken by the prophet Joel, And it shall come to pass in the last days, saith God, I will pour out of my spirit upon all flesh ; and your sons and your daughters shall prophesy, and your young men shall see visions, and your old men shall dream dreams : and on my servants and on my handmaidens I will pour out in those days of my Spirit ; and they shall prophesy : and I will show wonders in heaven above, and signs in the earth beneath ; blood, and fire, and vapour of smoke : the sun shall be turned into darkness, and the moon into blood, before that great and notable day of the Lord come.'' (Acts ii. 16–20.) Thus Peter expressly declares that what they saw on the day of Pentecost was the fulfilment of this prophecy, and that it was ''in the last days.'' Ought not this to be a key to the interpretation of all such language when used by the apostles, especially by Peter ?

In the interpretation of Scripture, if one part of a statement is taken literally the whole ought to be. If it is said that the moon shall be turned into blood, we must accept that as a literal fact if we do the other part of the statement. We ought to believe that the stars will fall upon the earth, even as a fig-tree casteth her untimely figs when she is shaken of a mighty wind, if we believe the other part of the statement, that the heaven will depart as a scroll when it is rolled together, and that every mountain and island will be moved out of their places. (Rev. vi. 12–14.)

According to the same principle, if we accept a statement of Scripture as referring to a particular event in one part of the Bible, it is reasonable to accept every similar statement in every part of the Bible in the same sense. If this is done I do not hesitate to say that it is impossible to prove from the Bible that the material universe is ever to be destroyed by fire. Some fact will always be found which cannot be brought to harmonize with the others. The doctrine or theory does not explain all the facts, and, consequently, either the facts or the doctrine cannot be true.

Now let us apply the doctrine of the New Church and her method of interpreting the Scriptures to those passages which are supposed to refer to the end of the world. The doctrine is this :

By the end of the world is meant the end or consummation of an age, or a complete cycle in the spiritual movements of humanity. The Jewish Church was one age, which came to an end when our Lord was upon the earth. The Christian Church was another age or distinct movement in the spiritual progress of humanity.

The Jewish Church was purely natural, and the representative of a spiritual church. The Jews had no hopes or aspirations beyond this world. They believed that the Messiah was to be a temporal ruler, like David and Solomon, who was to exalt them to the pinnacle of earthly power. Jerusalem was not a heavenly but an earthly city, the capital of their own kingdom, which they expected would become the capital of the whole earth. This life and this world bounded all their hopes and fears. There may have been some men who caught glimpses of something beyond, but this pure naturalism was the essential element of the Jewish Dispensation.

The Christian Dispensation took a distinct step in advance. It was a spiritual church. God was a spiritual being, and not a merely temporal king. Jerusalem was a church or a heavenly city. Righteousness did not consist in a scrupulous adherence to the ceremonial law, but in a life according to the commandments. The law reached the thoughts and intentions. But these truths the church received upon authority. The church has never had any rational knowledge of spiritual truth. All her doctrines are taught dogmatically, and are to be received by faith, as matters of belief, upon testimony. The essential characteristic of the first Christian age has been belief in spiritual truth and obedience to it ; but truth received upon authority and not rationally understood.

A church or age comes to an end when the essential principle which distinguishes it from all others ceases to be a living principle. Thus the Jewish world or age came to an end when they made the Word of God of none effect by their tradition, and when their national life and civil polity and ceremonial worship at Jerusalem ceased. The first Christian age came to an end when its love for the truth had grown cold, and its belief in the truth which constituted the church had been destroyed. This, we believe, took place about a century ago. It would not be difficult to show by the testimony of the church herself that all real belief in her doctrines had perished. You can hardly find two men now who think alike upon any of the essential doctrines of the church. Even if they use the same words, they do not attach the same idea to them ; and multitudes repeat the creed without attaching any idea to it. It is not my purpose to prove this truth, but simply to state it for illustrating what we mean in the New Church by the end of the world, or the consummation of the age. You will perceive that it is not the end of an organization, of dogmas and outward forms, but of inward life. A tree may retain its form for many years after it is dead. Wood may preserve its existence for many centuries and be applied to many useful forms after its life has come to an end. So a church may retain its outward organization and teach its dogmas for many years after it is dead. Indeed, it is the distinguishing characteristic of a dead church that it is scrupulous in paying tithes of the mint, anise, and cummin of creeds and ceremonies, while it neglects the weightier matters of the law, judgment, mercy, and faith.

Having stated what we understand by the end of the world or age, let us look at the terms in which that event is described in the Bible. The doctrines of the New Church teach us that the whole Bible is written according to the correspondence of natural with spiritual things. The sun represents the Lord ; its heat represents His love received and reciprocated by men. The moon represents the cool light of faith. The stars are bits of knowledge of heavenly things held in memory. The earth represents the church ; all things on the earth represent the truths or principles which constitute the church, and everything that occurs on the earth represents some form or activity of those truths and principles. Now let us apply this method of interpretation to some of the passages in the Word which relate to this subject.

The darkening of the sun means the loss from the church of that love for the Lord and of that sense of the Lord's love which are its very life.

The withdrawal of the moon's light means the gradual loss of all belief or faith in the truths of the church. Its being changed into blood denotes the destruction of all living quality in the faith of the church. It represents the loss of all charity or brotherly love. The falling of the stars from heaven denotes the entire dispersion and loss of all the knowledges of spiritual truth, by giving them a merely natural meaning. The spiritual mind is heaven compared with the natural mind. The kingdom of heaven is within us. When those truths which relate to the spiritual man are brought down and sensualized, when the church begins to lose the spirit and to think lightly of the life, and makes much of mere dogmas and ceremonies, which is the sign of a dying or dead church, then the stars fall from heaven upon the earth, even as a fig-tree, which denotes a development of merely natural good, casteth her untimely figs when she is shaken of a mighty wind.

When the light of Divine truth is darkened in the mind ; when the warmth of spiritual love grows cold, and all belief in spiritual truth is destroyed, and all true knowledge of its facts and doctrines is lost, then the heavens depart as a scroll when it is rolled together ; the spiritual mind becomes closed to all spiritual truth, and the end of the world draws near.

If we look at any particular church and note the changes that have taken place in her when she approached her end, we shall find that the changes which are said to take place in the earth represent them in every particular. Our Lord says that many will come in His name, claiming to be the Christ, and shall deceive many. This prediction means that many will claim to have the only message of Divine truth. How diverse the doctrines are we know, and how sharp the controversies and how bitter the persecutions which have arisen among their adherents. These are the wars and rumors of wars foretold by our Lord. The conflict of evil with evil and of falsity with falsity is described as nation rising against nation and kingdom against kingdom. Famines are caused by the lack of the bread of life, which is love to the Lord and the neighbor. The pestilences foretold are the moral and spiritual evils which corrupt the hearts and minds of men, and cause spiritual disease and death. The earthquakes are the commotions in the church, which shake it to its foundations and break it up into sects, as the earth's crust is shaken and broken into fragments by natural earthquakes.

In this manner we might take every passage in the whole Bible which refers to the end of the world, and show the special meaning of every particular, and its entire harmony with this doctrine and its bearing upon it. All these terms are not given a special meaning to adapt them to this particular doctrine. But they have this meaning everywhere, in the whole Word. The sun, moon, stars, and earth always have essentially the same meaning. The earth always means the church or those principles which constitute it. All the wars, famines, and pestilences mentioned in the Scriptures signify and represent spiritual conflicts, in which evils and falsities contend among themselves òr stand opposed to goodness and truth. And we are not compelled to remain in a general application alone. We can descend to the minutest particulars, even to the kind of weapons used in these conflicts, the people who carry on the wars, and the causes of defeat or victory. The farther this correspondence is carried, the clearer it becomes and the more universal its application becomes, so that the argument from the Word comes out in the clearest and fullest manner, satisfying every condition of humanity and every demand of the reason and every statement of Scripture. I have not attempted to do more than to give an outline of the argument and show the manner in which we read the sacred symbols to learn what the Word really teaches concerning the last days. I shall invite your attention now to some of the rational considerations which confirm the belief that the end of the world is a spiritual and not a natural event.

According to the doctrines of the New Church, the

material universe was created to be the birthplace of end-less generations of intelligent beings, who were to pass on into the spiritual world and make room for those who should come after them. It is the essential nature of love to create, to communicate itself as fully as possible to others. As the Lord's love is infinite, this essential ele-ment of His being can never be exhausted. He must have the same reasons to-day for creating intelligent beings that He had for creating the first man ; and there must be the same reasons millions of years hence for creating new souls to become the recipients of the Divine love and blessedness that there are now. It must, there-fore, be contrary to the essential nature of the Lord that He should ever cease to create.

It has been proved by modern astronomers that our sun with its attendant planets and the myriad visible stars are moving in vast orbits around some common centre. This orbit of our solar system is so vast that it could complete only a small part of a revolution in six thousand years. How absurd to suppose that a Being of infinite wisdom would create a universe and set its worlds re-volving in their orbits, and then destroy them before they had completed one revolution ! A little child is not guilty of so great a folly who builds a house of cards and throws it down for the pleasure of seeing it fall.

But again, the ratio between the smallest grain of sand and our earth is greater than the ratio between our earth and the whole of the material universe ; can any supposi-tion be more absurd than that the Lord would destroy the whole material universe because some beings who dwell upon this grain of sand have broken His laws?

The act of a man who burned his barn to kill a rat was wise compared with such a destruction of the universe. You cannot find anything in the childish ignorance or fitful spite of men so absurd as this. How irrational, then, to call it by no worse a name, to attribute such folly to infinite love and wisdom! Suppose the Lord has been disappointed and His purpose in some respects defeated by sin, is that any reason why He should complete the defeat of His ends by a universal destruction? But it cannot be that He has been defeated or disappointed. Omniscience saw the end from the beginning, and infinite wisdom provided the best means. The Lord can make no mistakes. Sin has only served to bring out the manifestations of His love in larger measures and in a greater variety of forms. There is no more cause for the destruction of the universe than there was to prevent its creation in the first instance. There is the same reason for its continuance, and must forever be, that there was for its creation. The Divine nature as it is in itself, the end for which the universe was created, the whole order and method of the creation and human reason, all teach us in unequivocal terms that the material universe will never be destroyed until infinite love grows cold and infinite wisdom fails to provide the ways and means for carrying into effect the purposes of infinite love, and infinite power becomes exhausted; and when that crisis comes there will be no God and no universe and no human beings. We infer, therefore, that the destruction of the natural universe is contrary to the Divine nature, to the purposes of the Lord as declared in the creation, and to human reason.

The idea held by some, that the earth will be remade, that the Lord will give to man a better body at the resurrection, and that the new earth, if it is a material one, will be a better earth than this, practically accuses the Lord of folly, of not doing the best for His children that He could, and that is to say that His love and wisdom are not perfect. If it is replied that man finds the earth very imperfect and is constantly improving it, the answer is that it is one of the perfections of the earth that man can improve it,—it is one of the conditions of life essential to his intellectual and spiritual development. If he had no occasion to call forth his faculties they would lie dormant. If he saw no room for improvement, or found it impossible to make improvement, he would have no stimulus of hope, and all motives to exertion beyond what was necessary to support life would be taken away. Man's nature is self-adjusting to all the conditions of life. Infinite wisdom is embodied in the creation, and when men try to improve upon the methods of infinite wisdom they show their ignorance and folly.

But the doctrine that this earth or any part of the material universe is to be made over into a new world and become the future dwelling of man after the resurrection is materialism. This result cannot be avoided. Man's body is not a spiritual body after all, and instead of going to heaven and dwelling in one of the mansions in His Father's house according to the promise, he must remain forever in this world. He is not essentially a spiritual being, but an earthly one, and however perfect his condition may be as a material being, he can never hope to attain to the glory and blessedness of a purely spiritual life.

But the whole theory that this world is to be the eternal home of the redeemed is contrary to the oft-repeated declarations and promises of the Word. "My kingdom is not of this world," the Lord says. "I go to prepare a place for you ; and if I go and prepare a place for you, I will come again, and receive you unto myself ; that where I am, there ye may be also." The whole tenor of our Lord's teachings was directed to prepare men for life in another and spiritual world which is not to be created at some future time, but which was already in existence, and when the Lord spoke was the home of all those who had passed from earth.

When we understand the term "world" as meaning not the natural ground but the world of human life ; especially when we give the Greek word which is translated "world" its strict meaning of "age" or "dispensation," how simple it all is ! Within historic times the world has more than once passed away and a new world has been created. The Europe which the Roman conquerors knew is gone. The America which Columbus found is passed away and a new America has come into being. And turning our thought to the spiritual states of men, of which the Bible always directly speaks, the world has been destroyed and a new world created as often as one system of religious truth has lost its vitality and its power over the lives of men and a new system has been raised up by the Lord. Not to go back to remote antiquity, the world was in comparatively recent times made new when the Christian Dispensation displaced the Jewish at the coming of the Lord ; and in our own day is taking place before our very eyes the destruction and new creation of the church which the Lord Himself predicted. And all the while our faithful planet keeps steadily on its way fulfilling the purpose for which the Lord created it, as a nursery of human beings, where they may awaken to consciousness and learn their first lessons of obedience to the Heavenly Father, then to pass on to His eternal home. As saith Ecclesiastes, "One generation passeth away, and another generation cometh ; but the earth abideth for ever."

v

THE SECOND COMING OF THE LORD.

" They shall see the Son of man coming in the clouds of heaven with power and great glory."—MATTHEW xxiv. 30.

THE necessity for the Second Coming of the Lord is due to the mental and spiritual condition of humanity at the time of His first advent. All true knowledge of the Lord and the spiritual world had long been lost. Men were in a natural and, for the most part, in a sensual state. Their ideas of God, of heaven, of His kingdom and power and glory, and of their relations to Him were purely natural. The disciples, in common with the Jewish people, understood all the prophecies and promises naturally. The Lord was literally to occupy the throne of David ; the enemies over whom He was to triumph were the Romans and the other nations who had made war upon and subdued them. The "peace on earth" was not a spiritual, but a civil peace. The blessings the Jews expected from the Messiah were temporal, and limited to their own nation.

It was an immense advance from such natural and strictly national ideas to the acknowledgment that the Lord's kingdom and blessings are spiritual and universal. It was only by slow and painful steps, with many doubts and misgivings, and by the influence of the Lord's resurrection and subsequent appearance, and the miraculous powers conferred upon the disciples by the gift of the

322

Spirit, that they gained a full and clear conviction of the spirituality of His kingdom and the fundamental doctrines which constitute it.

But these doctrines were received as a matter of faith, upon Divine or human authority, as truths to be believed and obeyed. And this has been the teaching of the Christian Church in every age. "We walk by faith." "We see through a glass darkly." The fundamental doctrines of Christianity are acknowledged to be a mystery, and in their reception the reason must be kept in subordination to faith. The Lord has taught us certain truths in the Sacred Scriptures, and we must believe them, whether they accord with our reason or not.

A church based upon this principle must come to an end, not because the principle itself is not true as far as it goes, but because the human mind is so constituted that it cannot rest in simple obedience. Admitting that the doctrines taught are true, as long as men are contented to obey them simply, they will go right ; but the moment they begin to reason, to think for themselves, there must arise diversity of opinion, and consequently doubt, especially when language in which those principles are taught is capable of so many interpretations. Discussions, differences of opinion, dissensions, perversions, doubts, disbelief, and ultimate rejection of the truth itself necessarily follow. And as man has no means in himself of gaining the truth concerning spiritual things, the Lord must interpose and provide some way to save him. He must come again in some form adapted to man's state, or he would utterly perish. There are many other subordinate causes which rendered the second advent necessary.

Every principle in man's character and all his relations to the Lord increased and modified this necessity. But it is sufficient for my purpose to present this principal cause. I next invite your attention to what the doctrines of the New Church teach concerning the manner of the Lord's second coming.

The second coming is described in various ways in the Sacred Scriptures. In the twenty-fourth chapter of Matthew and thirtieth verse it is said, "They shall see the Son of man coming in the clouds of heaven with power and great glory." As we understand these words, they contain an exact description of the manner in which the Lord will come. By the "Son of man" we under-stand the Divine truth of the Lord; by the "clouds of heaven," the literal sense of the Word; by the "great glory," the spiritual sense of the Word, or the Divine truth as it really exists when stripped of all natural ap-pearances; and by "power" we understand true spirit-ual power, power over the minds and hearts of men, the power which true knowledge always gives.

I do not ask those who are not familiar with the doc-trines of the New Church to assent to this. You cannot assent to it until you see it to be true. All that I ask is that you will admit it as an hypothesis or supposition. If the Bible is acknowledged to be such a book as our doc-trines teach us that it is, I am confident that this doctrine of the second coming will also be seen to be rational and true. I shall not argue the question,—my limits forbid me to do that,—but simply state the belief of the New Church.

Our doctrines declare that the Sacred Scriptures are

Divine truth itself. They contain a precise, connected, and logical statement of all spiritual and Divine laws and principles. They are to man's spiritual nature, to the spiritual world and the Divine nature, what a book which contained a perfect physiology would be to the material body, or what a perfect work upon mathematics would be to all numbers and geometrical forms. That is, the Word contains a perfect spiritual and Divine philosophy and a perfect spiritual history of the human race from its first creation, and a perfect prophecy of its future. This history is not limited to this world, but it extends. to the spiritual world, and gives us a complete and clear idea of the nature of that world and of all its inhabitants. When this spiritual truth is seen, it carries with it the same conviction of its absolute certainty that mathematical truths do of their certainty when they are seen.

This spiritual truth is as distinct from the natural truth contained in the letter of the Word as the soul is distinct from the body. Indeed, the spiritual sense bears the same relation to the literal or natural sense that the soul bears to the body. The Bible was not given to man to teach him in what manner or order or time the earth was created, to give him a history of the Jews, or to tell him how or when the world would be destroyed. What is said upon these subjects may be literally true or it may not. It is of no consequence to the real purpose for which the Word was given to man whether it is naturally true or not. It is of no more consequence that the history of the Jews should be true in every particular than it is that the parable of the Prodigal Son or of Dives and Lazarus should be an exact statement of natural events that really occurred. The only essential requisite in the letter is, that the natural object or action shall correctly represent the spiritual idea, as a man's actions, looks, and voice, when spontaneous, truly represent his affections and thoughts.

The literal or natural sense is used to embody and convey or express spiritual truth, as the body is used to express the various states of the soul,—that is, the natural events, images, and actions of nature, animals, and men are employed as symbols to express corresponding spiritual truths. The natural sense is, therefore, called the covering or cloud, which in some places entirely conceals, and in others only partly reveals the real meaning. The objects or events narrated are natural ciphers or hieroglyphics. The natural image bears about the same relation to the spiritual idea that the printed word does to the natural idea. But the difference between natural and spiritual things is so great that but little spiritual truth can be directly expressed by the natural image. We all know how difficult and often impossible it is to express our affections and thoughts fully by words. The real meaning struggles through them like light through a cloud. How much more impossible must it be to express spiritual and Divine truth in all its fulness and clearness in natural forms !

If the Word is written in symbols, it is plain that the only way to get its true meaning is to know what spiritual truths the natural images represent. For example, we can never learn how the Lord is coming, or what the signs of His coming are, if we think only of wars, earthquakes, clouds, and material things, any more than we could learn what wars, earthquakes, and clouds are by looking at the printed words without imagining even that they had any meaning. When our Lord said to the Jews that they must eat His flesh and drink His blood, they understood Him naturally, and they were astounded at the assertion. " How can this man give us his flesh to eat?" " This is an hard saying ; who can hear it?" "From that time many of his disciples went back, and walked no more with him." They would not follow a man who told them such absurd things. There are many persons at the present day who reject the Bible for the same reason, and many more who draw entirely erroneous conclusions from it.

Now, we believe the key to this cipher has been given to men, and that by means of it they can ascertain with perfect certainty what spiritual and real truths the natural symbols of the Word represent. We are able to open the covering, the cloud, and the Son of man, the Divine truth, comes to us. But He comes to us in the cloud. The letter of the Word is the instrumentality, the vehicle in which He comes ; we do not get the truth by rejecting the letter, but by understanding it. By means of this key, therefore, we gain access to the infinite treasures of spiritual truth.

The first effect of this knowledge is to give us a clear understanding of the nature of the Word itself, and to save us from all the doubts and difficulties which have obscured and troubled readers of the Bible for many generations. We are no longer troubled because we find that the natural sense does not agree with geology or any other science. The discrepancies and contradictions contained in the letter do not disturb our faith in its claims to be the Word of God, because we know it was not given to us to teach natural science or the history of nations. The fact that a great part of it is occupied with trivial details, or prophetic visions which have no consistent natural meaning, does not diminish our estimation of its Divine origin and infinite value, because we know that these details, trivial in themselves, and this prophetic imagery, are natural symbols of spiritual things. I regard it as I should a rough casket full of the most precious jewels. I do not stop to criticise the outside. I proceed at once to open it and feast upon the beauty and glory within. I regard it as I should a present of fruit if I were hungry. I do not stop to find fault with the hard and bitter shells. I open them and satisfy my want with the sweet and savory substances within. It is a letter from my Father in heaven, written in cipher, because He could not get it to me in any other way. And in it He tells me all about Himself; what He has done and is doing for me, what a beautiful home He is preparing for me, in what forms He is coming for me to receive me unto Himself, and what I must do to meet and receive Him and follow Him. I do not complain because it is written in cipher. I do not reject it or receive it with doubt because the meaning is not all expressed upon the surface. I am filled with delight rather at the glorious revelation of Himself, and the precious promises I find in it.

Again, by means of this key we get from the Word a clear, consistent, and rational doctrine concerning spiritual things and the Lord ; a doctrine that fully satisfies the reason and all the wants of the soul, that reconciles all the apparent contradictions in the letter of the Word, that shows how the unity and the trinity are perfectly consistent with each other, and presents the Divine character in such a light that we can see how every attribute and relation is in perfect harmony with the Divine love. The opening of the Word removes all doubts concerning those fundamental questions which have been debated for eighteen centuries, and which by the usual methods of interpretation are no nearer their settlement now than they were when they first arose.

But the spiritual understanding of the Word not only settles satisfactorily and rationally all the doctrinal questions which have agitated the Christian Church from its early history, it elevates and indefinitely enlarges the field of knowledge. We gain a clear and rational knowledge not only of the existence, but of the nature of the spiritual world and of man as a spiritual being. By drawing aside the veil of the letter a new world and a new life are revealed to the reason and the heart.

Every one knows what clouds of doubt and uncertainty and utter darkness surround death and all subjects connected with the spiritual world. Many persons really deny its existence ; most persons practically do so ; and it is regarded as a very high attainment in spiritual progress when there are no fears of death and no doubts about the future, when all those momentous subjects which concern our eternal welfare are regarded as matters of faith, and we are willing to shut our eyes and push off into the unknown dark. But in the spiritual sense of the Word these subjects are revealed in clear

light.   Those whose understandings are elevated into
this light not only believe, they know, that the spirit is
the real man, that death is a step in life, that the spiritual world is a real world ; and all the laws of that world
and the nature of human beings in it, their social, civil,
and spiritual relations to one another, their modes of
life, their sorrows and their joys, are so clearly revealed
that they can see them and understand them as fully as
they can any natural laws.   They come home to them
with the conviction of certain knowledge.

We not only gain certain knowledge upon spiritual
subjects, which were the mere objects of faith before, but
this spiritual glory sheds a clearer light upon all material
things and earthly interests ; it gives a new meaning to
all material things and to all human relations ; it removes
the curse from labor ; it lifts the burdens of life from the
heart; it solves its enigmas ; it takes the sting from care
and death, and gives a new zest to every joy ; it throws
a new light upon every path ; and what is of far more
importance, it shows how all human, earthly paths open
into spiritual ones.   This is its great, inestimable service,
because it is by means of this that it performs all others.
It shows the intimate relations between this life and the
life beyond, between earthly and spiritual things.   In its
pure light we see clearly that natural things are not for
themselves alone.   The labor, the wealth, the skill, the
art, the science, the beauty, the graces, the joys, the
power and glory of this life are not for this life alone or
primarily ; they are only the wonderful means to a more
glorious end.   They are so rich, various, complex in
their forms and relations ; they so far surpass all human

wisdom that men have mistaken them for the final end instead of the means to it. The scaffolding is so complex, so beautifully finished, so spacious and in itself desirable, that men have regarded it as the building itself. They cannot conceive how the Lord can be so prodigal of power and riches as to spend so much for a mere temporary purpose. But when He comes in the glory of spiritual light, they see that He leaves nothing undone, even for the momentary good of His children ; and that the most beautiful things of this life, even the human body which is a universe in itself, are only the coarse and hard coverings and rough doors which open to the real mansion and the real world within.

While, therefore, this new glory corrects our estimate of all earthly things, and shows that they are mere instruments to higher things, the steps by which we enter the mansions of our eternal home, it does not in the least diminish their value. It increases it rather, because it shows their true use. The value of every instrument is not in itself, but in the good it helps us to attain. Measured by this rule and in the light of spiritual truth, we can see that gold has more value than the worldling and the miser put upon it. Knowledge is worth inconceivably more for its spiritual than for its natural use ; and civil power is a greater good than the most ambitious ever believed it to be. Even poverty and pain and disappointment may have an inestimable value, and death itself is but the open portal to an endless life.

Again, this coming of the Lord not only throws a new light upon man and nature ; it is a new light in him. So long as the truth remains in the book it gives us no light ; the images must be transferred to our own minds. Then the clouds and the glory are both there. The understanding becomes elevated, enlarged, illuminated, and purified. The intellectual eye is opened to discern spiritual truth, and the whole mind is illuminated with a new light and comes more directly under the influence of the Spirit of truth ; the Divine promise is fulfilled, "He shall take of mine, and shall show it unto you."

The gradual and ultimate effect of this clear, rational, spiritual light must be to settle all theological disputes concerning the fundamental doctrines of religion, and consequently it must produce that unity in the church which every good man knows to be so desirable, and which the church has sought to effect by external and arbitrary means. This unity will be obtained through the largest freedom of investigation and discussion ; it will come from within. This new spiritual light must change the whole character of social, civil, and industrial life, because it changes the ends or purposes of life. It brings humanity under the special guidance and control of infinite wisdom, because the coming, the power, and the glory are in the clouds, in the Divine truth in natural forms, as they exist in human minds. So the Lord's kingdom which is within us comes, and His will is done on earth as it is in heaven. Surely no one can deny that such a coming of the Lord must effect such results. Does it not also involve the exercise of the greatest power and redound the most fully to His glory ?

The common ideas of power are very natural and sensuous. We judge too much by the noise and commotion and the vast array of means, by those effects which strike the senses. We think of the earthquake which topples down the firmest structures of man and shakes continents, of the cataract sweeping along in its restless current every obstruction and dashing it into its abyss, of the ocean and the storm. But these are not the true types of even physical power. If the force which rifts and rends and sweeps from its foundations is so great, what must that power be which draws all things to a common centre and binds them together? There is more physical power exerted in a mild May morning by the force of attraction in growing grass and blossoming flowers and by the balmy heat that penetrates everywhere and permeates every grain of mould and every germ-cell of every plant than in earthquake and ocean, cataract and storm. The power that destroys is exceptional, local, temporary, while that which creates, sustains, and saves is omnipresent and ever operating. The sun coming in the summer clouds, in the power of heat and the glory of light, is the perfect physical type of the coming of the Son of man, in the power of His love and the glory of His truth. As the sun dissolves the bonds in which frost holds the earth and bids the imprisoned rivulets go free on errands of love and use ; as it opens the closed cells of leaves, blossoms, and fruit to gladden the eye with their beauty and feed the world with their substance ; as it visits every particle of mould and every cell of plant and animal and gives to each according to its needs the power to perform its use, so will the Son of man come to every imprisoned mind, to give freedom to every thought and affection, power to perform its appointed use, and guidance to attain its end.

We make the same mistake in our estimate of civil power. We think of mighty armies marching with resistless might to subjugate great peoples, of vast fleets sweeping over the sea and sinking the commerce of nations in its waves ; we think of the power to overcome enemies, to subjugate, to imprison, to destroy. But that is not true power. He who operates on others only from without, by restraints, by fears, by compulsions, may restrain their external movements, but he does not control their affections and thoughts. True civil power consists in guiding the will of the people ; in making their power yours by their own choice. Every mind you can control in this mild, unobtrusive, invisible way increases your power by the amount of its own. A king or president who could so win the confidence and love of a great people would have in his control a power unknown to any tyrant that ever lived upon earth. Not only the hands and physical strength of the people are his, but those higher faculties of knowledge and skill and art and intelligence and will.

The same principle applies to moral and spiritual power. The church has been and still is an immense power in the world, and the ruling minds have sought to extend it by external means, by compelling assent to certain dogmas and conformity to certain external rites. Suppose the Pope sitting in the seat of St. Peter could burn every book and silence every voice which did not speak the shibboleth of Rome, would that be true power? Would he not destroy more power than he exercised? Would he not put out the lights of the world? Would he not obstruct and thwart and make useless the mightiest forces that are now awakening man to new life? And yet how imposing such a power would be! Conceive it to extend over the whole earth! An edict issued from Rome reaches every man and woman and child upon the earth, dictates to them what they shall think and do, how and when they shall pray. Awful power! What grandeur of architecture would be embodied in the churches! What beauty and splendor of ornament would adorn them! What pomp of ritual and form would characterize the worship! What unity and peace would everywhere reign! But would there be as much life and power in humanity as there is now? Would human faculties have the same free scope and the same incentives to activity? If they would, then the history of humanity is a lie. No, with all our distractions and collision of interest and opinion, there is inconceivably more power exercised for human good than could be in such a state of forced uniformity and external restraint.

It is said that some of the icebergs are truly grand and beautiful. They rise hundreds of feet above the ocean and cover many roods of its surface. They are so compact and solid that they seem capable of resisting every force. They crush the strongest ships when caught in their embrace as easily as the bark canoe. They lift from their beds and carry to remote distances immense rocks which no human power could move. And yet there are unseen forces playing upon them and penetrating them above and below, which gradually dissipate their form and substance and bear their particles on invisible wings aloft into the sky and scatter them in dews

and showers over a continent. Now they carry sustenance to the plant, refresh the thirsty, gather in streams
and drive the wheels of power, or, vitalized with heat, move
vast engines, bearing man's burdens and doing his work.
Such is the difference between a government or a church
crystallized into imposing ceremonies and dead formal-
ities, and the human faculties set free from restraint and
vitalized by pure affections and employed in multiplied
specific forms for human good. Such is the difference
between apparent and real power.

The same principles apply to glory as to power. The
true glory of a king does not consist in the pomp and
splendors of his court, the magnificence of his retinue,
and the obsequious honors of the multitude, or the fame
of his exploits, but in the wisdom and beneficence of
his government ; in the direction he gives to the common affairs of his kingdom and the provision he makes
for all his subjects ; the freedom he secures for them ; the
avenues he opens for the development of every faculty
and the attainment of every good. It is not the outside
splendor and show, but the quiet, unobtrusive, genuine
worth that constitutes true human glory. This has been
and must ever be the verdict of humanity. The glory
of truth outshines the splendors of the sun.

Now let us apply these principles to the coming of
the Lord. If, as He Himself declares, He is coming in
power and great glory, shall we look for power and
glory in their lowest and most external forms?

According to the common idea, He is coming in the
clouds that float over the earth. He is to be attended
with a magnificent retinue of angels flying to every part

of land and sea, to awaken the sleeping dead with the terrible blast of their trumpets. · He will establish His throne in the heavens, from which will issue terrific lightnings ; the earth will quake and tremble at His presence ; the sun will grow dark in the splendors of His glory ; the moon will not give her light, the stars will fall from heaven, and the powers of the heavens will be shaken. The whole material universe will be in wild commotion and rushing madly to ruin. And man and timid woman and fearful childhood, trembling, affrighted, aghast at these awful commotions, will, it is thought, be summoned before the dread tribunal ; the wicked to hear their awful doom, the righteous to be introduced into their eternal homes. Would that be a greater exercise of power than it requires to keep all these shining worlds in perpetual and harmonious play? Would it be more glorious to make all knees tremble than it would to give them strength to go on their errands of duty and · love ; to paralyze all hearts with fear, than to fill them with the quiet joys of home or the holy aspirations of heaven?

Or suppose the earth to be regenerated and the Lord to have established His throne upon it and to be the glorious King of the righteous? The whole earth has become a paradise, and the comparatively few who 'have believed on Him are enjoying its beauty and peace, and will continue to do so forever. Is that as great or benevolent an exercise of power as it would be to make the earth the gradually improving home of successive generations of immortal beings forever ; of beings who are to be transferred in a few days or years at the most to a world whose perfections are inconceivably greater than those of a material world can ever be, and whose means of development and capacities for happiness surpass all our conceptions? I do not see how there can be but one answer to this question.

View the subject, then, in whatever aspect we please, how can we resist the conclusion that if the Lord is coming in person to the natural sight of men, according to the literal understanding of the Scriptures, He is not coming in the highest, but rather in the lowest degree of power and glory.

But it may be asked, Is it not equally or much more absurd to suppose that nothing more is meant by the Lord's coming—a coming which we must believe, if we believe anything about it, is to work the greatest changes upon the earth and in all human conditions—than that men are to get new truths from a book? Let us look at the question a moment and see whether it is absurd or not.

The true object of the Lord's coming must be to effect the greatest good to humanity. This no rational mind can deny. It is to exercise the most power over the understandings and wills of men. The question is, Which would effect His purposes the most fully, a personal coming, or the revelation of new and higher forms of spiritual truth?

If the Lord comes to destroy the earth and to put an end to the creation of human souls, it is self-evident that He puts a limit to the exercise of His power at once. But suppose He should come and establish His throne here, and govern men directly. Suppose He should come as many Christians expect Him, with irresistible power, with great magnificence, with the richest rewards for His friends and the most terrible punishment for His enemies. Suppose He were to establish His government over the nations of the earth to-day. There is not a mercenary politician, or an offiee seeker, or a contract hunter that would not hasten to His courts and seek His favor. The stock exchange and legislative and congressional halls would be changed into houses of prayer, and Jew and Gentile would vie with each other in devotion. Why? Because they would be suddenly converted to a love for truth, justice, purity? Because they are humble and penitent for the past and sincerely desire Divine aid to assist them in overcoming their evils and living a heavenly life? No, but that "thrift may follow fawning." And Christians themselves must be much changed before they could bear such power and favor, or all observation and history are false. If you say, the Lord would be omniscient and know the hearts of all men, and would spurn from His presence all hypocrites, that does not alter the result. Suppose He spurns them from His presence, or sends them to hell, the result is the same. He loses His power over their understandings and hearts. He fails in the very object of His mission. He could control outward actions by external power, but the will and the understanding cannot be forced. The mind must be instructed, the will and the affections must be led and gradually developed by their own exercise. Even man's physical powers cannot be forced beyond their own strength. Samson could not compel an infant to walk. It can gain the strength or acquire the skill to do it in no other way than by walking. The wisest teachers cannot force the mind beyond its own capacity. The attempt to do it often injures its delicate organization. The Lord has all knowledge and all power, but the human mind can only receive according to its capacity and the laws which the Lord has implanted within it. No, every fact of human experience, every natural, spiritual, and Divine law, leads to the conclusion, that by coming in person with display of power and glory the Lord would defeat the very ends for which He created and sustains humanity.

Suppose, on the other hand, that the Lord has given to man a Book embodying His will, the principles of His own being, the modes of His life, the existence and nature of the spiritual world, the joys of heaven and the sorrows of hell, and pointing out clearly the way in which man may escape the one and attain the other. These Divine laws and principles of human life are so expressed that they are adapted to every state and condition of society, giving natural truth to the natural mind, and rising and opening as man advances, supplying milk for babes and meat for men. When at length man is prepared for it, the Lord gives him a key which opens a distinct plane of spiritual truths that satisfy the reason, illuminate the understanding, and feed with the bread of heaven every want of the heart. Has He not embodied His power and glory in the most benignant, the wisest and most efficacious form ?

According to our belief, there are signs in that Book which represent every principle in the Divine being, and every mode of Divine and human operation. As education and civilization advance, the Book can be multiplied and introduced into every home and imbue the life of every inmate within. The traveller can take it on his journey ; the lonely prisoner in his cell can learn the way to gain true spiritual freedom ; the sick man in his chamber can find in it a physician which will cure every spiritual disease. As its true principles become known, and the lives of men are formed after their laws, these principles will rule in the marts of commerce and in the halls of legislation ; they will guide the hands of civil rulers, and human laws will be the outward and natural expression of Divine laws. The graceful courtesies and sweet charities which they inculcate will rule in social life, and every home will be modelled after the heavenly home which they reveal. By means of these spiritual truths the Lord will come to every understanding, illuminate it with the light of heaven, and guide it in perfect freedom according to the laws of His own life. He sits upon His throne and establishes His kingdom, not in one place alone, but in every heart. And there He dwells in all the fulness of the heart's capacity to receive Him, constantly expanding every faculty and making more room for Himself. He takes the helm of every individual life in His own hand, and steers its course towards heaven.

As men yield more implicitly to the Divine guidance, and come more fully under these principles, the heavens open, the spiritual world becomes the great reality. In their clear vision men see it shining through every natural form and human use. They know that they are already in it, and while they do their duties with cheerful hearts and willing feet, they look forward to the time when the Lord shall call them home, with subdued patience but unspeakable joy.

This is the New-Church doctrine of the Second Coming. True or not, can you conceive of any other form in which the Lord could come with so much power that reaches to the centre of human life and places humanity so fully under its beneficent control, and with so great glory to Himself and blessing to His children?

HOW TO GET THE MOST GOOD OUT OF LABOR AND THIS WORLD.

" I pray not that thou shouldest take them out of the world, but that thou shouldest keep them from the evil."—JOHN xvii. 15.

RELIGION has generally been regarded as something foreign to man's nature and hostile to this world, as something to be superinduced upon him or added to him to supply a want which is not inherent in his nature. It is not regarded as an outgrowth and normal development of his faculties as he was created in the image of God, but rather as something to get, as a criminal obtains a pardon and a release from the penalty of crime, or a favor which he receives as a gift. It is regarded as something distinct from his daily life. It is a sentiment, or a creed. Religion is not infrequently spoken of as especially useful to woman and adapted to her nature and wants, while men have not so much need of it, implying that it is not an essential factor of human nature. Its essential use is supposed to consist in obtaining a remission of the punishment of our sins and securing our happiness in the future life. It looks more to the future than the present, mainly to the spiritual world rather than to this world. Its exercises and duties have only a remote connection with the common labors, duties, and enjoyments of this life.

What help does religion give to the great majority of

Christian people in their daily labor? Does it sustain them in it? Does it make useful labor honorable? Do its doctrines, as they are generally understood and taught, tend to make the ordinary duties of life pleasant and a means of expressing our love for others?

On the contrary, is it not true that useful labor is generally regarded as a curse? that there is thought to be something ignoble and degrading in it? and that those who are able to live without it are the favorites of fortune? How is a woman regarded who is compelled to support herself by sewing or teaching or domestic service? Compare her lot with the lot of one who is under no necessity of doing useful work ; whose delicate hands are never soiled and hardened by contact with the implements of domestic service, and whose face is never exposed to the sun unless in travel, or lawn tennis, or some form of amusement ; who spends her time in reading novels, or embroidery, or chatting with companions about the last party or the next one. How fortunate and enviable is the position of such a one compared with her poor sister ! She has escaped the primal curse. Like the lilies of the field, she toils not neither does she spin, but is delicately dressed.

How often we hear it said of a young man who has money, that he is independent! He is not laid under the necessity of doing any useful work. He is in perfect freedom to go where he pleases. He can travel ; he can amuse himself. He has no exacting necessities, no hard taskmaster to call him up early and compel him to work late. He, too, has escaped the curse of useful and regular labor with his hands. This is the verdict of the world, of the poor as well as the rich, of the saint as well as the sinner. A laborer spoke the general sentiment when asked what he would do if a fortune were left him, when he said, "I would throw down my spade and never do another stroke of work." Consider the meaning of the word "fortune." One man has lost his fortune ; another has become heir to a fortune. Does it not mean riches, freedom from the necessity of daily labor for a living, freedom from obligation to perform any use to others except it may be some polite social service ?

The church is in a great measure responsible for this mistake and its unhappy consequences. It teaches that labor is a curse. The error originated in part in an entire misunderstanding of the curse pronounced upon man, " In the sweat of thy face shalt thou eat bread," and of the meaning of labor and rest in the Scriptures. Labor is supposed to mean useful work, and rest cessation from it. But this is not their meaning. If it were, could our Lord have said, " My Father worketh hitherto and I work" ? By labor is meant conflict between good and evil in our minds, and by rest the cessation of the conflict. But the Christian world has understood rest to mean cessation from all useful service. Consequently heaven is regarded as a state of eternal idleness, only relieved by the diversion of song, and possibly by some social intercourse between the shadows of human beings in the shadow of a world. This freedom from the necessity of all useful action is regarded as the highest ideal of happiness. One of the common and absurd misconceptions of the doctrines of the New Church is, that they teach that we shall pursue the same employments in the other life that we do in this world. That would be impossible in the nature of things. But we do believe that the widest held will be opened for the exercise of every good affection and orderly intellectual faculty ; that every one will have some employment in which he can perform some use to others and make it the means of expressing his affection and of communicating and receiving delight. I can conceive of no more terrible fate than to be compelled to eternal idleness, or to feel the stirring and impulse of immortal affections with no power of expressing them in useful service. All delight, all happiness consists in some form of action. The reverse of conscious action is death.

The same fatal error has been made in religious teaching concerning the material world as in respect to labor. It has been regarded as a poor, mean, bad world, hostile to man's highest interests, a world to be despised and rejected and trampled under foot. Yet the very act of departure from it, which men call death, is thought to be the greatest curse and the severest punishment ; there· are few who are eager to leave the world. But there is no imperfection in the world. When the Lord created it He pronounced it very good. It is perfectly adapted to the purpose for which it was created. It is not the world that is at fault, but the people who dwell in it, and the misuse they make of it. Religious teachers have mistaken the material world for the supreme love of it, the Lord's hostility to error and sin for hatred of the sinner, and the immutable principles and methods of the Divine wisdom for an arbitrary and almighty wilfulnesss. The Lord is represented as being above law, which is impossible in the nature of things, because He is law in its origin, and to act contrary to it would be to act contrary to Himself.

These mistaken views of the Lord's character and relations to men, and the purpose of man's life in this world, have cast a gloom over human minds. They have filled the heart with groundless fears. They have reversed the true order of all man's relations to the world and to the Lord. They have robbed man of his best Friend and the most powerful means of gaining his highest good. They have mixed bitterness in the cup of all natural delights, turned light into darkness, confidence into distrust, hope into doubt and despair.

The New Church entirely reverses this mistaken view of life in this world. It corrects groundless misapprehensions and places them where they belong ; it dispels baseless fears and reveals the true cause for real ones ; it shows man his true relation to the Lord and the Lord's aspect to man. It dispels the appearances and illusions of the senses, and shows man how to get the greatest good out of this life and at the same time prepare for future happiness. It gives him the knowledge and power to get rest out of labor, comfort out of suffering, joy out of sorrow, a substantial and permanent good out of transitory possessions, help even from his enemies, success from his failures,—in a word, to make all things and all beings work together for his highest good. Let us see in some particulars how the New Church helps us to find light in darkness, blessings in curses, friends in enemies, and good in everything.

First let us look at labor, which is generally regarded

as the primal and bitter curse. By labor I mean every form of it, from work with the hands to work with brain and heart. How much of it is basely servile! How much of it is done from compulsion! How much of it is repulsive to natural taste and feeling! The limbs are weary, the heart faints, the brain aches, and body and mind pray for rest. The chief attraction of heaven is its promised rest.

How can the curse of labor be escaped? Not by abolishing labor. The most miserable beings in the world are those who have no useful and steady employment. They lose their health for the want of regular exercise, or from dissipation and excesses into which they plunge to find relief from the monotony and weariness of an idle life. The mind becomes weak, the purpose aimless, the thoughts confused, and all the faculties of mind and body become so relaxed and weak that a grasshopper is a burden. It requires then more effort to step into a carriage than it would for a person in robust health to walk a mile. So essential is physical labor in some form to health and happiness, that when men and women are not compelled by necessity to engage in useful labor they will seek exercise in sports, in travel, in hunting and fishing, in playing ball or tennis, or in other ways which they tax their ingenuity to invent. The history of the world shows that no human being can be happy without labor in some form, whether it is from the necessity to gain a subsistence, or an effort to escape from monotony and find pleasure. Action is a law of life and the essential means of happiness. Idleness is a curse from which every one seeks to escape.

Useful labor is more conducive to happiness than that

which is sought merely to escape from *ennui* or in the pursuit of pleasure. To carry stones from one pile to another and then carry them back again would weary one more than to build them into a useful wall. To water a garden and see the freshness and beauty of the growing plants would give one more pleasure than to draw water from a well and pour it back again. Exercise for the sake of exercise, without the stimulus of some delight and the reward of something accomplished, is dreary work. It is better than inertness, but it lacks the present pleasure, which is a great stimulus to action. The pleasure which labor gains from the enjoyment of some present or future good, however, only in part relieves the burden. The pleasure is not so much in the labor as in the reward we hope to gain. Most persons would prefer the reward without the labor.

But the way to take the whole curse out of labor and to make it an unmixed blessing, is to perform it from love to the Lord and man. We must put a spiritual and heavenly love into it. The desire to do good to others, to be useful to them and to contribute to their comfort and happiness, must be the primary and central motive of our action. This does not mean that we are to have no regard for ourselves, and are not to receive a just compensation for our work, but it does mean that the supreme and governing motive and aim that enters into all our employments must be the desire of being useful to others ; and they must be so conducted, as far as possible, that there will be use in the performance of them as well as in their results. Let us look at some of the common and useful employments as illustrations of this principle.

30

Take agricultural pursuits of every kind as an example. The farmer can till his ground and raise his crops from love to the Lord and the neighbor. He can plough and reap and gather his harvests with the distinct purpose of co-operating with the Lord in carrying His purposes of love to man into effect. The Lord has so constituted man's material body that it must be constantly supplied with food, and He has provided the means of supplying it. He has created ground composed of elements suited to this purpose; He has provided the seed, and the sun to quicken it into growth with its heat and light; He sends the rain to dissolve these material substances and present them in a proper form to feed the hungry plant and quench its thirst. He causes it to grow, "first the blade, then the ear, after that the full corn in the ear." But He needs the co-operation of man to prepare the ground, to plant the seed, to cultivate the soil, to gather the harvest and prepare it for the market.

Suppose the farmer, while he is engaged in his work, keeps this fact in his mind. The Lord has honored me, he says, by taking me into His counsels, by permitting me to assist Him in carrying His purposes of love into effect. Would not this elevate his labor from the exercise of mere animal strength, like that of the horse and the ox, to a spiritual and human plane of life and make it honorable? He is co-operating with the King of kings and Lord of lords, in building up His kingdom on the earth, and forming His heaven in the spiritual world. Can you call the labor of this use a curse?

While the farmer sees his corn and wheat and fruit

growing in the sunshine and the rain which the Lord sends, suppose he thinks of the use to his fellow-men which this food will render. How much hunger it will appease! How much physical strength it will give to men and women to render a service to the Lord in some other form! It will satisfy the keen appetites of the children, whose cheeks will grow rosy and whose limbs will grow strong with the nourishment which he has been an essential factor in providing. Would not his own heart grow warm with this love of the neighbor? Would not his brown face grow bright with the thought that the currents of the Lord's love had flowed through his heart, softening, enlarging, and enriching it, and that he had been an instrument in the Lord's hands of distributing His bounty to men, women, and children? Is such a position mean, degrading? Is such labor a curse? If it is a curse for man to render this service, must it not be a curse for the Lord to do His part of the work? If it is love, mercy, grace, and kindness in the Lord to provide food to supply human wants, does not man partake of the same nature by freely co-operating with Him?

As another example, take mechanical employments of all kinds. What does the mechanic do? He takes the woods and metals and earths, which the Lord has created for human use, and builds houses to give shelter from cold and storm, and to be a home for infancy and childhood, for the culture of domestic affections, and to be the theatre of quiet and exquisite joys. He constructs implements for his neighbor to use in cultivating the ground; he weaves his cloth and makes his garments. He constructs engines to carry men and the products of their

labor over land and sea and bring the wealth of all climes
to every door. If the miner in the dark chambers of the
earth, the smith and tailor and shoemaker in their shops,
the merchant in his store, the sailor on the sea, and the
cook in the kitchen, could know and acknowledge the
grand truth that they are helping the Lord to carry out
His purposes of love and mercy and tender regard for
men, would it not lighten their labor and make it a joy
rather than a task? They are doing a work which the
Lord cannot do directly with His own hands. He can
create the wood and the iron, but He cannot build the
house and construct the engine. He can create the corn,
but He cannot grind it and make it into bread. He can
cause the flax and cotton to grow and the silkworm to spin
its fine thread, but He needs our help to prepare the fibre,
to weave the cloth, and to make the garment. He has
given to man the ability to do this work, and made it the
means of the development of his intellectual and spiritual
faculties, and of filling his heart with delight. He has
placed us in the midst of these manifold uses, given us
the ability to perform them, and rewards us in doing
them, with health and strength and increase of capacity to
receive more life from Him, and crowns us with honor for
doing them. Here, as in the work of the husbandman,
every one can gain the comfort and receive the delight
of knowing that he is rendering a service to the Lord and
to man. He is clothing the naked, he is feeding the
hungry, he is healing the sick, he is carrying the weary
on his journey, he is providing homes for the homeless,
he is instructing the ignorant, he is contributing to the
common good according to the kind and measure of his

use, and the knowledge of this fact will strengthen his arm and encourage his heart.

Take the employments of woman as another illustration of the principle. Many of her employments are monotonous and in themselves contain but little to awaken interest or call forth intelligence. Her work is perpetually recurring. When one meal has been prepared and the wants of nature supplied, another must be provided. The cook and the chamber-maid and the mistress go the daily round with little variety and apparently with little permanent result. Wants perpetually recur and must be perpetually supplied. What does the labor amount to if it is performed from necessity? What permanent reward is gained for the care, the weariness, the anxiety, the frequent failure, if there is no purpose but simply to do what necessity compels? I am not surprised that women grow weary and feel life to be a burden. Many of them are loyal to duty and natural affections. But what help do they get from their religion? Do Christian women bear these burdens more cheerfully and find more comfort and delight in their work than others? On the contrary, are they not taught that their labor and care and sorrow are a curse which they inherit from the first mother?

Now, suppose they grew up under the influence of the truth that all their employments and relations are forms of use and are means of calling spiritual affections, love to the Lord and man, into exercise. Suppose the mother and the nurse and the cook and the teacher and the seamstress thought and felt that they are working for the Lord and co-operating with Him in accomplishing His purpose in creating the human race, would not that

x   30*

thought fill their hearts with a peaceful and heavenly pleasure? Would not they see that every word spoken, every meal prepared, every garment made, every provision for health and comfort and the development of the physical, intellectual, and moral nature has a permanent value? The deed is ended, but the effect remains. The burden of life is lifted, and the sense that some permanent good is accomplished fills the heart with satisfaction and delight. Working so, we are not working merely for to-day. We are laying up treasure in our own minds which neither moth nor rust can corrupt. We are doing a permanent good to every one to whom we minister in these natural things. If we put love to the Lord and man into our work, if it be no more than giving a cup of cold water to one of the little ones, we cannot lose our reward. The heavenly motive glorifies the work. The heavenly worker glorifies the Lord. "Herein is my Father glorified, that ye bear much fruit." The Lord glorifies us. We are working for the Lord and with the Lord. We are doing His work here in this world; but it is the same in final purpose that He and the angels are doing in the spiritual world. We are working for humanity and placing ourselves in such relations to the Lord and the angels and all good men that they can work for us. There is unity of purpose and unity of interest which draws us together, which ennobles the most trivial deed, and sanctifies the heart.

All the principles and doctrines and the whole spirit of the New Church tend to this result. It is a maxim of the New Church, that all religion has relation to life, and that the life of religion consists in doing good. We do not mean by this that we are rewarded for our good works with heavenly joys, as men receive money for their work. We are not rewarded in an arbitrary way for what we do, but the reward is in the doing. We are rewarded in the heavenly affections called into play, in the heavenly characters formed, in cherishing the unselfish affections, in thinking truly and acting kindly. The daily duties which we perform with our hands minister to our spiritual and eternal good, because we put a spiritual and heavenly motive into them.

Finally, the doctrines of the New Church give us a true conception of the nature of this world and of the purpose of the Lord in regard to it. It is a grand and beautiful world, and perfectly adapted to man's nature in the first stages of his existence. It is our home for a few years, and our Heavenly Father has furnished it in the greatest variety and abundance with all the means necessary for our support, our instruction, our comfort, and our delight. How lovely it is! How varied and beautiful its forms! How glorious the colors in which He has painted it! How delicious the substances He has provided for the nourishment of the body! How nicely adapted its forms and forces to call into play the latent possibilities of our affections, our intellectual and spiritual faculties, and all those powers and qualities which will fit us for our eternal home in the spiritual world!

You know how much is said against the world. It is generally regarded in the churches, at least by the doctrine of the churches, as hostile to man. Religious devotees flee from the world, or try to do it, by shutting themselves up in cloisters, by denying themselves its pleasures, and despising its beauty and manifold uses. But this is a great mistake. The Lord probably knew what He was about when He made the world. It is not the world that is wrong. It was created to supply our needs and minister to our delights. It is not the love of the world that is wrong. The Lord made it to be loved, and He gave man the capacity for loving it. It was necessary that it should be lovely and charming to attract our attention and call our natural and spiritual faculties into play by its delights. It is not the love itself of the world that is wrong and deadly in its influence, it is the *supreme* love of it. It is when the world becomes the end, instead of the means of gaining a higher end ; it is when we make it our god and the object of our worship that it becomes a deadly curse.

This distinction the doctrines of the New Church clearly teach. While they show the danger and the fatal consequences of making the world and its possessions and delights the object of supreme affection, more clearly and forcibly than any other doctrines have ever done, at the same time they teach us that its good ought not to be despised. The Lord created the world for our instruction and delight, and it is as ungrateful and wicked to despise and reject His natural, as it is His spiritual, blessings. Innocent amusements and social pleasures and natural delights are good and useful in their place ; the enjoyments of the earth are as harmless and useful in their place as the enjoyments of heaven. We can eat and drink to the glory of God.

From this point of view, and in the light of these principles, this world has a new meaning, a new use, and a new glory. Everything which ministers to our comfort, instruction, and delight is a form and token of the Divine love. The power to see the beauty and enjoy the good which the Lord provides is also a provision of the Lord's love. In the light of this truth we can appreciate His blessings more fully. It gives a keener relish to our food ; it fills our social and domestic life with a more interior delight. It gives a new beauty to the flowers, and a new glory to the heavens. We are the children of our Heavenly Father. It is His love which creates, His wisdom which forms, His hand which brings us these tokens of His love, His loving thought and tender care which provide them for us to-day. These doctrines bring the Lord near to us ; they tend to call forth our affections and our gratitude, our trust and confidence, and a sense of security from harm while we remain under the shadow of His wings. They show us the deadly evils of the supreme love of self and the world ; they give us power to resist temptation, patience and hope in trial and suffering ; they make our labor an honor and a delight ; they give us a just estimate of the value of this life and a foretaste of the life to come.

Suppose, when you go to your work to-morrow, you say to yourself, " I am going on an errand for the Lord ; I am going to do a work which He has commissioned me to perform ; I am going to render a service to one of His children ; I am His agent ; I am employed in His office ; I am commissioned to assist Him in His work." Would not such thoughts and the consciousness of such a purpose fill your heart with delight? It is of but little consequence what your mission is, so it is a useful one.

Would not the thought throw a splendor over the day? Would it not give you a supreme motive to do your work well? Would you not be happy in it? Would you not feel it an honor and a joy to help the Lord and to add to the comfort or alleviate the suffering or minister to the wants of a human being? Try it, and you will see and know by blessed experience how such a purpose will lighten the burden of labor, how it will raise it from a drudgery and a curse to the high level of an honorable service for the Lord and the neighbor. And in doing it you will find that the Lord is working for you, and rewarding you with enlarged affections, with keener perceptions of His goodness and mercy. You will find all your spiritual faculties expanding and growing into the beauty and harmony of the Divine order, because you are doing a heavenly work ; for every work is measured by the love we put into it.

All the doctrines and principles of the New Church tend to raise us up to this high plane of action. They teach us the principles of this life of heaven upon the earth, and they show us how to put them in practice. They reveal the Lord as a Being who loves us with an infinitive love, and who has no thought or purpose with regard to us but to save us from sin and sorrow and bestow upon us eternal life. A knowledge of these doctrines and a life according to them will help every one in every condition to get a higher good out of daily duty, and will prepare him for greater happiness through eternity.

PEACE IN THE LORD.

"Peace I leave with you, my peace I give unto you: not as the world giveth, give I unto you."—JOHN xiv. 27.

WHAT is this peace which the Lord promised to the disciples in His farewell words,—promised as His most precious gift, and as the fruit of His finished labors? We have some knowledge of peace on the material and natural planes of life. Natural forces are at peace though these bright worlds are moving with inconceivable velocity, because each one keeps in its orbit and flies on its shining way in the path ordained for it. Natural forces give us most beautiful and impressive types of peace when they act in harmony : a river gliding along in a smooth and silent current ; the wind bending the waving corn, playing with the dancing leaves, rippling the smooth surface of the lake which sleeps among the hills, and bringing coolness and refreshment on its wings. A spring morning when new life is beating in the heart of nature and quickening every vegetable form into new activity is a most impressive exhibition of immense forces moving in orderly ways to accomplish the Divine purposes. How silently the tender leaf emerges from the coarse bud ! How gently the blossom opens its prison doors and smiles in beauty upon the world ! There is no noise, no confusion, no struggle with opposing obstacles. The murmuring winds, the vernal warmth, the opening flower, the growing harvests, with united voice say, Peace. Invisible influences melt into the soul with the benedictions of peace. Such is the voice of the Lord in His works ; such are the hints of the nature of peace, which He gives us on the lowest plane of the creation, and from them we may get a suggestion of the origin and nature and blessedness of the peace which He desires to give us in the higher realms of the spirit. Let us look up then from nature to the Lord's direct teachings concerning the origin and nature of His peace. "My peace I give unto you."

" By peace," says Swedenborg, "are signified all the things in the complex which are from the Lord, and thence all the things of heaven and the church, and the blessedness of life in them. These are of peace in the highest or inmost sense. It follows ·from this, that charity, spiritual security, and internal rest are peace ; for, when a man is in the Lord, he is in peace with his neighbor, which is charity ; in protection against the hells, which is spiritual security ; and when he is in peace with his neighbor, and in protection against the hells, he is in internal rest from evils and falsities." ("Apocalypse Revealed," No. 306.)

Let us consider this instruction in regard to the essential nature of peace.

First, observe what is said of its origin. It is from the Lord. All its constituents in their aggregate are from Him. What are we to understand by their being from the Lord ? All life, all power, all capacity to love, to know, to act, to suffer, are from Him, but the order may be disturbed, their nature changed, in coming to us. Peace results when these constituents of life are received by us in the same form, order, and harmonies in which they exist in the Lord. Love and truth are united and become one in act. They go forth in the form of use to others. Truth does not remain a cold and separate thing in the understanding ; love is not an aimless and helpless impulse in the will. They become one. Each gives itself to the other, and hand in hand they go forth to serve and bless. They move in the paths of the Divine order, and in the harmonies of the Divine life. There is no struggle with obstacles, no conflict with hostile forces, no resistance, no doubt, no fear ; there are no clashing and distracting influences. All the faculties are lifted up and borne onward to attainment by the gentle attractions of the Divine love. The will and the understanding are in the Lord,—that is, they are in the sphere of His love, they are in the harmonies of His order. The will is vivified with His life, the understanding is illuminated with His truth, and all the faculties move in accord with His creating and sustaining energies. This is the condition into which the Lord created us, and these are the relations which the Lord desires us to sustain to Him. In such a state of the soul there can be no jar, no discord in the harmony of life, no failure in the attainment of the highest good. "In me," says our Lord, "ye shall have peace." Such is peace in its aggregate. Let us consider its three essential constituents.

The first is charity ; "for, when a man is in the Lord, he is in peace with his neighbor, which is charity." Charity consists essentially in loving the neighbor as ourselves. It consists in putting his interests on a level with our own, and in doing to others and thinking of others and in regarding them in all respects as we desire to have them think of us and do to us. When we are in this state we are at peace in ourselves with others. They may think evil of us, but we do not think evil of them ; they may try to injure us, but we do not try to injure them ; they may hate us, but we do not hate them. We do not make others an excuse or an example for ourselves. Our minds are serene whatever storms of passion may be raging in the minds of others. The Lord gives us His peace when we abide in His love.

Suppose every member of a family to act from this principle of charity. Would there not be peace in that house? Each member of the family is looking to the good of all. Each one is trying to contribute to the comfort and happiness of all. Consequently all the members are serving each one. This is the heavenly order. To every family living in this order the Lord comes with the Divine benediction, "Peace be to this house."

When the members of social, civil, or religious societies think and speak and act from this principle of heavenly life the kingdom of God will come to them. They will be societies of heaven upon the earth. Suppose every member of the various societies that are founded for social, civil, industrial, or religious purposes should regard every other member as he or she wished to be regarded ; suppose we all thought of others with the same kindness, consideration, and good feeling with which we desire others to think of us ; suppose we all spoke of others with the same tenderness, the same scrupulous regard for the truth, the same desire to do them no harm, the same desire to help them, with which we wish others to speak of us ; suppose we were in the constant effort, according to our ability, to give strength to the weak, courage to the timid, light to the ignorant, and in all kind, wise, gentle, and useful ways to help the needy, as we, who are all needy in some respects, desire to be helped by others, would not such societies be heaven upon the earth? The Lord's peace would reign in them. There would be union, harmony, activity, strength, help for each and all, peace and happiness beyond our present conception of the possibility of attainment in this life.

Another constituent of the peace which the Lord gives us is "spiritual security" from the assaults of all the influences which tend to disturb the harmony of life. This is an essential factor of perfect peace. However deep and full and exquisite might be our peace, it would still be imperfect if its harmonies could be disturbed by any corruption from evil desires or assaults from false principles. The Lord gives us His peace according to the immutable laws of His Divine order. The soul stands in them, is lifted up by their attractions. It is borne onward in the currents of the Divine forces. They environ it on all sides ; they flow into it from within ; they encompass it from without. It takes refuge under the wings of the Almighty. There is no possibility that any disturbing influence can gain access to it. The love of self and the world has become quiescent, and we yield ourselves without any reservation or reluctance to be led by infinite love and guided by infinite wisdom. The promise is fulfilled : "Thou wilt keep him in perfect peace, whose mind is stayed on thee, because he trusteth in thee."

When the Lord gives His peace unto us we come into the clear and steadfast light of Divine truth. The darkness of error cannot cast a shadow over us. Darkness cannot approach light. Darkness comes by the absence of light. Fill a room with light and you cannot get any darkness into it. Illuminate a mind with genuine truth and error can find no place in it, a falsity cannot approach it. Cold cannot exist in the presence of heat. The most delicate plant is perfectly secure against frost in a warm and genial atmosphere. So the love of self and the world cannot approach the love of the Lord and the neighbor. They are opposites and cannot dwell together. When the heart is full of heavenly love there is no room for hatred. The conditions on which we gain heavenly peace secure us against its disturbance and loss. The reason why our peace is so often disturbed and destroyed now is because we live so much in the world, under the influence of selfish and worldly desires. We have not gained the peace which the Lord gives to all who will receive it. We have not yet gained the heavenly mansions ; we are in the border-land between heaven and hell, and we are the subjects of contention between the heavenly and the infernal hosts. We are troubled, distracted, drawn in opposite directions. But the Lord bids us be of good cheer, because He has overcome the world and has gained a position in which He can help us to overcome it. When by His Divine aid this is accomplished, we shall be where no falsity can find us and no evil disturb the serenity of our peace. We shall gain "spiritual security."

The third essential of peace is "internal rest." While we live in the world,—that is, in the love of it and in the thought of it,—we shall look to it for peace. This is the condition of the mass of humanity, and we are all more or less in this state. We are looking without for peace, to our external and natural relations for rest. If we can gain sufficient wealth to satisfy our wants and gratify our desires, then we vainly think we shall be contented and happy. But we forget that our wants increase with our means of supplying them. Our desires grow faster than our means of gratifying them. Then, too, there is no security against the loss of any possession. It has become a maxim of worldly wisdom that it is more difficult to keep wealth than it is to gain it. The consequence is that those who possess it and set their hearts upon it must be disturbed with anxieties and fears for its safety. Those who look for happiness in domestic and social relations and who are the most delightfully situated in these respects have no security for the permanence of these possessions. The relation of husband and wife, on which more than on any other depends our happiness in this world, is liable at any time to be severed by death. Parents and children must part ; the most intimate friends must separate ; families are broken up and dispersed ; homes are forsaken and become desolate. There is no worldly, no natural possession that is permanent. There is no place on the earth where we can lay up a treasure of any kind in which it will be secure. There is no natural relation or possession, no knowledge, no affection, no honor, no power, no personal tie that is safe from harm and loss. Consequently every state and condition of the natural mind is subject to doubts and fears and anxieties and disappointments. "In the world ye shall have tribulation." This is a truth to which there are and can be no exceptions. But by the world is not meant the material world, but the world of the natural mind, the world of thought and affection that relates to this life alone. So long as we limit our thoughts and affections to a purely natural life, and in the degree that we do so, our hearts will be troubled with fears and cares and anxieties. We shall be subject to disappointment and sorrow. It lies in the nature of things that it should be so. There is nothing substantial and permanent and fully satisfying in a worldly life or in worldly knowledge, in worldly thoughts and possessions of any amount or kind. They are useful in their time and place ; they are as the husk to the corn, the chaff to the wheat. They are instrumental to a permanent and substantial good, and when they are regarded as instrumental means to the attainment of something better than themselves they are estimated at their true value and do not disappoint us.

This is a difficult lesson for us to learn. How hard, almost impossible, it was for the disciples to believe that the Lord would be more fully present with them, and in a position to do more for them after His ascension than while He was with them in the material body ! And yet it was so. How difficult it is for us to believe that those to whom we are bound by the most intimate and tender ties, ties which can never be severed, are nearer to us and dearer to us, and we to them, and can render us a more precious service now that they have awakened to the spiritual life than when they dwelt with us in the world! And yet it is true beyond all possibility of mistake. How difficult it is to get out of the world in our thoughts and affections and regard ourselves as spiritual beings, as citizens of the spiritual world, and all our permanent possessions and relations to others as spiritual! But only in the degree that we do this shall we come into "the peace of God which passeth all understanding."

Internal rest is peace of the soul. It is the harmony and orderly activity of the inmost and purest faculties of our nature. It lies beyond the reach of all the changes of time and space. Its home is in the serene heaven above the clouds and storms, the doubts and fears, the disappointments and sorrows of a natural, worldly life. Internal rest! Quiet, peaceful, trusting, satisfied affections! Clear, distinct, tranquil thoughts! Secure from every disturbing influence; secure from harm and loss; every treasure of the heart safe and assured; no more severed ties; no more partings. "There the wicked cease from troubling; and there the weary are at rest." This is what the Lord promises us.

But this is not all, and consequently it is not enough. There is no assignable limit to the Lord's peace. It is more than rest; it is more than security from any disturbing force; it is more than possession of any present attainment; it is more than home and life with loved ones; it is more than we possess or can ask at any assignable point in our progress.

Peace is not a quiescent, passive state. It is a most active one. It is caused by the inflowing of the Divine love into the inmost affections, vivifying them with life and awaking them to harmonious and delightful activities. This love comes by means of the Divine truth, the truth of peace, which affects universally all in heaven, and makes heaven to be heaven. For peace contains in it a confidence that the Lord governs all things and provides all things and that He leads to a good end. When a man is in the faith of these things he is in peace, for then he fears nothing, and has no solicitude about things to come to make him unquiet. A man comes into this state in proportion as he comes into love to the Lord. "The state of peace which prevails in heaven," says Swedenborg, "is such as cannot be described in any words, neither can it come into the thought and perception of man, so long as he is in the world, by any idea derived from the world ; for it is then above every sense. Tranquillity of mind, content, and gladness on account of success are respectively as nothing, for these affect only externals, whereas peace affects the inmosts of all . . . and thus makes the mind of man a heaven." ("Heavenly Arcana," No. 8455.)

Such is the peace, so sweet with inmost blessedness, so full of every possible delight from the centre to the circumference of our being, which the Lord promises to leave with us and to give unto us. Such is the peace He offers to each one of us to-day. Such is the peace He will give unto us as fast and in as full measure as we are able to receive it. It is indeed the result of the awakened activities of the deepest and purest affections of our nature going forth to the attainment of their end ; it is the glow and glory of the highest intellectual facul- ties, acting in harmony with our affections, conjoined with them, married to them, and working with them for the attainment of our highest good. It is rest in action ; it is certainty in the attainment of the highest good we can conceive ; it is the fruition of our highest hopes ; it is possession without the possibility of loss. It is more than these ; it is elevation into clearer light and into a finer and larger power ; it is the opening of the doors of every intellectual faculty to be illuminated with the light of Divine truth, and of every affection to be thrilled with the Divine love.

y

BOOKS BY THE REV. CHAUNCEY GILES.